W9-AEH-886

SHORT COURSE SERIES

**WORLD
TRADE
PRESS®**

Professional Books for International Trade

A SHORT COURSE IN

International Business Culture

Charles Mitchell

World Trade Press
1450 Grant Avenue
Novato, California 94945 USA
Tel: (415) 898-1124
Fax: (415) 898-1080
USA Order Line: (800) 833-8586
Email: worldpress@aol.com
http://www.worldtradepress.com
http://www.globalroadwarrior.com

A Short Course in International Business Culture
By Charles Mitchell
Illustrations: Tom Watson
Editor: Jeffrey Edmund Curry
Short Course Series Concept: Edward G. Hinkelman
Cover Design: Ronald A. Blodgett
Text Design: Seventeenth Street Studios, Oakland, California USA
Desktop Publishing: Edward G. Hinkelman

Disclaimer
This publication is designed to provide general information concerning aspects of international trade. It is sold with the understanding that the publisher is not engaged in rendering legal or any other professional services. If legal advice or other expert assistance is required, the services of a competent professional person or organization should be sought.

Library of Congress Cataloging-in-Publication Data
Mitchell, Charles, 1953–
A Short Course in International Business Culture:
/ Charles Mitchell.
p. cm. — (Short course in international trade series)
Includes bibliographical references.
ISBN 1-885073-54-2
1. Corporate culture.
I. Title. II Title: International Business Culture. III. Series.
IV. Series: Short Course in International Trade Series.
HD58.7.M567   1999
302.3'5--dc21   99–32547
                                                      CIP

Printed in the United States of America

A SHORT COURSE IN

International Business Culture

Charles Mitchell

World Trade Press
1450 Grant Avenue
Novato, California 94945 USA
Tel: (415) 898-1124
Fax: (415) 898-1080
USA Order Line: (800) 833-8586
Email: worldpress@aol.com
http://www.worldtradepress.com
http://www.globalroadwarrior.com

A Short Course in International Business Culture
By Charles Mitchell
Illustrations: Tom Watson
Editor: Jeffrey Edmund Curry
Short Course Series Concept: Edward G. Hinkelman
Cover Design: Ronald A. Blodgett
Text Design: Seventeenth Street Studios, Oakland, California USA
Desktop Publishing: Edward G. Hinkelman

Disclaimer
This publication is designed to provide general information concerning aspects of international
trade. It is sold with the understanding that the publisher is not engaged in rendering legal or
any other professional services. If legal advice or other expert assistance is required, the services
of a competent professional person or organization should be sought.

Library of Congress Cataloging-in-Publication Data
Mitchell, Charles, 1953–
A Short Course in International Business Culture:
/ Charles Mitchell.
p. cm. — (Short course in international trade series)
Includes bibliographical references.
ISBN 1-885073-54-2
1. Corporate culture.
I. Title. II Title: International Business Culture. III. Series.
IV. Series: Short Course in International Trade Series.
HD58.7.M567 1999
302.3'5--dc21   99–32547
                                                    CIP

Printed in the United States of America

TABLE OF CONTENTS

TABLE OF CONTENTS

CHAPTER 1

Understanding Cultural Differences

THE ONLY TIME WHEN TRUE SUFFERING OCCURS IS

WHEN TWO CULTURES COLLIDE. — HERMANN HESSE

ANYONE WHO HAS done business internationally knows that dreadful feeling brought on by the blank stares, the forced half-smiles, the murmured comments in a language that seems indecipherable—when what you say doesn't connect, and when something seems missing. The paranoia is inescapable. You had your checklist of cultural do's and don'ts and followed them religiously. You broke no taboos, committed no cultural faux pas, insulted no one—yet you failed to break through. Why?

Distance and time were once the biggest obstacles to doing business internationally. They are now among the least of concerns for any organization that has decided to go global. Today, international businessmen and businesswomen increasingly find themselves working in multi-cultural environments, dealing with real differences in everything from communication styles to social etiquette to core values. While many savvy international business travelers may not be able to give a textbook definition of what constitutes culture, they know it when they see it. And they also know they had better be prepared to deal with it beyond a superficial level. After all, winning acceptance from foreign colleagues and turning cultural differences into a competitive advantage means more than making sure you know how to properly accept the business card of a Japanese colleague or avoid serving cocktails to a Moslem banker. People

from different cultures process information in different ways, value different traits and measure the concepts of time and space in dramatically different fashions.

Why is cross-cultural knowledge and understanding so important? The American statesman and inventor Benjamin Franklin wrote that time is money. Globe-trotting businesspeople would add that being aware of cultural differences and sensitivities is money, too. Failing to grasp the subtleties that lie beyond such public cultural displays like greeting rituals and seating arrangements can make the difference between a truly successful international business transaction and one that fails to connect. Culture affects the most basic forms of personal and business interaction from decision making to management style. National culture, in turn, determines corporate culture, affecting a firm's internal structure, its marketing behavior and its view of foreign business partners and contracts. The business world is littered with "international" projects that failed to overcome cultural barriers. If you have doubts that cultural insensitivity can translate into business problems on a megascale, consider the case of The Disney Corp's French adventure—EuroDisney.

Monsieur Mickey

Bringing the wonders of Disneyland to a foreign country must have seemed like old hat for Disney. After all, only a few years earlier the company had successfully opened a Disney theme park in Japan, bridging the enormous differences between Japanese and American cultures. EuroDisney, at least initially, proved to be another story entirely. The company, it seems, failed to do its cultural homework on everything from French business negotiating styles to employee flexibility and dress habits to consumer spending patterns and eating preferences. The company had a system that worked in the United States and Japan—two very diverse cultures—and evidently saw no good reason to change it to adapt to European sensibilities.

Day one began with a nightmare. The French people, who tend to wear their cultural hearts on their sleeves, howled about Yankee cultural imperialism when Disney managed to buy 1,950 hectares (4,400 acres) of prime farmland for a fraction of the market price after the government used its right of eminent domain to find Mickey and friends a home. The farmers whose families had worked the land for centuries were bounced. French newspapers railed at the American invaders in a very public display of anger and insult. Before a single building foundation had been dug or a brick laid, the company had managed to alienate the community, partly because it had underestimated the attachment to the land of one segment of French society.

SENSE AND SENSIBILITY

Next, Disney offended French sensibilities and created a wellspring of ill will when it used lawyers rather than its executives to negotiate construction and other contracts for EuroDisney. It was simply not a French thing to do. In France, lawyers are considered a negotiating tool of absolute last resort. The use of lawyers early on in the process was a sign of mistrust and backhand rejection of French ways. Then, according to the French trade and popular press, the company insisted during the construction of Disney-run hotels that a sprinkler system be included. While required under American law, such a system was unnecessary under French law which demands only adequate fire escapes and alarms and access to an emergency water supply. Disney's insistence on the sprinkler system was perceived as a negative comment on French safety standards and an assertion that the "American way" was better. The battle ruffled the feathers of Disney's French partners and management, generating even more ill will made public in a stream of negative press reports.

In terms of operations, Disney's ignorance of European culture and French working norms caused more problems. The company, which prides itself on the squeaky clean All-American look of its employees, instituted a strict dress code for its local employees, barring facial hair, dictating a maximum length for fingernails and limiting the size of hooped earrings. The staff and its unions rebelled at this perceived attack on everyday French fashion. Morale plunged.

THE DEVIL IS IN THE DETAILS

Disney got several other important details wrong. For example, the company believed that Europeans do not generally have sit-down breakfasts. Relative to the normal workday lifestyle of the European commuter, they were correct. But the exact opposite is true when Europeans vacation. As a result of this incorrect notion, hotel dining rooms at Disney hotels were kept small, creating logjams and angry customers when the overcrowded rooms that seat a maximum of 400 guests tried to serve upwards of 2,500 sit-down breakfasts every morning. Lunch times inside EuroDisney also bordered on disaster. While Americans visiting Disneyland prefer to graze, that is, eat at irregular intervals, as they wander the park confines, Europeans are used to set lunchtimes. As a result, the park's restaurants became jammed at the lunch hour as everyone tried to eat at once and were empty the rest of the day. Customers complained of long lunch-time lines and pressure to eat quickly. The staff complained of being overworked at lunchtime and underworked during the rest of their shifts. To top it off, Disney, in keeping with the "family friendly" theme, barred the serving of alcohol—perhaps the ultimate insult in a country where the consumption of wine at mealtimes is a birthright.

HOSPITALITY HEADACHES

The company committed other marketing foibles. While the park did hit its initial attendance target of more than 10 million visitors in the first year, its revenue projections were way off. The reason: unlike Americans or Japanese visiting Disney parks in their home countries, the European visitors to EuroDisney did not spend money on souvenirs. Europeans, it seems, are more used to taking month-long vacations and as a rule do not go on short spending sprees like the Americans and Japanese when they visit a theme park. Finally, Disney found that checkout at its official hotels had turned into a nightmare because of different consumer patterns. Unlike the Americans or the Japanese, the European visitor to EuroDisney tends to stay only one night at a hotel, not the three or four nights common at other Disney parks. The result: the hotels had too few computers to handle the irate guests as they all tried to check out of the hotel at the same time after a single night's stay.

"It was so unlike Disney to get so many details so wrong," says one U.S.-based securities analyst who follows the company. "Maybe it's not such a small world after all. The company's cultural insensitivities cost it a lot of money and goodwill.

I think it is a good reminder to any company or individual doing business in another country—the devil is often in the cultural details. They can make or break you." But for Disney at least, all's well that ends well. After making some significant "cultural adjustments," EuroDisney is no longer the economic drain it once was on company coffers.

CULTURE CAUTION: It should be noted that for all of Disney's faults the French government was more than happy to have them set up shop. The government also bears some responsibility for not making Disney's transition smoother. The French have claimed for centuries that Americans have no culture but nowadays, it seems, they believe Americans have too much and need to export some.

What Is Culture, Anyway?

It may seem obvious but culture is what makes the Japanese, Japanese; the Germans, German; and the Brazilians, Brazilian. The noted Dutch writer and academic Geert Hofstede referred to culture as "the software of the mind"—the social programming that runs the way we think, act and perceive ourselves and others. In other words, your brain is simply the hardware that runs the cultural programming. The implication is that culture is not innate. There is no gene that forces Americans to treasure individualism and brashness, or Germans to value rigid order. It is learned behavior and hence can be changed. Just alter the internal programming and you, too, can think like a Yank, a Brit, or a Kuwaiti. While this is certainly a useful and encouraging metaphor for anyone dealing in global business affairs, it is more difficult to implement than it sounds. It takes study, a keen sense of observation, and, above all, a willingness to learn and relinquish the notion that one's native culture is superior. When was the last time you heard a foreign colleague admit that their way of doing things is inferior to yours? It doesn't happen. When dealing in a multi-cultural environment the "adapt or die" philosophy is a good one to remember.

A more formal definition is that culture is a set of learned core values, beliefs, standards, knowledge, morals, laws, and behaviors shared by individuals and societies that determines how an individual acts, feels, and views oneself and others. A society's culture is passed from generation to generation, and aspects such as language, religion, customs and laws are interrelated—that is, a society's view of authority, morals and ethics will eventually manifest itself in how an individual does business, negotiates a contract or deals with a potential business relationship. Understanding the cultural context and mindset of a potential foreign business partner or competitor can help in developing sound strategy for negotiations and deal-making. What once seemed mysterious may become more predictable—and can ultimately be used to your advantage.

Cultural Components

Viewing a national culture from the outside can be intimidating. But breaking it down into its components and understanding how each component is related to the whole can help unwrap the enigma and provide some logic and motivation behind behaviors, including business behaviors. The three most important cultural components that relate to business transactions are:

LANGUAGE

Often, it's not what you say, but what you don't say, that counts.

Language is more than just spoken and written words. Non-verbal communication, gestures, body language, facial expressions all convey a message. When two people do not speak a common language and are forced to use an interpreter, this non-verbal form of communication is the only direct contact and method available for individuals to take a direct read of each other. By failing to understand the cultural context in which such non-verbal communication occurs you run the risk of not only failing to read your colleague across the table but of actually sending the entirely wrong signal.

This can be true even in situations where two people speak the same (almost) language—as in the following case involving an American businesswoman and a British businessman.

"We seemed to get along great on the telephone. It was a relief after several years in Eastern Europe to actually be doing business with the British. At least we spoke the same language," says the American businesswoman. "We thought alike. I trusted him."

All went well until the American traveled to London to meet face-to-face with her British colleague to sign a research and development contract. The first meeting did not go well. "There was something that didn't seem right," she says. "Throughout the presentation none of the Brits, not even the guy I had developed a phone relationship with, would look us in the eye. It was like they were hiding something. After a lot of internal discussion, we decided to sign the contract, but many of us still felt uneasy. Even when we talked on the phone later I just couldn't get that failure of them to look me in the eye out of my head. It almost ruined the relationship and sunk the deal."

All that doubt could have been avoided if the American had been cognizant of one subtle cultural difference: Whereas Americans believe that looking someone directly in the eye during negotiations indicates honesty and sincerity, the British believe such a gesture to be a mark of rudeness until a more familiar relationship is established. "I guess I shouldn't have taken it so personally," says the American. "I understand it now, but I still don't like it."

RELIGION

God may have a deeper influence on business strategy than you think.

The dominate religious philosophy within a culture can have a much greater impact on an individual's approach to business than most people expect—even if that individual is not a devout follower of a particular religion. In the Arab world, conversations are sprinkled with the phrase *Inshallala*—if God wills. The deference to a higher power, a lack of control over many matters here on earth and the general what-will-be-will-be attitude that the phrase epitomizes carries over into everything from the airline schedules to the pace of business negotiations.

Take the case of a German investment banker recently sent to negotiate a finance deal for a manufacturing plant in Vietnam—a country that may follow a communist social philosophy but is heavily influence by a centuries-old Confucian philosophy that emphasizes consensus and places a premium on harmony. After all, lighting incense at a family shrine is as much a part of contemporary Vietnamese life as watching videos or attending local Communist Party meetings.

"My contact proudly boasted of his Communist Party affiliations but at the same time proclaimed himself a man of the 1990s, tuned into Western business ways. The negotiations seemed to drag on for months and it was impossible to find anyone prepared to make a decision. I just put it down to communist inefficiency," says the banker. "I began losing patience. They didn't seem to understand that this deal could mean a lot of money for their factory, for my bank and for me. I was shouting trying to make my point. I banged my fist. I was out of control. Days later the Vietnamese broke off the talks and suggested I leave. Typical communists, I thought. They just don't get it."

But it wasn't communism or even third world inefficiency that sabotaged the mission. It was the failure to fully understand the influence of Confucian thought on Vietnamese perceptions. Decision making is slow in Vietnam partially because Confucian beliefs dictate decision by consensus. Adversity—and contract talks— is faced with calm and patience. Lastly, the Vietnamese have little respect for anyone who loses patience (the German banker's first mistake) or appears selfish (banker mistake number two—by highlighting how much money he could make from the deal). A little more homework and understanding of the cultural context in which the banker was dealing and the deal might have been saved.

CULTURE CAUTION: The Vietnamese, like other communist and post-communist societies, have little understanding of the capitalist concept that buyers and investors are in a more powerful position than sellers and those seeking capital.

CONFLICTING ATTITUDES

Obviously, cultural values have an enormous impact on the way business is conducted. Two of the most basic value differences to be considered are whether a culture emphasizes individualism, like the United States, or collectivism like China, and whether societies are task-driven—like the United States or Canada— or relationship-driven—like Latin America. (Individualist and collectivist societies are discussed in more detail in Chapter Two.)

The cultural values that are manifested in daily life are not only reflected in business but are sometimes exaggerated. Failing to understand the cultural basics can translate into a deal killer even before the negotiations begin. Often visitors will be left scratching their heads as to why things have fallen apart.

A talented young Canadian representative of a consumer products company ran into just such a situation in China. Keen to make his mark, the Canadian was sent to Shanghai by his company to begin talks about setting up a sales and manufacturing distribution network in China. The investment was worth hundreds of millions of dollars. In their initial correspondence, the Chinese appeared eager to participate. A group of high-level executives visited the Canadian company's headquarters and were warmly feted by the CEO and senior management. The mistake came when they assigned the young executive to travel to China to hammer out the details.

"I could tell by their written correspondence that they were eager to do business and when I arrived I was treated like royalty," the Canadian says, "but a few days into the trip, their attitude seemed to turn cold. They began treating me like just another foreign nuisance. The difference in their attitude was night and day between their visit to Canada and my visit to China. I just didn't understand it." The mystery was solved when a group of concerned Chinese middle managers took the visitor aside and explained. They told him that despite his qualifications, the senior management of the Chinese firm believed he was simply too young to do such important business. "They explained that in Chinese culture, age and experience are highly valued and Chinese business leaders look down on young negotiators. They cannot take them seriously. They said, that because I was the one chosen to come to China—someone so young—that our home office somehow had devalued the deal and the relationship."

The damage was repaired and the deal salvaged when headquarters flew a more senior—and older—executive to China to act as a front for the business and to deal with senior Chinese executives. The younger executive still ran the show on a day-to-day basis but kept a lower profile.

CULTURE CAUTION: This example illustrates how a lack of understanding on both sides can cause confusion. The Chinese must also understand that Western culture is based in meritocracy and that young executives in the West are given far more training and responsibility than their Chinese counterparts.

Other Key Components

Familiarity with these other basic building blocks of culture can provide insight into what to expect at the negotiating table as well as in relationships with foreign colleagues or partners. Each piece contributes to the whole that is a national or regional culture. Many of the most obvious clues can simply be discovered by reading some history, current publications, and through general observation. Some of the best lessons about cultural mindset are available free—on the street— if only you train yourself to observe and then put these observations into the proper context.

MANNERS AND CUSTOMS

Basic rules of etiquette, how much physical contact is acceptable, how much physical space do people expect, how formal are greetings—clues to all these manifestations of a national cultural mindset are available the minute you step off an airplane in a different country.

THE ARTS

Drama, music, literature and architecture are all manifestations of a cultural mindset that can provide insight into the thought patterns of a society and, in turn, of an individual that you might be dealing with. Clues to evolving attitudes and tolerance levels can often be found in current pop culture.

CULTURE CAUTION: Don't make the mistake that some people do by trying to figure out American or Indian cultures simply by reading books and watching movies. The entertainment industry does not always reflect reality.

EDUCATION

Some cultures place greater value on formal education than others. Understanding this attitude and tailoring a presentation or even designing a business card (listing academic qualifications and higher degrees) can win instant respect. However, if you boast of such qualifications in a business culture that cares little for such credentials, you run the risk of being labeled a pretentious windbag. Understanding how a society values education can also help determine how a business partner processes information and how you might need to construct a presentation or sales pitch. A company from a society that values education is also likely to be interested in the type of special training a foreign business can offer.

HUMOR

Some societies are simply more lighthearted than others and have a larger capacity for humor. Clues to the length of the national funnybone are often reflected in local advertising campaigns and the media. For example, British television is laden with situation comedies whereas this genre is relatively sparse on German airwaves. Cultural Indicator—the British may appreciate a touch of levity in their business dealings. Germans believe business is far too serious a matter for humorous asides.

SOCIAL ORGANIZATIONS

The formality of government, the basic organizational chart of a corporation, the propensity for individuals to join groups and how these groups are led can reveal much about a culture's decision making process. These in turn can give you insight into how you can expect business decisions to be made and how much autonomy your counterpart may have in negotiations. A highly structured culture usually means longer decision time and less autonomy for a negotiator.

Do Cultures Evolve?

A society's culture is far from stagnant; rather, it is forever evolving and re-inventing itself. While certain cultural traditions may remain constant, a society's tolerance level and the application of deep-seated, long-standing beliefs do change. What was forbidden in a society a decade ago may be accepted practice and the norm now. Perhaps the most sweeping and rapid change in business culture attitudes to take place this century is currently under way in Russia. Meanwhile, in Japan, there are increasing signs of change in attitudes and traditions concerning business and employment that have been hallmarks of the society for centuries.

THE MOSCOW MORPH

In Russia, only a few years ago, the central government *was* business. It owned everything from armaments factories to retail stores. Now, the sale (some would contend, giveaway) of the century is almost done. More than 120,000 state-owned enterprises have been privatized, including 75 percent of manufacturing firms and 85 percent of wholesale and retail trade. New millionaires have been created along with a new class of poor Russians.

Today, the "you eat what you kill" attitude of Russia's new market economy, coupled with the frontier mentality prevalent in major cities that says anything goes, especially in money and sex, is essentially contrary to previous mores under communist rule. By 1991, virtually overnight, the social order of the past 70 years in Russia vanished. What were previously crimes—economic speculation and private ownership of property—are now virtues. The ability to think and act independently, traits that even ancient Russians shunned, are now the essence of not only success but survival. It is difficult to find a foreign businessperson who has not experienced difficulty in doing business in Russia. The confusion and the chaos of the basic cultural transformation that dominates Russia today may not necessarily mean that Russians are bad at private enterprise, just that they are new to it.

Those involved in commerce are the new elite, replacing the coddled and heavily subsidized intellectuals, the "haves" of previous eras. The writer, the professor, and the thinker led a charmed life of special shops with imported goods, summer dachas and high respect in Soviet society as in earlier Russian society. Today, these people are near the bottom of the social heap.

"What is happening in Russia is well beyond a change in economic or market systems. It is a change in the very fabric of what defined the Russian character and Russian culture," says an Italian businesswoman who has resided in Moscow since the early 1970s. "This is an all-out assault on the culture, even on the language, on perceptions of such basic concepts as good and evil. The Russian value system has changed; formal education—unless it is an MBA from some European university—used to be a ticket to respect and even relative material wealth. Now the admired aren't writers or dancers, they are the businessmen," she says.

"The Russian culture that I studied and lived with for several decades has vanished. To be honest Moscow is getting to be pretty much the same as any other big European city, right down to the McDonald's."

IN JAPAN, TOO, "THE TIMES THEY ARE A-CHANGIN'"

No country today is immune from the fallout of the globalization of the world's economy. In Japan, a country whose business foundations rest on the principle of *giri ninjo*—a sense of honor, loyalty and empathy—the approach to business and employment is showing signs of creeping Western, or rather global, values. One of the hottest management buzzwords in Japan is "ability-ism." No longer will workers be promoted solely according to longevity or seniority or age (the latter being a reflection of the country's Confucian respect for the elderly). Rather, promotions and salaries in many businesses and industries are to be based on merit and skill. While this has long been the norm in capitalist countries outside of Asia, it is truly a new and radical development in Japan.

Another sign of change: the demise of the small retail shop. Such stores—Japan with half the population of the United States has twice as many retail shops—are the backbone of the economic structure. Although they are inefficient and charge relatively high prices, Japanese consumers have long supported local shops, even in the purchase of big-ticket consumer goods like stoves and refrigerators, out of their sense of giri ninjo. Now, even that is beginning to change, with more and more Japanese turning to new superstores, large retail outlets (a concept imported from the United States and Europe) that sell at discount prices. The result has been the closure of a large number of small retail stores. A more subtle sign of the changing times is the growing reluctance of younger Japanese workers to wear the corporate pins that once proudly identified their place of work and their loyalty. This reluctance signifies how younger workers are beginning to distance themselves from the traditions of their elders, at least as far as employment expectations are concerned. At least three of Japan's best-known companies— Bank of Tokyo, Mitsui, and Mitsubishi—have stopped issuing the pins altogether or no longer require them as part of the corporate uniform.

Since the end of World War II the Japanese have been stereotyped world-wide as workaholics, devoted to job and company. That, too, is beginning to change. A 1998 survey by the Dentsu Institute on Human Studies found that compared to other Asian cultures, Japanese workers are far less work-obsessed than, say, the Chinese or the Thais. Only 28 percent of Japanese workers said "they live for work" but 74 percent of workers in China, 70 percent in Thailand, 49 percent in Indonesia, and 48 percent in India replied that they indeed are toil obsessed and "live for work."

"We are witnessing some very subtle but fundamental shifts in Japanese work and business culture," says an American business executive who travels frequently to Japan. "Don't get me wrong, the business cultures are still miles apart but the need to be competitive on a global scale is truly affecting businesses and business culture here. Government regulation can no longer protect Japanese businesses as it used to. Forcing these firms to compete means they have to have a viable cost structure. Companies can no longer carry inefficient employees and reward those that are not the most productive. Many Japanese are sorry to see this practice go, but they also realize it is the way of the world now and Japan is part of it."

A COUNTER POINT

Do people exaggerate the impact of cultural differences when it comes to making an international business deal? Is this the classic consultant's scam— invent a problem that doesn't exist, create paranoia within the business community by emphasizing the impact on the bottom line and then earn a fortune consulting the paranoid out of harm's way?

When it comes to international business, cultural differences can often be the universal fallback excuse. The danger does exist that companies and individuals will not look beyond the excuse of "cultural differences" to discover the true root of failure. A European business consultant tells the story of an Asian manufacturer that opened a small consumer electronics plant in Eastern Europe. The Asian expatriate manager of the plant lasted a year before being transferred because of poor quality and low productivity. "The manager explained his problems by saying the Asian and Eastern European cultures and work ethics were simply too different. The workers didn't understand the company's message and policies," says the consultant. The truth was that this manager did an awful job of communicating policy and showed little respect for the workers themselves. There was quite simply a failure to communicate—period. This was not a failure to communicate across cultures. This manager would have failed even if the plant had been populated by people all of the same nationality and cultural background working in their home country. This manager was not a bad cross-cultural manager; he would have been a bad manager in any culture.

THE PROOF

The Asian manager's replacement, also an expatriate from the company's home country, had the plant up and running at impressive production and quality rates within 18 months. Indeed, there is a body of evidence that suggests people often do subconsciously look for and then exaggerate cultural differences. Often when we view the behavior from someone within our own culture we attach no great significance to it, but if we see the exact same behavior from someone from another culture we somehow apply profound cultural differences to explain it.

Just as being willing to blame cultural differences for all of one's international business problems is ridiculous, so is the other extreme in denying that real and profound cultural differences do not exist and do not have any impact on global business transactions. The cultural differences are indeed very real. Ignore them and you take a great risk. Exaggerate the differences, and the result will be equally risky.

Coping with Another Culture

One British journalist covering Africa in the late 1970s and early 1980s had a simple mantra for coping with and surviving the myriad of cultural differences found on that continent: "Never show fear—and speak the local language." WAWA, or West Africa Wins Again, was another pet phrase that seemed applicable when in a country like Nigeria, where few things seemed to run right. If your flight was canceled days earlier and no one at the airline bothered to tell you, repeating WAWA was essential in accepting differences in culture and avoiding a fight. Accept it—and learn from the experience.

Too often people emphasize the differences rather than the similarities in cultures and view these differences as threatening and negative rather than as opportunities for creative solutions. It is an easy trap to fall into. Remember, anyone can cope successfully with cross-cultural relationships with the proper mindset. All you have to do is change your mental computer disk and reprogram yourself.

CULTURE CAUTION: Relating to the example above, naturally it is the duty of the Nigerian government to make an effort to remedy the inefficiencies of their society if they wish to attract foreign investment and capital. They cannot afford a WAWA attitude in the long term.

Religion and Islamic Banking

After centuries of hibernation, Islamic banking has re-emerged in recent years and has gained increasing acceptance in the Middle East and parts of Asia. It is one of the few areas of international commerce where a religious philosophy actually dictates the terms of the business relationship. Islamic banks now handle more than $100 billion in assets worldwide and asset growth at Islamic banking institutions has been well over 10 percent per year in the 1990s. Even some large Western banks such as America's Citibank now have Islamic branches.

Islamic financial products and services are based on profit-sharing principles so as not to break the Islamic prohibition on *riba*, or usury. The essential feature

A Checklist for Coping

Differences exist. Accept that and move on. Priorities and perceptions differ between cultures. What you deem as a reasonable or logical reaction to an event may seem quite the opposite to someone from another culture. What seems like an important detail to you may be considered minor by another.

- Fear and lack of confidence are common feelings when an individual is introduced to a different culture. Do not let these feelings dictate the outcome of your business. Work to overcome them.
- The discomfort you may feel in dealing with an individual from a different cultural environment is often mutual. Don't assume that the other person is at ease and on top of things.
- Change your expectations. You may have to raise or lower them depending on the circumstances. Cross-cultural relationships by their very nature are complicated. Progress is in direct proportion to the similarity of the cultures.
- Keep an open mind. Not everything your culture does is the best or most efficient.
- Don't neglect to do some formal study of a new culture to increase your understanding. Language is important but personal experience is still the best way to learn about any culture.
- Cultural awareness is an ongoing learning experience. You can't learn everything in a day, a week or even a year.
- Expect to be viewed stereotypically—at least initially—and expect to encounter stereotypes; they often possess some validity or they wouldn't exist. But try and judge people on an individual basis. There are, after all, zany Germans, reserved Americans and ill-bred Britons. Look out for the exception to the stereotype.

of Islamic banking is that the payment of interest is forbidden by the Koran, the Islamic holy book. In general, Islamic law requires that risks should be shared between the financier and the entrepreneur. Islamic scholars argue that the concept of Islamic banking contributes to a more equitable distribution of income and wealth, and increased participation in the economy by common people. Islamic banks do not pay regular predetermined interest to depositors nor do they charge predetermined interest rates to borrowers. Rather, the banks take a share of the profits (or losses) which are again shared with depositors. What makes profit sharing, unlike interest, permissible in Islam is that only the profit-sharing ratio, not the rate of return itself, is predetermined.

ECONOMIC ORDER

The concept of Islamic banking is part of what Middle Eastern scholars call the Islamic Economic Order which is based solely on the teachings of the Koran. It strives to build a society based on social justice, equity, and moderation. All activities must conform to Shariah—the Islamic legal code. Under Shariah, all resources available to humans must be put to optimum use, and no one—not even the government—has the right to hoard them, waste them or let them lay idle.

Islamic banking relies on four basic techniques to keep economies and commerce moving: Murabaha, Musharaka, Ijara and Mudaraba.

The most common is *Murabaha*, which is basic cost-plus financing. It involves a three-party contract between the bank, its client and a purchaser for the sale of goods with a profit margin agreed upon by all parties. Most Islamic banking operations are based on Murabaha.

Musharaka is simply a partnership deal in which all parties contribute toward financing while profits and losses are shared according to equity input.

Ijara is a leasing agreement in which the bank buys or leases equipment or other assets to the business owner for a fee.

Mudaraba is an agreement between two parties in which one party provides 100 percent of the capital and the other party manages the venture. Profits are distributed according to a pre-set ratio. Losses are borne only by the lender.

THE RULES OF ISLAMIC BANKING

The rules regarding Islamic finance are quite simple and can be summed up as follows:

- Any predetermined payment over and above the actual amount of principal is prohibited.

- The lender must share in the profits or losses arising out of the enterprise for which the money was lent. Islam encourages Moslems to invest their money and to become partners in order to share profits and losses in the business instead of becoming creditors. Translated into banking terms, the depositor, the bank and the borrower should all share the risks and the rewards of financing business ventures. This is unlike the interest-based commercial banking system, where all the pressure is on the borrower.

- Making money from money is not acceptable in Islam. Money is only a medium of exchange, has no value in itself, and therefore should not be allowed to give rise to more money, via fixed interest payments. The human effort, initiative, and risk involved in a productive venture are more important than the money used to finance it.

- *Gharar* (speculation or unnecessary risk) is prohibited. Under this prohibition any transaction entered into should have only those risks associated with normal business development. Contracting parties should have perfect knowledge of the counter values intended to be exchanged as a result of their transactions.

- Investments should only support practices or products that are not forbidden by the Koran. For example, no Islamic bank would finance a brewery or a casino.

CHAPTER 2

Basic Cultural Types

THE GREAT LAW OF CULTURE: LET EACH BECOME ALL

THAT HE WAS CREATED CAPABLE OF BEING.

— THOMAS CARLYLE

HOW PEOPLE AND cultures define themselves has a great impact on their business practices. Consider the case of Japan, where group goals and needs are almost always placed ahead of those of the individual. In Japan, the classic American hero—the self-made man or woman who blissfully and boastfully looks out for "number one"—is hardly an ideal. There the individual gives way to the group. Decisions are made on a consensus basis and group harmony is the desideratum—to the point that even when visitors are thought to be dead wrong, the Japanese will never tell them that they are. The Dutch researcher and business consultant, Geert Hofstede, has developed a useful framework that illustrates the four major issues that define and classify national cultures. Each issue ultimately has a very real effect on how people process information and interact, either personally or with business colleagues.

One: Individualism versus Collectivism

Does a society cherish rugged individualism, the independent thinker, the person who values personal success over group success? Or does it function in an orderly fashion only when individuals cede their needs to those of the group? The values that a society embraces will determine how an individual defines himself or herself—as free agent or as a member of a group, organization or company. Determine the answer to this most basic of questions about a society's cultural values and you will obtain a  valuable clue as to how to proceed in successfully concluding a business negotiation and managing a business relationship in the future.

Societies that rely on a collectivist mind-set value conformity and seek to control the behavior of the individual through external sanction—shame or expulsion from the group. The expressions "the nail that sticks up is pounded down," long associated with Japanese society, and "the highest blade of grass is always the first to be cut" that governed the attitude of the "have-nots" in the former Soviet Union are valid reflections of collectivist societal attitudes. Both express society's intolerance of the placement of personal success over that of the group. Though group pressure controls behavior in collectivist societies, control in individualist-oriented cultures depends on self-generated sanction, namely, guilt.

The practical implications of this contrast between the group and the individual are clear for business. While decision making in an individualist culture may be more rapid, the implementation of a change in policy, such as a new manufacturing process or a new company ethics code, will be perceptibly slower than in a collectivist culture. The reason: in a society that values individualism, workers will question the new method and probably not sign on until they figure out how it will directly impact them as individuals. It may take longer to come to a consensus in a collectivist environment but once the decision is made, implementation is generally quicker. The individual's ceding of self-interest to the group and identifying and defining himself or herself through the organization will not stop to ask "what's in it for me" and will in turn go along with what is best for the group with no, or at least very few, questions asked. The mind-set is that everyone else is going along so it is important for me to conform.

THE MONEY FLOWS UP

There are other subtle examples of how individualist versus collectivist thinking plays out in national business cultures. Take the example of attitudes toward executive compensation. The ratio of annual compensation for executives compared to line employees in the manufacturing sectors of highly individualistic cultures such as the United States and South Africa is far more disproportionate than in highly collectivist societies like Japan. In the United States executive pay is 28 times that of the average manufacturing worker and in South Africa it is 24 times. In Japan the top executive earns only about 10 times the average worker's pay. American executives measure their success through pay and perks; Japanese executives through the overall health of their company and the contentment of employees. The Japanese concept of the role of the company chief executive dates back to the days of the shogun who did not directly engage in commercial activity but rather encouraged underlings to do so. These rulers lived frugally and left the administration of their territories to their subordinates, just as the ideal Japanese CEO now leaves much of the day-to-day business affairs of his company to trusted managers. Individuals in a collectivist culture derive their status relative to others within the society and each person accepts the obligations that come from one's position in the hierarchy. To take monetary advantage of one's position would be shameful. This ancient social contract is the basis of most Japanese business organizations.

LOYALTY IS AS LOYALTY DOES

Most businesses in Arab societies—where the collectivist culture is dominant—place far greater value on the loyalty of employees than they do on efficiency.

One British consultant visiting a small family-owned Saudi Arabian lighting manufacturer investigating the possibility of becoming a public company was both impressed and exasperated by the family's devotion to the business's loyal employees.

"The company's ownership faced some hard choices if they wanted to go public and tap into overseas capital," the consultant said. "The workforce was terribly bloated and inefficient. Output and revenue per employee was embarrassingly low. When I explained this situation to the owners, they only shrugged. 'There is not much we can do. Most of our employees have been here for many years,' they said."

"They balked at the idea of layoffs and firings. Their solution: cut pay across the board and reduce everybody's hours. The workers understood. No one complained and many even thanked the owners for saving their jobs. I was stunned. I mean could you imagine that sort of idea flying with a German union or an American manufacturer?" The lesson learned: when dealing in a highly collectivized culture it may be wiser to trim the pay of all workers in a downturn rather than lay off individuals. The workers themselves may actually want it that way. The case is an excellent example of how a different cultural mind-set can present creative solutions to universal business problems. Multinational corporations and expatriate managers should take notice.

Two: Power-Distance

This cultural dimension describes how individuals within a society view power and, consequently, their role in decision making. In cultures with a low power-distance profile, individual employees will seek a role in decision-making and question decisions and orders in which they had no input. By contrast, high power-distance societies are such that employees seek no decision-making role. They accept the boss's decision simply because the boss is the boss and is supposed to give orders. Employees in high power-distance cultures need direction and discipline and they look to management to provide it. In low power-distance cultures, workers will accept more responsibility. Low power-distance cultures tend to be more individualistic in nature.

The practical implications for managers are straightforward: In high power-distance cultures, it may be impossible to micro-manage employees. But be prepared to defend decisions in low power-distance countries where workers will expect you to justify yourself and seek their input. In high power-distance cultures, managers can expect little personal initiative from employees. Any North American or Western European expatriate manager who has attempted to recruit or motivate a workforce in that bastion of high power-distance culture, Russia, will attest to the difficulty when a low and high power-distance culture clash. In fact the Russian verb "sidyet" (to sit) is still often used to describe the perfect job—one with no responsibility and no need for individual initiative.

THANKS, BUT NO THANKS

The reason behind the Russian worker's preference for shunning responsibility has little to do with an ingrained work ethic or character flaw but rather owes its prominence to the dominant culture of the past 70 years, namely, communism.

Russia's old command economy left decision making to a small cadre of high-ranking individuals in each government-run firm or ministry. Today, despite the move toward a market economy, responsibility has been slow to filter down to the rank and file. And, exhibiting the classic signs of a high power-distance culture, many employees simply don't want it.

"Once given a specific task or goal, many Russians will tackle it with bulldog determination," says the U.S. manager of a service industry firm in Moscow. "But it is up to the employer to show the Russian employee how his role or task is connected to the big picture and the future success of the company. Trying to involve employees in decisions so they feel they have a stake in the success and profitability of the company has been difficult. It is something they never had before. It may take some convincing of the employees to accept this type of responsibility and involvement but it will be worth the effort, I hope." One has to wonder, though, if the U.S. manager really understands that he is actually trying to change a fundamental of the culture rather than a simple workplace attitude.

There is another basic fact that an observer from a low power-distance culture needs to remember when visiting a high power-distance society—the element of status and formality in business proceedings is much more important in a high power-distance country. Because of this culture's ingrained respect for authority, a visitor's formal title and status within an organization count for much and are important to being taken seriously or even in winning an introduction.

CULTURE CAUTION: Even when characteristic of a national culture, such power relationships are not necessarily present to the same degree in every firm throughout the country.

Three: Uncertainty-Avoidance

A Swiss business colleague often told a joke that he said summed up the attitude of the Swiss toward uncertainty-avoidance. Buses and taxis taking visitors from Geneva's airport to town would repeatedly broadcast the following announcement: "Welcome to Switzerland. Have a good time and remember that in Switzerland everything that is not mandatory is forbidden." The tale explains why Switzerland ranks high on the list of countries with high uncertainty-avoidance which is a measure of a society's ability to tolerate ambiguity and uncertainty. While the Swiss are noted for being ambiguity-averse by nature, the neighboring Germans may be the ultimate kingpins of uncertainty-avoidance in Europe. The Germans so hate the idea of uncertainty that there is actually a set of laws (known as *notstandsgesetz*) which would come into force when all other national laws break down. Germans obviously know something about redundancy planning and how much their culture uses rules and dictated behavior to avoid any uncertainty.

The cultural dimension of uncertainty-avoidance is profoundly exhibited in the workplaces of all societies. Take Japan, for instance, where the high penchant for uncertainty-avoidance translates into a trade-off of individual freedom and mobility in exchange for a guarantee of lifetime employment. (Indeed, the recent recession has begun to erode this social contract to some extent, creating what some sociologists believe to be an increase in national anxiety linked directly to society's need to avoid uncertainty). Societies that have a low measure of uncertainty-avoidance generally value achievement over security, exhibit a less structured and more free-flowing style of management, and have fewer workplace rules than societies with a high measure of uncertainty-avoidance. As would be expected, countries that exhibit low measures of uncertainty-avoidance experience high rates of employment turnover and job mobility.

CHANGE IS A RISKY BUSINESS

The United States is the quintessential risk-taking society. This helps explain why U.S. executives might do little formal preparation in advance of a key meeting preferring to rely on wit, charm, acumen, and the ability to think on their feet to carry the day. It also explains why a Japanese executive will make painstaking preparation—down to a full dress rehearsal—for a similar meeting. While the Japanese may make a highly structured presentation, the American manager is more likely to be able to handle questions, interruptions, and agenda changes.

CULTURE CAUTION: Japanese companies have actually paid gangsters to help prevent interruptions at shareholder's meetings while U.S. executives pride themselves on being able to control the American version of these often chaotic meetings. The ability to handle risk and change has been cited as one reason why the West has, on the whole, been more economically successful than other regions.

The impact of uncertainty-avoidance can often be seen within a large multinational company that is introducing major changes in its work process. Quite simply the acceptance of change will vary considerably as will the need for employee assurances and explanations depending on the country's uncertainty-avoidance measure. Those working in high measure societies will tend to resist change and feel threatened by new ideas and processes.

"I couldn't believe it. It was like being in a time warp," explains one British accountant employed by a large multinational firm. "I walked into our Frankfurt office and its procedures were five years behind our London office. We knew there was some resistance to our new accounting rules but they were getting the work done in Frankfurt, albeit a little slowly. I wasn't prepared for their explanation though."

The manager of the German accounting department felt uncomfortable with the new system and ordered workers to keep two sets of accounts—one in the old system and one in the new. "He just said he was nervous and afraid that the new system wouldn't work and his staff had become anxious that they would be blamed for errors. His solution was to avoid the risk by keeping two sets of accounts. I found that extraordinary," the British accountant says.

ASSESSING RISK, ALLAYING FEARS

Negotiators and sales professionals from low uncertainty-avoidance cultures, dealing with executives from high-avoidance ones, need to alter their tactics and emphasis for the best results. High-avoidance people like to hear about a company's long-standing reputation, proven—not necessarily new—technology and solid financials, which indicate it will be around for years to come. Also, hearing details about the continuity of management and management style is reassuring for a high-avoidance executive to hear.

Of course, when you have to deal with cultures that thrive on risk, you will need to appeal to that aspect of their nature. Innovation, aggressive marketing, venture capital strategies are all topics that make up their daily business culture. The higher the risk, the greater the potential for profit. Everything that you would do to make uncertainty-avoidance types happy makes risk takers believe you are not on the "cutting edge" of business. Plan accordingly.

Four: Masculinity versus Femininity

This dimension speaks to both societal values and attitudes. Societies with supposedly "masculine" values appreciate aggressiveness and assertiveness while respecting the goal of material acquisition. The more "feminine" cultures value interpersonal relationships, put quality of life before material acquisition and actively express concern for the less fortunate.

The pace of business tends to be more pedestrian in cultures with a majority of feminine traits. Business hinges more on personal relationships—friends doing business with friends—rather than on pure efficiency and written contracts. Businesspeople from feminine cultures are often more reserved and less time-driven than those from masculine cultures where achievement—closing the deal, the next quarter's financial results—is more important than building a long-term relationship. In masculine cultures, success is the function of the individual and society is made up of leaders and followers. If you are a success—or a failure—it is the result of your own actions. Business is a more efficient process than in feminine societies and people plan on enjoying their retirement rather than the present working day.

Few societies have all masculine or all feminine traits. The concept is more that of a spectrum with a variety of mixes in between the two extremes. Governments can be a solid indicator of where a society lies on the masculine/feminine spectrum. A government that promotes a comprehensive social welfare system represents a highly feminine society that demonstrates concern for the downtrodden. As governments move away from higher taxes and welfare systems it could be said that they are exhibiting a more masculine approach to social responsibilities.

CULTURE CAUTION: While it should be obvious that the more successful economies are masculine in nature—or heading that way—it should not be construed as implying that only male government officials espouse a masculine economic agenda. A brief review of Margaret Thatcher's policies should dispel this notion.

Time: Polychronic versus Monochronic

Culture also dictates how individuals within a society process information, set priorities, manage time and interact with other individuals. Americans, for example, will refer to someone who is less than bright as an individual who "cannot walk and chew gum at the same time"—implying that someone who is unable to handle two tasks at once is deficient. Oddly enough, when you compare Americans to people from Asian cultures, it is the Americans who like to do things one at a time. Compare that attitude with a Chinese executive who can talk on the telephone, write a memo to a colleague and continue to listen to a visiting businessperson all at the same time without appearing to miss a beat. The Chinese are considered highly polychronic, that is, they can—and prefer to—do multiple tasks simultaneously.

To an individual from a monochronic society, time is used for ordering one's life, for setting priorities, for making a step-by-step list for doing things in sequence, for dealing with one individual at a time. Americans—and most Western societies—are monochronic. They believe in linear time that, because it is limited, must be used efficiently. They plan their work and work their plan.

Most polychronic societies believe that time is circular and therefore eternal. What does not get done in this life will be taken up in the next. Time is used to attempt to accomplish whatever presents itself in whatever order it appears. Efficiency is not as important as the process. Polychronic groups plan little and accomplish less.

A diplomat from Norway recalls how during a visit to Thailand he became offended by what he thought was a rude brush-off by a government official during an informal lunch at a rather posh restaurant.

"My counterpart's cell phone rang at least a half dozen times during the lunch and he engaged in several extended conversations. On one occasion, a man who introduced himself as the official's accountant came over to our table to discuss an outside business matter. It turns out he had been invited to drop by. Finally another business colleague of the official joined us for coffee. The invitation had been issued earlier in the day. I was offended. I really didn't think he had heard a word I said during the lunch," the diplomat says.

"It was only after several more trips to Thailand that I learned this is how the Thais handle their business affairs. I have to admit that in the end it seemed a pleasantly social if rather chaotic way to do business. But what amazed me the most was that after that first lunch, despite all the distractions, this man was able to restate my presentation almost verbatim. I was impressed."

CULTURE CAUTION: The reader should note that the behavior the diplomat received is not solely an indicator of how an Asian society approaches time usage. The same behavior is used to remind foreigners who is in control. It is also used in some South American societies for the same reason. Economic downturns in both regions and the accompanying exodus of foreign capital will presumably call for a reassessment of this form of cultural power play.

High-Context versus Low-Context

People from different cultures process and disseminate information differently. Low-context cultures are much more precise in their communication, providing mountains of detail, groping for the correct word or phrase to summarize an event. They assume a relatively low level of shared knowledge with the individual they are communicating with and thus feel a strong need to explain all in great detail. Low-context cultures, such as the United States, Britain and the Scandinavian countries focus more on what is being said, rather than on who is saying it. Body language, hand and facial gestures are secondary, if not entirely ignored, to the message itself. Business can be conducted successfully by letter, telephone, fax or e-mail in such cultures. It is not necessary to meet face-to-face with a colleague to get things done.

High-context cultures are the exact opposite. Communication tends to be imprecise and as much attention is paid to the person delivering the message as to the message itself. In high-context cultures—most of Latin America, Asia, the Middle East and Africa—personal encounters are essential before business can begin. These people need as much ancillary information as possible. They pay more attention to physical surroundings, how a business colleague is dressed or coiffured—the general ambiance of the negotiations—than individuals from low-context countries. Body language, facial gestures and voice inflection are important methods of communication. The physical surroundings for a meeting or a business meal are just as important as the substance of the discussion.

CULTURE CAUTION: Low-context business cultures tend to have strong legal frameworks for commercial transactions and rarely rely on personal interaction as the driving force behind a business deal. Legally binding contracts make for a more efficient use of time and an increase in the potential number of deals that can be transacted.

Relationship-Driven versus Task-Driven

This classification deals more with the business culture within a society but it does have application to societies as a whole. Cultures, especially in reference to business dealings, are either relationship-driven—which, under Hofstede's theory, would classify it as a feminine culture—or task-driven, the masculine side of Hofstede's theory. Knowing which side of the fence your potential business partner sits on, will allow you to prioritize your presentation and give you a fair estimate of the time frame needed for closing a potential deal.

Task-driven cultures are usually low-context cultures, while relationship-driven cultures are high-context ones. When giving a presentation to an individual from a task-driven culture, the main concerns will be price, quality and guarantees associated with a product or service. A sale can be closed on the first meeting. When presenting to people from a relationship-driven culture, you're doomed to failure unless you have established a personal relationship. The product could be the greatest thing since the invention of the wheel but until you are trusted, they won't want to hear about what you have to sell until you have sold yourself.

Conversely, attempting to rely solely on friendship in a task-driven society is of minimal use. While your friendship will not be rebuffed, your presentation and deal structure had better be organized and to the point.

Concepts of the Future

Every culture has an internal clock. For some it ticks loudly, urging action. For others, it ticks softly, being more a stage for performance than a motivator. Some people simply move through time; they are not controlled by it. How a culture views time and time horizons is critical in how business relationships are formed and contracts negotiated.

Some cultures place greater emphasis on "time past" than others, valuing the continuation of tradition and established practices (The Chinese are a good example of such cultures). Others, like Americans, live more in the present and have a view towards the future. Their time horizon is relatively short—like the next business quarter—and they plan for the immediate future rather than dwell on the past. They value speed over endurance.

Finally, there are those cultures that include in their view of time an expanded future orientation. The Japanese, for example, while valuing tradition, have a much longer time horizon and see themselves as travelling through an historical continuum. In business, they are willing to absorb short-term losses in exchange for long-term gains—and tend to move at a relatively slow pace. Often their business plans will include detailed long-term scenarios that play out over a decade. Time is the true test for business relationships and there is no way to quickly conquer the Japanese business world.

A CLASH OF CLOCKS

The practical implications of a clash of time horizons are clear. When a present-oriented company deals with a future-oriented concern, the conflicting time frames cause tension, a muddling of clear-cut objectives and a strategy that may work at cross-purposes. The more future-oriented negotiators may feel they are being pressured by the present-oriented team which not only prides itself on getting the deal done, but getting it done quickly.

"We were investigating getting involved in a joint fishing venture with a Japanese firm in the Russian Far East," says an executive from an Alaska-based fishing and canning company. "The Russian fleet was pretty rundown, barely seaworthy but with a little help we thought their boats would be a nice addition. We crunched the numbers and figured that with a few million in repairs and some time in dry-dock, we could have them out catching fish. Hell, the whole thing could turn a profit in a year or two." But the Japanese executives were thinking very differently than their American counterparts. "They said, 'What is the point in having to keep repairing these boats and never be sure how many can operate in any given year'. Christ, they wanted to build boats for the Russians. One Japanese executive told me, 'The fish have been in this ocean since before we arrived and they will be here long after we are gone. With new equipment this will be a very profitable operation in years to come, if we plan correctly'. He had a point. But their outlook on capital return was stretched out over a much longer horizon than mine. I can't say I agreed with that outlook, but I understood. In the end we walked away from the deal. My company just wasn't willing to wait a decade for the deal to be profitable. I understand they still aren't making money on the deal and that was four years ago."

CULTURE CAUTION: Not all of the Japanese approach to business deals is driven by their concept of time. The highly vaunted Japanese corporation paid very little for investment capital during the 1980s and early 1990s (less than 2 percent) while U.S. counterparts were paying over three times as much. The Japanese could wait three times as long to turn a profit. Patience is easy when the finance terms are right.

Promptness

One's philosophical view on the meaning of time translates into either an obsession with promptness (when was the last time you ever heard of a German businessman being late for a meeting?) or a much more relaxed and casual attitude towards punctuality (the Nigerian businessman who shows up on time probably got his schedule mixed up). As a general rule of thumb, societies that are monochronic value punctuality. Societies that are polychronic are very ambivalent about promptness. Punctuality is valued only when it serves the polychronic's purpose—as on payday. For all professionals in any culture, however, punctuality is the best recommendation.

CULTURE CAUTION: Some individuals and societies believe that "power makes you wait" and use tardiness as a means to show who is in charge of the proceedings. This can only be used from a buying or investing position. Sellers that are late usually arrive to find an empty room.

Time Passages

SOME EXAMPLES OF GLOBAL FLEXTIME

- When South Africans are asked to do something they are likely to give one of two responses which, while sounding similar, are as different as night and day. One is "I will do it now-now" the other is "I will do it just now." "Now-now" carries a sense of immediacy and it means a task has been given top priority. "Just now" is the South African equivalent of *mañana*. It means that a task is of low priority and it will get done at some unspecified time in the future. However, if the truth be told, there is no guarantee it will get done at all.

- If you ask an Israeli employee if he or she has completed an assigned task you are likely to hear *Yihiyeh b'seder,* which loosely translated means "not to worry, everything is fine." The expression probably means the task has yet to be started. Only in a crisis does time take on serious meaning for most Israelis.

- Kenyans have a similar expression which reveals a highly relaxed attitude toward time. When you hear the expression *hakuna matata* (Swahili for "no problem") do not expect anything to happen too soon.

- Indonesians have a term for their flexible attitude toward time that virtually makes it impossible to be late because no one ever expects you to arrive anywhere near the appointed time anyway. *Jam karet* literally means "rubber time."

- In France, time is a flexible concept. The French see time more as a gift to be used for many things—preferably all at once. They rarely identify themselves with their job and believe that personal time is by far the most valuable. Long lunches and long vacations are the norm, not the exception.

Profiling Your Foreign Partner

Building a basic cultural profile of your potential business partner can help you better anticipate and understand potential differences. Perhaps his or her behavior will not seem so strange if you have at least some idea of what to expect and why. Then you can turn all those potential negatives into positives and deal from a position of strength and knowledge. Among the questions you need to ask:

YOUR PARTNER'S HOME CULTURE:

- Do they follow a particular religious philosophy that spills over into the business culture?

- Does the society put much stock in non-verbal communication, such as body language and facial expressions? Are you aware of the potential negative signals your body language can send?

- Do they value formal education? Should you make them aware of your own educational background?

- Do they value a sense of humor or is business considered too serious a matter to make light of?

- Does the culture appreciate independent thinking or is the status of the group more important?

- Do they have high respect for authority?

- Do they prefer a more rigid structure and value security over individual achievement?

- Does the culture value material acquisition or is the collective welfare of the group a priority?

- Will they stick to a schedule or use time simply as a rough framework?

- Will they expect highly precise communication loaded with detail that leaves little room for doubt?

- What kind of time horizon will they have when it comes to business?

- Is it a meritocracy or an age hierarchy?

MANNERS AND CUSTOMS:

- How formal are greeting procedures?

- Is there much physical contact at the start and end of meetings?

- How much physical space is required? Will your contact be in your face or keep a distance?

- What level of eye contact is appropriate?

- Will socializing be considered part of all business dealings?

- Is the exchange of gifts part of standard business protocol?

Cross-Cultural Success Tips

- **SHOW EMPATHY** Try walking a mile in their shoes. It will make you more tolerant of their view and also reveal just how much your own cultural background influences your perceptions and view of ideal social interactions.

- **BE FLEXIBLE** Not all Europeans are the same, nor are all Africans, or all Asians. Not only do cultures vary dramatically within a single geographic region, they may be wildly different within regions of a single country. Be ready to adapt.

- **MANAGE YOUR RESPONSES** It is far easier to manage your responses than to change those of others.

- **DON'T GO NATIVE** Going native, becoming "one of them," can damage your image and make you look silly. Be proud of your own cultural identity but by the same token don't shove it down anyone's throat, either.

- **RESPECT LOCAL CUSTOMS** Making jokes or light of any aspect of local practices or traditions is a sure way to offend your hosts.

- **BE AWARE OF NON-VERBAL COMMUNICATION** With a language barrier, picking up on non-verbal forms of communication may be your only direct way to assess your partner.

- **DEVELOP TRUST BY COMBATING MISTRUST** When cultures collide there is an inordinate amount of mistrust between parties, at least initially. Take the initiative to break down that barrier. Reassure your partners that you have trust in them. (But don't be so foolish as to reveal important matters until a mutual trust has been established.)

- **BECOME INVOLVED** Be it a dinner, an opera, a ball game or a drink at the bar, participate, even if you have to force yourself. Try the chopsticks, the fried dog, the Coney Island hot dog, the chili, the chilled vodka. Don't drift off to the sidelines. It will be perceived as a snub of the home culture and a sign that you are feeling quite superior.

CULTURE CAUTION: While it is certainly wise to meet your counterparts, you should not feel obligated to participate in activities that might violate your personal moral codes or endanger your health. If you must decline, do so respectfully.

CHAPTER 3

The Impact of Culture

THE PERPETUAL OBSTACLE TO HUMAN ADVANCEMENT

IS CUSTOM. — JOHN STUART MILL

SO YOU HAVE DONE all your homework on a particular culture and you feel that you have your counterparts and their culture figured out? You are confident that you know what they think, how they act and even what they like to eat. Yet, when you arrive to meet them you find that they fit very few of the cultural stereotypes that you have uncovered in your research. In some ways they are like what you expected and in other respects they are almost polar opposites. The reason for this discrepancy is that within any culture there are regional differences that can be as dramatic as those between nations.

Regional Differences

Too often, even internationally savvy businesspeople forget to take the concept of regional differences into consideration. They have a broad understanding of a national culture but fail to take account of the subtle—and often not-so-subtle—differences within a national culture. Often, these differences go well beyond the superficial aspects of cuisine and etiquette. Language is one obvious area of regional difference but it often extends to whole approaches to philosophy, time, religion and business. Failure to be aware of these differences can be costly.

SOME REGIONAL DIFFERENCES THAT ARE OFTEN OVERLOOKED

- **THE UNITED STATES** The world loves to stereotype Americans, but the type of composite picture it comes up with—materialistic, aggressive, violent, superficial and insincere—tends to describe an urbanite rather than someone who lives in a rural area. The attitudes, industries, accents and foods of America's four basic regions (Northeast, South, Midwest and West) vary by geography, climate as well as the history and culture of those who settled these regions. Business can be conducted in a very different manner and pace depending on where you are. Almost 150 years after the American Civil War, there remains a distrust between North and South and even rampant prejudice based on such superficial regional cultural traits as an accent. Northern Yankees still look down upon Southerners as "hicks and good ol' boys." As the cultural epicenter has moved west, wealthy Californians consider the Eastern seaboard to be "the old country."

- **CANADA** The rift between Canada's English and French cultures is often underestimated by non-Canadians and requires great sensitivity so as not to offend. The dominant culture in Québec is, of course, French, and the use of the French language in all correspondence with companies in this region is virtually mandatory to avoid insult. The difference between Ontario and the Yukon is enormous. Whatever you do, don't typecast Canadians as ersatz Americans.

- **EASTERN EUROPE** Often it seems that businesspeople from developed economies view the former Soviet bloc nations of Eastern Europe as virtually homogeneous—which can be a fatal error. In fact, Europe is really now divided into Western Europe, Central or Middle Europe (Poland, Hungary, the Czech Republic, Slovakia, the former Yugoslavia) and the true "Eastern European" nations of Russia, Bulgaria, Romania, and Albania. Also, the Baltic nations of Latvia, Lithuania, and Estonia are very different from their neighbors to the west. Business attitudes vary greatly as do the views on everything from religion to politics to materialism.

- **RUSSIA/CIS** Confederation of Independent States: The most common error in dealing with the 15 countries that once made up the Soviet Union is the attempt to speak Russian everywhere. Speaking Russian, a language viewed as that of the oppressor, will get you nothing but a cold shoulder and snub in Ukraine, for example. Former Soviet republics like Uzbekistan and Kazakhstan more closely resemble their Moslem neighbors to the south than they do the Europeans of Russia. Moldavia views itself as more Romanian than Russian. Also, the Russian Far East is much more Asian than European and functions as virtually an independent nation. It is more familiar with business overtures from Japan, South Korea, and China than it is from those of Germany or the United States.

- **BELGIUM** Few foreign businesspeople seem to realize that Belgium is home to the Flemish people in the north (about 5.7 million) and the French-speaking Walloons (about 3.1 million) in the south. This split dates back centuries to when the tribes inhabiting the country split into Roman and Germanic camps. French became the language of the educated "upper crust" and Flemish, which is similar to Dutch and Afrikaans, became the language of the peasants. When doing business in Belgium, it is important to ensure that all non-English business correspondence is targeted in the proper language. It is no accident that this nation of polyglots is home to the government of the European Union.

■ SWITZERLAND This is a country with three fairly distinct cultures, divided between the French-, Italian- and German-speaking Swiss. The regional differences are profound and any one of the three languages may be used in doing business.

The Value of Cultural Stereotypes

Culture dictates how people generally think and interact with each other in society. A stereotype is really a composite of the cultural mores of a society and in many cases can be narrowed to a specific region. To stereotype is to formulate a standardized image of a group that assigns that group a number of characteristics that helps to simplify what would otherwise be a very complex task of identification. By looking at the cultural components and traits, an accurate model—a stereotype, if you will—of how an individual from a certain culture is likely to act can be constructed. Stereotyping makes reality easier to deal with.

Of course, there will be exceptions to the stereotype rule—people are, after all, individuals—but by and large a businessperson from Japan or Germany is more likely to conform to the model than not. The key is to avoid a slavish adherence to stereotypes and to leave room to evaluate individual behavior in an overall cultural context. There are, of course, independent-minded Japanese, rebellious Germans, shallow Russians and task-driven (as opposed to relationship-driven) Arabs—but these would truly be exceptions and when seen in their native cultural context might very well be viewed as rebels in their own right.

As a general rule, stereotyping of cultural traits works when applied to large groups, even whole societies, but may not stand up on an individual one-to-one basis. It is important to remember that you, too, will likely be viewed or profiled by others according to their stereotypes of your culture. If you stop to think about it, you may be surprised about the high number of national cultural traits that you exhibit. Accent the more endearing traits and try and leave the less unacceptable ones at home.

CULTURE CAUTION: It is always fair to use someone's stereotyping of you as a negotiating tactic, but be aware that the same tactic may work in reverse.

Sensible Stereotypes

Not all stereotypes are negative; in fact, forming cultural stereotypes is a kind of shorthand for helping an individual deal with the complexities of another culture. And—you can probably already hear the howls from the adherents of political correctness—they do have some basis in fact. Stereotypes do evolve and can help us trace the evolution of cultures—both the one being stereotyped and the one forming the stereotype.

An example would be the way the Japanese have been viewed by most Western nations. Prior to the 1930s, they were seen as mysterious, quaint, and backward. Then as WWII approached, they became fanatic evil conquerors out to dominate the world. In the Cold War era, they were stalwart anti-communist allies in Asia. Then in the late 1960s, 1970s, and 1980s, they were considered a nation of superefficient workers, a global success story and a dangerous competitor to American interests. Finally, by the late 1990s, with the country in the throes of a major recession, and an economy plagued by an outmoded way of doing business, the Japanese executive became a person to be pitied rather than feared as a competitor. Nowadays, it is viewed as a culture suffering from a self-inflicted decline.

While it is important to make individual judgments about your business partners, it is also important to remember that cultural stereotypes will play a valuable role in forming your judgments. To an English manager, an Italian businessman may seem disorganized, chaotic and more concerned about forming personal friendships than in doing business. But to a Spanish or a Greek business partner it would all seem perfectly normal, since their societies share the same basic cultural traits. And it is these cultural traits that give the stereotype a certain degree of validity. There is a reason that Germans act like Germans and Americans like Americans—they are reflections of their own cultural values and societal pressures. In many ways, we all see whatever part of that reflection best fits our expectations.

The Cause of Stereotypes

Stereotypes make more sense when you consider the cultural roots of the group being stereotyped. For example:

NATIONALITY: GERMAN

STEREOTYPE: The Germans are usually seen as rigid, somewhat humorless and obsessed with order and formality. A smile does not come easily and business is taken seriously. They are particularly focused on detail.

NATIONAL CULTURAL TRAITS: Low-context culture that values precise communication. Focuses on what is being said rather than who is saying it. Monochronic, that is, they have a very linear concept of time and prefer to do one thing at a time. The German culture is one of very high risk-avoidance.

NATIONALITY: AMERICAN

STEREOTYPE: Brash, materialistic. A cowboy culture where individuals are obsessed with time and deadlines. A society plagued by crime and violence.

NATIONAL CULTURAL TRAITS: American culture is task-driven and places great value on individual achievement and thinking. Monochronic, with a very low risk-avoidance, which allows Americans to speak without thinking—and often act without thinking, sometimes in a violent manner. It is a very masculine culture, which means that society appreciates assertiveness while respecting the goal of material acquisition.

NATIONALITY: JAPANESE

STEREOTYPE: Very group-oriented. Quiet, shy, reserved and highly respectful of status and position. Negotiates in groups or teams and avoids criticism of partners or proposals. Japanese will work their whole career at a single company.

NATIONAL CULTURAL TRAITS: The Japanese culture is collectivist by nature, that is, group achievement and harmony comes before that of individual fulfillment. It is a high power-distance culture where workers do not seek personal decision-making powers. It is high risk-avoidance.

NATIONALITY: FRENCH

STEREOTYPE: Romantic, fond of good food, good art, and not overly concerned about doing great business. More eager to argue politics and art than to do business.

NATIONAL CULTURAL TRAITS: A highly feminine culture which values interpersonal relationships, putting quality of life before material acquisition and applauds concern for other individuals. Also high-context, which means that the medium is the message and not overly concerned about precise detail or communication.

NATIONALITY: ITALIAN

STEREOTYPE: Excitable and seem to relish chaos. Not very detail-oriented when it comes to business, which seems to take forever to conclude. They are romantic and seem to shake hands with and kiss visitors forever. Very demonstrative and physical.

NATIONAL CULTURAL TRAITS: Italians are polychronic which means they prefer to do several tasks at one time in no particular order. Their concept of time is non-linear. It is also a high-context, relationship-driven culture.

NATIONALITY: BRITISH

STEREOTYPE: Stuffy, prim and proper. Business is done through an "old boy's network."

NATIONAL CULTURAL TRAITS: Low-context, low risk-avoidance, monochronic, mixture of relationship-driven and task-driven cultures.

NATIONALITY: CHINESE

STEREOTYPE: Like the Japanese, they always seem to travel in groups. They are quiet, reserved and never lose their temper. But at times they can seem chaotic and unfocused.

NATIONAL CULTURAL TRAITS: The Buddhist philosophy plays an important role in business dealings and the approach to life. It is a collectivist, high-context, polychronic culture.

NATIONALITY: NIGERIAN

STEREOTYPE: Gregarious, outgoing and eager to please. Seem never to say "no" and enjoy physical contact but are never on time for anything. Great schemers.

NATIONAL CULTURAL TRAITS: A polychronic, high-context, relationship-driven society.

NATIONALITY: ISRAELI

STEREOTYPE: The Israelis are brash and rude wheeler-dealers who always seem to have something to say about just about everything.

NATIONAL CULTURAL TRAITS: Polychronic, high-context, individualist culture, that features low power-distance—i.e., society members insist on having decision-making power.

NATIONALITY: SAUDI ARABIAN

STEREOTYPE: Quiet, thoughtful, almost meek, with great respect for power and money and hierarchy.

NATIONAL CULTURAL TRAITS: Islamic religion influences business values, high power-distance, collectivist society that features many masculine traits, including a touch of materialism. A relationship-driven culture that does not bother to separate the individual from the business he is conducting.

NATIONALITY: INDIAN

STEREOTYPE: Reserved, philosophical, lacking confidence, self-effacing, but very bright.

NATIONAL CULTURAL TRAITS: Feminine qualities, high-context, polychronic society that places high value on group harmony. It is a relationship-driven society with high risk-avoidance. Religious philosophies play a key role in everyday life as does the value that society places on education.

NATIONALITY: AUSTRALIAN

STEREOTYPE: Loud, boisterous and materialistic. Ill-mannered and ill-bred.

NATIONAL CULTURAL TRAITS: Individualistic society with low power-distance, and very low uncertainty-avoidance that allows them to not worry about embarrassing themselves in public.

NATIONALITY: ARGENTINEAN

STEREOTYPE: Chaotic, slow-paced. Business based on an elitist network of families.

NATIONAL CULTURAL TRAITS: Polychronic with a non-linear approach to time, high-context society, relationship- rather than task-driven but places high value on individualism. Also a culture with a low power-distance rating.

The Effects of Culture Shock

One of the realities of working in a different culture is culture shock. Like death and taxes (at least in most countries in today's free market world) it is inevitable. The definition is simple. Culture shock occurs when everything that was once familiar to you—language, food, currency, values, beliefs and even such take-for-granted incidentals as traffic patterns, mealtimes and sleep patterns—vanishes. All the verbal and non-verbal cues you have spent a lifetime learning become useless. In the extreme it is like being an infant again. You cannot speak the language or read the newspapers. Culture shock is exemplified when a successful and respected businessperson at home becomes, in essence, a functional illiterate, dependent on others (in this case, a translator) for the most basic forms of communication. The frustration, like that of a child unable to communicate to its parents, builds. The effects of culture shock are cumulative—and sometimes even go unnoticed as they creep in with each minor irritation (ordering the wrong meal at a restaurant because you couldn't read the menu), each failure of self-expression (unable to ask for directions on the street), and each business setback (another appointment canceled).

FIGHTING OFF THE EFFECTS

Obviously, some travelers handle culture shock better than others and it is usually a function of experience. But there are many cases of an individual becoming virtually dysfunctional, unable to work at their best or remain focused on the goal while negotiating a business deal. Often it is because they are harboring resentment and anger against their own foreign business partners or counterparts.

The effects of culture shock can be compounded when individuals find themselves working in a culture where physical differences are obvious, say, a German working in Japan. A South African accountant, a very tall female, spent a year in Taiwan and never could get used to the stares—most of them focused on—of all things—her breasts. "It started out as a joke to me, something I figured would pass, but in a few months I just couldn't stand it. I hated going out in public. When I would walk on the streets I would tower over everyone. All I could see was the top of heads—and all those male faces gawking," she says. "I never felt so self-conscious in my life—and I am sure I never will again. I couldn't do my job, I didn't want to do my job. My original assignment was three years. I left after one. It was a mutual decision. The quality of my work slipped badly. My boss back in Johannesburg never understood. I couldn't tell him anyway. They would have thought I was crazy. But let me tell you, I won't even go to a Chinese restaurant now."

SYMPTOMATIC, AUTOMATIC

The symptoms of an individual suffering from culture shock are easy to spot, when you know what you are looking for. Cynicism about the host culture is one subtle sign. The physical symptoms include depression, lethargy, over-sleeping, over-eating, substance abuse; psychological symptoms might include withdrawal where one desires to become a hermit, declining invitations and preferring to stay at home to read a book or watch videos shipped in from back home.

Even an expatriate working in a foreign land never really gets over culture shock. It is cyclical in nature and characterized by a series of highs and lows that can take years to play out. For the short-term visitor, the cycles of culture shock can be compressed during a week-long visit. The initial phase is a general disorientation which is understandable considering that everything is new, different—and somewhat intimidating. Next comes a honeymoon phase. You may have picked up some of the local language, become familiar with a few restaurants or other public places, maybe conquered the taxi or public transportation system. Basically, you have familiarized yourself and become comfortable with some of the more obvious differences between your home culture and the new one.

Suddenly it seems less scary—and less odd. Often at this time all you can see is just how boring or provincial or inefficient your home culture has become. You flood family and friends at home and work colleagues back at the head office with gripping and fascinating tales (at least to you) of your new home and discoveries.

Then the cycle starts again. You raise your goals, you become, perhaps, over-confident and then whack! You smack into your limitations again. You realize you will never be an insider. Your communications skills level off. Suddenly it seems like an awful lot of effort just to finish routine tasks. The cumulative effects of just trying to cope can explode without expectation. And, if you are not prepared, it's back to cynicism and depression.

AN EXAMPLE: NO TIME FOR CHANGE

An American journalist who had worked in the Soviet Union for three years—and felt he had really acclimatized to the Soviet way of doing things—recalls how just a small incident can set off an explosion of years of frustration—frustration that you may not even be aware had built up. "For three years I had shopped in the hard currency store in Moscow (at that time only foreigners and high-ranking Communist party officials could legally possess foreign currency such as dollars or deutsche marks and there were special well-stocked stores for this elite). Every time I shopped, they never had any change to give you. Instead they gave you candy or gum to make up the difference. It was the way things were done and it didn't seem to bother me much. Finally after three years, I was buying a bottle of whiskey and as they had done hundreds of times before, the cashier said there was no change. I don't know what caused it but I hit the roof. I refused to move until I got my 65 cents—in cash. I cursed, I swore. Colleagues, journalists, diplomats waiting in the queue asked me to forget about it. One even offered me a U.S. dollar out of his pocket if I would just move on. Finally after more than half an hour I left—without my change and with a reputation in the small expatriate community of someone who had gone off the deep end. In a few minutes I had damaged a reputation that took three years to build. I knew then it was time to go. I was in a terminal stage of delayed culture shock."

AFFECTING THE BOTTOM LINE

Culture shock can have a real effect on the outcome of a business undertaking—often in ways that the head office may never know until they see the fine print of a contract. The most obvious negative is antagonism toward a foreign business partner. As mentioned earlier, the antagonism and cynicism that can build towards the representative of another culture can have very public manifestations that result in a failure to achieve business goals. But there is another and often more subtle danger: rather than becoming resentful toward the new culture and business partners and blowing the deal, an individual will become far too eager to please, to go along with almost anything, just to return home and escape the pressures. This loss of patience and perspective can result in something even worse than a failed business deal—a bad business deal, a nightmare contract that leaves your company with a huge disadvantage. Realizing that culture shock does indeed exist and can have a major impact on individuals in many different ways is the first step in coping with what is truly an inevitability of working in different worlds.

Countering Culture Shock

1. CULTURE SHOCK IS CYCLICAL Expect highs and lows but guard against the euphoria of the highest highs and the depression of the lowest lows. Try and keep a middle perspective.

2. MAINTAIN A SENSE OF ADVENTURE You are having experiences that most people will never have. Enjoy them. Treat life as an adventure.

3. AVOID CYNICISM It is a defense mechanism, and an easy trap to fall into, but a cynical attitude wins no friends and allies.

4. BE A PARTICIPANT Resist the urge to vegetate, to go back to your hotel or your home to avoid contact or dealing with the new culture. Avoidance will only amplify limitations and ensure that you will never grow in comfort with the new culture.

5. EXPRESS INTEREST IN LEARNING If you say you want to know more about the local scene, people will be more than willing to show off their home turf. It's a matter of local pride.

6. KEEP A JOURNAL Recording your experiences and impressions will help you focus on learning about the new culture and keep you motivated about personal growth.

7. TAKE CARE OF YOUR PHYSICAL HEALTH Do stress-relieving exercises both physical— breathing control, muscle relaxation—and mental—peaceful-imagery techniques, meditation, anticipation, and uncertainty-reduction strategies—to reduce the strain of culture shock.

8. TAKE WALKS—LOTS OF THEM Walking is not only good physical exercise but it will help you get more familiar with your surroundings. Assuming the area is safe and secure, walking will permit you to observe the nuances of the culture in your new setting.

9. JOIN A HEALTH CLUB Anyone on a medium-to-long-term assignment should consider joining a local health club as an outlet for stress.

10. MAKE A HOME If you are going on a long-term assignment bring familiar things from home. Pictures, a piece of furniture, familiar bed sheets can all turn a soulless dwelling into a home away from home and alleviate another potential area of depression.

Reverse Culture Shock

Culture shock can hit you both coming and going—something many individuals and companies take little notice of. In fact, the return home for many businesspeople who have had extended tours in a different country and culture can be far more disorienting and debilitating than the foreign assignment itself. Part of the reason: individuals are returning to a personal and business environment they view as secure, comfortable and probably unchanged— something that in reality it is no longer likely to be. Plus, the perspectives of the returning individual have also changed.

Thus, as a culture shock survivor you will probably end up experiencing similar feelings once you return home as you did when you first arrived in a new culture. There will be stress, uncertainty and anxiety. You will be happy to be home, but also sad about leaving behind friends and colleagues. Also, it is likely your value systems will have changed some as you absorb those of the culture you have lived in most recently. Your new life may seem dull compared to your foreign adventures. There is also coping with changes in social status and personal finances—both of which are often adjusted downward on returning home.

AN EMBARRASSMENT OF RICHES

One British businesswomen who had been living in Moscow for several years during the Soviet era recalls how on a trip back to London she burst into tears when she hailed a cab at the airport. The reason for the emotional breakdown—getting the cab was too easy compared to the daily street battles in Moscow. "I suddenly realized just how much stress I had been under. How everything was different. Here I was home and I couldn't cope. I couldn't walk into a supermarket. All the choices were overwhelming. It was depressing to have to make such minor decisions about what cereal or coffee or soap I wanted to buy. I had become Russian without really noticing it. My friends in England didn't understand at all and that was the most depressing part of all. They all seemed so boring, so disinterested and uninteresting. Over there everyday life was a challenge. You lived by your wits, you were on edge. Back home life just seemed so boring."

GOING NATIVE

An American executive who had worked for an American airline in Argentina for five years says he became increasingly depressed and angry at his colleagues in New York once he returned. "They were just so American, so different from what I had become. They had little respect for our operations in Buenos Aires and they just didn't understand that I felt the Latin American way of doing business had several good points over the American way. I mean, here were all these people in New York working themselves to death—and for what? They never took any time to enjoy life. It was their loss and I felt sad for them. I actually looked down on them and felt my experiences had made me superior. My new boss just thought I was being difficult, but I couldn't relate. I withdrew. I mean, it was like I was in a foreign country and these people didn't even speak the same language anymore. At least in Argentina I was different in a good way. Back in New York I was different but I wasn't supposed to be."

RIGGED FOR RE-ENTRY

The failure to realize that culture shock is a two-way street can have a negative impact on a business. According to a survey by Runzheimer International, a U.S.-based management consultancy, U.S. companies can expect to lose almost a quarter of returning expatriate staff within the first year. Similar studies in the United Kingdom found the turnover rate to be slightly less but well above the expected. Part of the problem: companies have no formal reintroduction program for staff to help them cope with re-entry culture shock. In the Runzheimer study, 73 percent of companies admitted to having no formal re-entry program and of those that did, 60 percent said the duration of their program was three days or less. One encouraging note: Companies that did have a formal re-entry program for expatriate workers, regardless of length, suffered a much lower turnover rate (less than six percent) than companies that did not.

The Expatriate Comes Home

Basically the same skills and coping strategies you used when you first took a foreign assignment will pay dividends when you return home. Look after your physical and mental health and fight the urges to withdraw. Participate—don't watch from the sidelines.

1. Expect people to react differently to you on your return but don't take offense. Give them time to re-discover who you are.

2. Remember, not everyone will be anxious to hear your "war stories" about life in a different culture. Don't bore them with endless remembrances. Seek out some new friends who have had similar and more worldly experiences. It will help you keep your balance. Offer to lecture on your experiences at local schools or before business groups who may appreciate your personal experiences more.

3. You will face new pressures at your job. Don't try and apply everything you learned in your foreign assignment immediately. Take time to become re-acquainted with your home culture and don't compare one way of doing business with the other—at least publicly.

4. Think of ways that you can incorporate all the skills you learned into your new assignment—both the professional skills and the personal coping skills. Remember, you have probably grown enormously as an individual. Seek a position where your new understanding of a different culture—and any language skills you may have picked up—can benefit your company and your personal position.

5. Find a mentor who can guide you through the "new" old corporate culture you are returning to.

The Company Can Help

1. Institute a formal and professional repatriation program that includes giving the returning staff member a general overview of current home office activities, a reorientation to the community and ample time to get acquainted with new procedures and staff.

2. Ensure that senior management understands the psychological stress that a returning employee faces and provide ways to help management cope with the special pressures. Let them know what to look out for when it comes to stress.

3. Begin the repatriation program a good six months in advance of the actual return date of the employee. Job options for spouses, financial planning, and tax assistance can help, as well as career counseling. Don't forget that the employee's family will also need help adjusting. This can help ease the strain on personal lives.

4. Have a plan on how to take advantage of the new skills of the returning employee. Set up a career path system for returning expatriates that underscores the value of their new skills and also reassures them that the time they spend working in a different culture did not hamper their career development but rather has helped it.

5. Provide a mentor for the returning expatriate. A personal one-to-one relationship can go a long way in retaining a returning employee.

6. Make them feel special and welcome. Poor treatment of returnees sends a signal through a company about the relative value of an overseas assignment.

CHAPTER 4

The Globalization of Business

ALL TRAVEL IS A FORM OF GRADUAL SELF-EXTINCTION.

— SHIVA NAIPAUL

GLOBALIZATION, FOR BETTER OR FOR WORSE, has changed the way the world does business. Though still in its early stages, it is all but unstoppable. The challenge that businesses and individuals face is learning how to live with it, manage it, and take advantage of the benefits it offers. The International Monetary Fund defines globalization as the growing economic interdependence of countries worldwide through increasing volume and variety of cross-border transactions in goods and services and of international capital flows, and also through the more rapid and widespread diffusion of technology.

Cross-Country, Cross-Border

The current era of globalization—the world saw a similar global business push on the eve of World War I but technology and communication restraints were obvious limitations on the scope of globalization back then—began shortly after the end of World War II with the victorious western powers supporting a worldwide "open" trade and investment policy. The idea was slow to catch on.

The number of companies that now deal across borders has mushroomed, as has the volume of international trade. The International Chamber of Commerce (ICC) cites statistics that show the international trade in goods and services stands at more than US$6 trillion. Global capital flows have exploded. Foreign Direct Investment, which involves the control of businesses or property across national borders, is at an all-time high in dollar volume. The accumulated stock of foreign direct investment was more than US$3 trillion in 1997, compared to just US$735 billion just ten years ago. Cross-border sales and purchases of bonds and equities by American investors have risen from the equivalent of 9 percent of gross domestic product in 1980 to more than 170 percent in the mid-1990s. Daily foreign exchange turnover is up from US$15 billion in 1973 to US$1.5 trillion by 1995. The volume of cross-border currency transactions in London, Tokyo and New York alone was US$1.5 trillion per day in 1997 more than twice what it was just five years earlier.

TECHNOLOGY RULES

Technology is one reason for the globalization phenomenon. Computers, which have eased telecommunication burdens, are cheaper now than they have ever been—and more powerful, too. In fact, the cost of computers has fallen on average 17 percent a year over the past twenty years even while processing power has increased dramatically. One example of their impact on global communications: A one-minute telephone call from New York to London was $300 dollars (in 1996 dollars) in 1930. Today it costs all of one dollar. New technology will lead to even further global business integration, as the Internet becomes more accepted as a business medium worldwide.

Technology has helped small- and medium-sized companies take advantage of the new markets that globalization presents. It is these companies, unencumbered by large head offices and bureaucracies, that can exploit global niche markets. Computers, faxes and e-mail have replaced large parts of the traditional office structures. Smaller companies can operate more efficiently on a much wider geographical basis with less overhead than ever before. The only barrier is the imagination of the entrepreneur.

MARKETS OPEN

Those who argue that globalization is a good thing say that companies dealing on the world stage will eventually become that much more efficient as they benefit from large economies of scale. Productivity will be boosted and living standards everywhere have the potential to rise as the world becomes richer and more prosperous because of globalization. There is ample evidence to support the benefits argument. According to the United Nations Development Program, total global wealth is growing faster than populations. The UNDP estimates that in the decade of the 1990s, 500 to 600 million inhabitants of the developing world have attained income levels above the poverty line and over the next 30 years another two billion should do likewise. Also, between 1965 and the early 1990s, the number of manufacturing and service industry jobs in both the developing world and the industrial world has more than doubled to 1.3 billion. And things should get even better as China, with a population of 1.2 billion—or one in every five inhabitants on Earth—opens itself to the global market economy. The fall of the Soviet bloc and economic liberalization in India has already brought an additional 1.5 billion people to the global consumer marketplace.

GLOBAL QUALITY

The naysayers take the opposite view, claiming that globalization has, in effect, triggered a "race to the bottom." Countries with low wages are attracting jobs from higher wage-paying nations, thus dragging everyone down to their level. The alleged "exportation of jobs" has surfaced as an important political issue in most industrialized countries. Nike, the US-based sneaker manufacturer, has been raked over the coals for paying Vietnamese 84 cents an hour to make $100 sneakers. In France, the issue has been a hot button in several parliamentary elections in the 1990s with unions claiming that upwards of 30 to 40 percent of France's more than 3 million unemployed were the victims of such "job exportation." In reality the number is less than 10 percent—and most of those were in inefficient government-subsidized industries that could not adapt to global competition.

Globalization creates more jobs than it actually destroys, but they are in different sectors and in different geographic regions. It takes more skill, education and mobility to be employable. The jobs lost in Europe and North America over the decades have generally been those requiring relatively uneducated workers. Indeed, wage differentials between the skilled and unskilled will likely increase. Both sides can point to ample examples to support their cases. But in the end, both are probably exaggerating to some extent. What is irrefutable is that the world economic pie is indeed bigger because of globalization—and it is being sliced differently than before.

The Globalization Paradox

The whole concept of effective globalization of a company presents a paradox: the more global a company becomes the more reliant it must become on local resources—people and management and marketing talent—to distribute its products or services to new markets.

The nationality of companies is becoming less important. British Airways is one of the first major global companies to recognize this trend. The airline has removed the British national flag from its aircraft livery and instead is using designs and art forms from across the world. The tailpieces of British Airways jets are now adorned with artist renditions of everything from Chinese calligraphy to Bushman paintings from the Kalahari Desert. The bulk of Toyota Camry automobiles—once the very symbol of the threatened Japanese dominance of the American auto market—are now made in the United States. Yet the Ford Motor Company's high-end Crown Victoria is actually an import from Canada.

GLOBAL COMMUNICATION

Successful companies, both large and small, are dealing with the globalization paradox by learning to think globally and act locally and by encouraging a diversity of management and giving subsidiary operations in different countries a higher degree of autonomy than ever before. However, no global strategy can be effective without a corporate communications program that drives the global theme throughout the organization and into the marketplace. This has fostered a broadening of perspectives and diversification of efforts—to think globally by acting locally.

One obvious impact of globalization is that the number of business travelers, and the amount of miles they fly to conduct business across borders, has exploded. Business travelers are constantly coming in contact with new and different cultures—but sometimes they find some awfully familiar sights to remind them of home. Some would argue that the globalization of trade is moving us toward a common international standard in many aspects of business—from accounting standards to unofficial dress codes. In many cases the quest for a "one-size-fits-all" set of standards for global business behavior has progressed quite far.

Moving Toward a World Standard

One expression of culture and national character is the way people in different countries drive cars. Nations take great pride in the vehicles they produce—it is a reflection of the state of engineering prowess. German technology earned a global reputation through the export of Mercedes-Benz and BMW motorcars. The French Peugeot and Swedish SAAB are household names throughout Africa. Now, the Ford Motor Company, based in Dearborn Michigan, has a better idea— one that it thinks will help it hit the global jackpot—a "world car" that can be manufactured anywhere on the planet and sold to anyone living on it. The goal: one million in global sales per year. Talk about economies of scale.

GLOBALLY ACCEPTABLE PRODUCTS

Ford has been trying to produce a "world car" for years. In fact, the Ford Escort was supposed to be that car but, in the end, the U.S., European and South American versions ended up so different they actually shared little but the nameplate. The biggest obstacle was differing regulations and customer preferences around the globe. But now Ford sees a narrowing of those differences, in essence, the surfacing of a global consumer, with similar tastes and safety requirements.

The emergence of a global market economy and freer trade has also cut down on the vast differences between government regulations on a country-by-country basis. This new attempt at a truly world car will be called the Ford Focus—and in fact was designed in Europe not the United States (Ford is one of those companies evolving into a truly global corporation) and was unveiled at an auto show in Geneva, Switzerland—not in Detroit. The Focus is part of Ford's grand plan called "Ford 2000" which aims to capitalize on global economies of scale to cut costs and prevent duplication of product development costs, such as design. The Focus will be built at Ford plants in Germany, Spain, Mexico and the United States.

But is this pitch of a world product toward a single global consumer the wave of the future? Not necessarily, at least not yet. But there are clear signs that companies are realizing that consumer preferences and product problems do have some commonalities and that pooling resources on a global basis can be highly efficient. The Italian automaker, Fiat, for example, is considering its own version of a "world car" for emerging markets. It brought together a design team of engineers from Argentina, Brazil, Poland and Turkey—all of whom had experience building and designing cars for populations who drive aggressively on absolutely lousy pot-hole filled roads.

LOCAL RESOURCES

Still, most consumer-oriented "world" products are victims of the globalization paradox. The more a company expands into the global marketplace, the more it relies on local resources and caters to local preferences. Take such global broadcasters as Cable News Network. While trading on its global reputation stemming from its coverage of American-oriented news events, it has earned a global following by tailoring its broadcasts to individual regions. ESPN, the American sports channel, is betting that the "couch potato"—the self-absorbed and sedentary TV viewer—has a counterpart somewhere in India and Asia. The network, which already operates 20 networks in 21 languages, televising everything from cricket to Australian-rules football, plans to launch an all sports network in India.

Few products can boast of beating the globalization paradox. Coca-Cola is one. Its formula, its logo and its packaging are the same virtually all over the world. It is one of the few exceptions to the prevailing rule of catering to local preferences. However, when it comes to soft drinks other than Coke, the company indeed manufactures to local preferences. Its Mello Yellow drink is called Lychee Mello in Japan. Meanwhile, Fanta, which most Europeans know as an orange-flavored drink, is peach-flavored in Botswana, passion fruit-flavored in France, and flower-favored in Japan.

But at least in one instance, even the giant Atlanta, Georgia-based company has been forced to bow to local taste preferences when it comes to its flagship cola. In India, Coke pushes a rival brand it owns called Thums Up over its own cola. Thums Up outsells Coke by a four-to-one margin. In no other country in the world does the company sell a rival to its own Coke. So successful has Thums Up been compared to Coke that the company has no plans to alter the marketing pattern. Coke will play second fiddle to Thums Up so long as Indians prefer the local brand.

CULTURE CAUTION: Coca-Cola had been asked to leave India many years earlier for refusing to reveal the secret to its formula. India did not like Coke's corporate culture. Thums Up was part of a compromise to get back into the enormous and thirsty Indian market.

Business Cultures Merge

However, in a number of important respects, the increased globalization of the world's major economies such as the United States, the European Union, Japan and China is beginning to elicit demands for more uniform and organized business practices—in other words, a global standard for such corporate practices as ethics, governance and accounting. The dramatic rise in cross-border capital flow and international investment has created a sense of urgency to reach such global standards. The information revolution and the Internet, along with improvements in telecommunications technology, has facilitated cross-border discussion on these issues as well.

CULTURAL CONFLUENCE

The globalization of economies has created a confluence of cultures when it comes to business practices. Meshing these cultures has proven difficult. For example, the United States government is spearheading a move to eliminate corporate bribery and corruption. Its Foreign Corrupt Practices Act, which forbids American companies from paying bribes to government or private sector individuals to win contracts, a common practice in most parts of the world, has been on the books for two decades. The U.S. Department of Commerce estimates the amount of business lost to American firms who are forced to play by a different set of rules compared to the rest of the world is in the tens of billions of dollars.

However, it has only been in the past few years following threats from the United States to move against foreign companies involved in bribery that other countries have agreed to take the problem seriously. Indeed, in such countries as France and Germany, the money paid for bribes to secure business overseas is a legitimate tax write-off. The Organization of Economic Cooperation and Development, which comprises most of the world's major industrialized nations, has formed a committee to investigate the extent of international bribery and its impact on business and to recommend a global standard of business ethics to deal with the situation.

PRIVATE INFLUENCE

In the area of corporate governance, it is the private sector that is pushing toward a set of global standards and practices. Corporate governance is a term that describes how those entrusted with the day-to-day management of a company's affairs are held responsible by shareholders, the community and employees. It is also concerned with communication and how a company presents itself to the wider world and the different corporate audiences, including shareholders, employees, potential investors and regulators. Governance structures are under pressure from cross-border investors to be more open and forthcoming.

U.S. investment institutions are becoming more interested in the rest of the world. As a result, American investment funds are taking a more proactive stance on governance issues, through one-to-one meetings with management and by initiating shareholder proposals. De-regulation of Japanese pension funds may also increase the extent to which foreign investors make their presence felt in other parts of the world. How strong is the sentiment for a global standard of corporate governance practices? A survey of major institutional investors found that 25 percent in the United States, 60 percent in France, 52 percent in Australia and 25 percent in Britain said that the realization of that goal was extremely important to them and considered a top priority.

THE EU: ONE ECONOMY, TWO CULTURES

Perhaps the most pressure for aligning corporate governance procedures is being felt in Europe because of the adoption of the Euro as a common currency and the increased flow of outside capital from the United States and Asia. Within Europe there is strong evidence of a convergence of corporate cultures which is the direct result of market forces. For centuries there have been two very different and competing business cultures present in Europe. The "Anglo-Saxon" model is characterized by large, liquid capital markets, a growing concentration of shareholding power by institutional investors, and a market for corporate control via takeover bids. The contrasting "continental" model is characterized by less liquid markets and a greater concentration of shareholder power in banks, families and governments. In France the business system is built upon an elite group of like-minded managers, most of whom were educated at the same schools and universities and who honed their business skills by serving for a few years in a government ministry. Italy has a similar structure of a business elite known as the *salotto buono*.

However, in recent years there has been a perceptible convergence of these two European cultures. In Britain the shift is away from short-term profit horizons on the part of management and investors and towards a commitment to enhancing long-term shareholder value. In continental European countries there is a gradual merging of long- and short-term aims caused by the need to raise external finance on world markets and by privatization programs. After centuries of very different business cultures, the fact that corporations are moving toward some standardization in the area of corporate governance practices is testimony to the impact of globalization. One of the first major continental European corporations to take the plunge was Daimler-Benz of Germany which has recently adopted American accounting standards in order to be listed on the New York Stock Exchange. Its recent merger with America's Chrysler Corporation is a major step towards a truly global scope.

Domination and Culturalization

Many international businesspeople will argue that when talking about the globalization of business standards people really mean the Americanization of such standards. In some cases this may be true. The area of corporate governance is one such case. However, this is not true in scores of other areas, from accounting to pollution standards to the finer points of human resources management. However, the current success of U.S. multinational companies has triggered global interest in American management practices. Many companies worldwide are adopting proven American management techniques. These include a strong customer and service orientation, streamlining of information systems, stock options for senior executives, and corporate stock buybacks.

One French company, Gemplus SCA, the world's largest manufacturer of "smart cards"—cash cards for consumers that store money and information on them electronically—was cited by the Wall Street Journal as a prime example of the global trend of the Americanization of management. The company is so pro-American it demands that workers speak English on the job. It even uses American consultants to advise on manufacturing processes.

CULTURAL COLONIALISM

However, there is a large school of global executives who believe that the Americanization of companies not only goes against the basic cultures of many nations, but that it is simply the latest management fad—not unlike the 1970s and 1980s blitz when everyone tried to copy Japanese management techniques.

"Management styles, governance styles, they come and go on a global basis," says one U.S.-based management consultant familiar with Asian and European management techniques. "But each time one of these management techniques comes into vogue and is copied, it brings the world closer to a global standard or really a global style of business management. People all over the world still use many of the techniques borrowed from the Japanese. And when the American fad ends, they will still use some of those techniques. Each time companies copy something from another culture, management styles on a global basis converge just a little more."

Though we will probably never see a single global management style, there are some basic principles being adopted. Local differences remain too large and few can agree on an absolute standard. Fears about Americanization are no more valid than those about Japanization a decade ago.

Global Accounting Standards

With the increase in international capital flow, it is becoming increasingly clear to international accountants, government regulators and global investors that if companies are going to be attractive to foreign investors, there is a need for a global accountancy language. Indeed, many European companies, again under pressure because of the introduction of the common currency in 1999, are beginning to see the benefits of adopting an internationally recognized accounting framework. The International Accounting Standards Committee (IASC) was formed in 1973 for the purpose of bringing into closer conformity all financial accounting and reporting standards on a global basis. The IASC has 14 voting members from various public accounting organizations, the International Association of Financial Analysts, and the business communities of various countries or groups of countries. Over the years, the IASC has issued in excess of 30 standards. Its recognition and acceptance are growing at an impressive rate.

GLOBAL STOCKS AND BONDING

The acceptance of a set of global accounting standards would mean that companies, regardless of where they are based, could list their shares on any capital market in the world. At present, each country has its own set of rules on disclosure and transparency that companies must meet in order to list shares on their markets. By the end of 1998 more than 50 nations—with the major exception of the United States—have welcomed these global accounting rules. The United States views the proposed global standards as too weak and less stringent than those already in place in the United States. However, a study of eight multinational firms using the international rules found that the results they produce are very close to those of the U.S. accounting procedures.

Of course, the actual achievement of a global ethics standard or a set of international corporate governance or accounting practices is probably still a long way off. The devil, as always, is in the details. So far, no nation has as yet been asked to give up much to achieve the global ideal. When they are, expect delays. Consider the European Union, the organization that is leading the charge on corporate governance issues. When the Union set up a commission in the early 1990s to come up with a common electrical plug for all Europe, the idea was met with great enthusiasm. But after six years of meetings, debates and engineering experiments, this same union has failed to agree on a standard plug because no one is willing to give up their current design.

So for now, international investors traveling to Europe to promote the notion of a set of global accounting and corporate governance standards would do well to remember the problem the European Union had in bringing about an electrical adapter to handle all the confusing electrical outlets and plugs. The reality is that despite many commonalities and a move toward global standards, there is still ample room for localization and assimilation.

CULTURE CAUTION: Membership in the World Trade Organization (WTO) requires members to adapt to a WTO standard accounting system. Nations with a fear of statistical analysis—like China—have found such accounting requirements problematic.

Global Business and Local Cultures

Globalization of national economies and business has had a great impact on capital, technology and trade flows but it has also had a major impact on national values, thought processes and the actions of people, organizations and institutions. The American fast food giant, McDonald's, is a dramatic example of how a company that does business around the globe can have an impact on local cultural traditions that seem totally unrelated to their main product—fast food. The company is also a prime example of how a company can think globally and act locally. In many countries—at least among the younger generations—

McDonald's is considered a local company. In these countries, McDonald's has been absorbed into the local communities and become assimilated. It is no longer thought of as a foreign restaurant—and in many ways it no longer functions as one. The company is about more than the globalization of hamburgers—it is about altering culture.

McDonald's opened its first restaurant in Des Plaines, Illinois in 1955. Today, the company operates more than 22,000 restaurants in 109 countries on six continents. McDonald's first began to expand internationally in 1967 with the opening of restaurants in Canada and Puerto Rico.

BURGERS AND CULTURE TO GO

During the first twenty years of its international expansion, McDonald's opened on average one restaurant in two countries per year. In the following ten years (from 1988 to 1998) McDonald's entered over half of its international markets, opening in 12 new countries in 1996 alone. In fact, from 1996-99, McDonald's has entered 31 new countries, bringing the running total to 109. The sun never sets on the Golden Arches. As a matter of fact, the northern-most McDonald's is at the Arctic Circle in Rovaniemi, Finland, and the southern-most McDonald's is in Invercargill, New Zealand.

THE RUSSIAN EXPERIMENT

McDonald's first restaurant in Russia opened in 1990 and since then more than 140 million customers have been served "Beeg Maks" at McDonald's restaurants there. But the company's contribution is much deeper than bringing the hamburger to Moscow. For most Russians, McDonald's was their first encounter with two basic consumer concepts—that the customer is king and that uniform quality can be guaranteed across a range of products and a range of stores. The concepts sound obvious to most consumers worldwide but in the Soviet system it was as foreign as, well, capitalism.

Russian consumers had always been on the short end. In the Soviet era, quality standards simply did not exist. Because of chronic shortages of consumer goods, it was the retail clerk, not the consumer, that was king. There was no certainty that if you bought a pair of shoes or a bottle of vodka from a retail store more than once that the quality would be uniform. Consistent quality and good service have finally come to Russia in the form of McDonald's.

"I don't think you can underestimate the impact that McDonald's had on the education of the Russian consumer," says a European advertising executive once based in Moscow. "The company introduced the concept of quality and reversed what had been the traditional relationship between buyer and seller on a retail level in Russia. Soon McDonald's quality and service were the standard by which every Russian retailer was being judged. Suddenly Russians could see what was possible, even in their own country and they were quick to demand more from retailers. They thought 'if Westerners can give us this, why can't our own people do it'. It was a cultural breakthrough."

CLEANING HOUSE

The company also set the standard for cleanliness in a country where customers had grown accustomed to the most abysmal conditions in public kitchens and toilets, even in better restaurants. Following its global guidelines for hygiene and cleanliness, the toilets at McDonald's were spotless. The kitchens, in full view of the consumer, were clean and efficient. Previously, most Russians felt they were better off not knowing how their food was prepared. If they were allowed a peek, they might never eat out again. Now, Russian consumers have come to expect a higher level of hygiene in all public establishments. "It's a small point," says the advertising executive, "but I guess you could say that McDonald's triggered a cleanliness revolution of sorts in public establishments. Before, the rest rooms were places to avoid at all costs. Kitchens were awful. Now, partially thanks to McDonald's imported standards, a lot of restaurants have really made improvements. I don't think that would have happened on its own. It took an outsider to come and change the culture."

CHAPTER 5

Customs Etiquette and Protocol

THE CHAINS OF HABIT ARE TOO WEAK TO BE FELT UNTIL

THEY ARE TOO STRONG TO BE BROKEN.

— SAMUEL JOHNSON

IN AN ERA OF GLOBALIZATION, understanding the basics of etiquette and protocol—that is, the type of behavior that others expect of you in both informal and formal settings—is an important skill. It can instill an individual with confidence to handle almost any situation in any culture and allow a businessperson to concentrate on the deal at hand rather than worrying about such peripheral distractions as which fork to use or which hand to use for passing food. Without an understanding of the basics of etiquette and protocol, you risk coming off as a boorish Neanderthal. You may even put your company's image at risk or risk potential failure in the formation of key business relationships that are vital to global success. Finally, a well-honed sense and appreciation of local customs, etiquette and protocol can make you stand out as a world-savvy individual in a competitive global market. The world may indeed be an oyster today for many businesses. The problem is that too many businesspeople are still, like Oscar Wilde, using the wrong fork.

The Ancient Art of Protocol

Etiquette—the codes and practices prescribed by social convention that govern correct behavior—and protocol—the form of etiquette and ceremony observed by diplomats and businesspeople during formal interaction—are really ancient arts. Ptahhotep, mayor of ancient Egypt's capital and vizier to Egyptian King Isesi around 2380–2340 B.C. (the vizier was ancient Egypt's highest appointed official) is widely considered to be the first (known) person to fully comprehend the importance of etiquette and protocol as business survival tactics. Sometime in the 24th century B.C., he put into writing a series of instructions for bosses and employees that amounts to what many scholars consider the first "how to" on organizational and management behavior.

Egyptian schools stopped using Ptahhotep's writings, known as the Instruction of Ptahhotep, as a text only around 1500 B.C.—more than 900 years after he penned it. Many of today's modern etiquette practices (the word etiquette is derived from the French word for "ticket") actually originated in the royal court of France between the 17th and 18th centuries. The behavior code spread throughout the royal courts of Europe and was eventually adopted by the wealthy upper classes across the continent.

Ancient Etiquette and Modern Protocol

Surprisingly, much of what the instruction of Ptahhotep had to say thousands of years ago is still relevant to the survival of today's international businessperson. He advises both management and employees to act virtuously, modestly, and with awareness of human needs. The following are examples of Ptahhotep's business survival etiquette tips that are now almost four thousand years old:

SCORING POINTS WITH THE BOSS:

"When sitting with one's superiors, laugh when they laugh."

ON CLIMBING THE CORPORATE LADDER

"Tell an important superior what is useful; help your superior to win acceptance by other people. This will also benefit you, because your livelihood depends on your superior's success, which clothes your back, and your superior's help protects you. When your superior receives a promotion, your own desire for rank progresses toward fulfillment, as your superior gives you a helping hand."

ON BEING A LOYAL EMPLOYEE

"Do not oppose the actions of important superiors; do not vex the hearts of the burdened. Opposition will rouse their ill-will, whereas support draws their love. Your superiors are your providers, along with the gods, and what they desire should take place. Pacify superiors when they storm in anger. Just as opposition engenders ill-will, support nurtures love. Pitiful is one who opposes a superior, for you live only as long as your superior is indulgent. Showing respect does you no harm."

TIPS FOR MANAGEMENT

On using consultants: "Don't be proud because of your knowledge, consult both the layman and the scholar."

Whose Proper Etiquette?

Proper etiquette in today's business world goes well beyond basic table manners (they are, after all, a given in most cultures) and common courtesies (allowing an esteemed colleague or superior to precede you through a doorway, for example). Think of all the elements that go into making a first impression. The list is lengthy. There is your manner of dress, your professional appearance, the color of your dress or tie, your body language, handshake, posture, amount of eye contact on introduction, where you put your hands, how you accept a business card and how you present yours as well as the actual content of the card—and you haven't even sat down to begin talks.

Many experienced international business travelers will advise you that "when in Rome do as the Romans do." While this may work if you are trying to figure out which fork to use or whether to bow or shake hands, it is, in most cases, far easier said than done. And besides, except in superficial areas, doing what the Romans do may be against your ethics, morals, company policy or home government laws.

Regardless of the culture, proper etiquette means maintaining your own values while respecting those of others. It does not mean slavishly following the rituals and practices of others to please your host. If you make an effort at the language, at understanding the basics of common courtesy, and avoid any flagrantly offensive or obnoxious acts, don't be overly concerned about the subtleties—at least the first time around. To be honest, not that much is really expected of the first time visitor to another culture, though a deeper understanding will be expected each time you visit. The real value in understanding etiquette and protocol is in the confidence it gives you and the impression it makes on colleagues.

The Name Game

Foot in mouth disease—e.g., when a newcomer to a foreign culture butchers the name of a business contact at first meeting—is more common in the international business world than most people think. There is probably no worse way imaginable to kick off a business relationship. Failing to show the proper respect or simply calling someone by the wrong name on first meeting is an avoidable mistake if you do your homework properly. Naming systems differ greatly and even within cultures there are subtleties that make guessing at a person's proper name and title a minefield. In most Asian cultures the family name or surname is given first. In Hispanic cultures most people will have two surnames, one from their father and one from their mother. There are also issues of formality.

There is no foolproof strategy for figuring out name order or even how formal a culture is when it comes to verbal address. One of the best strategies: be aware that there are differences in global naming systems and the differences can often be subtle. If you are not 100 percent certain, ask. Also inquire politely what the person prefers to be called to judge the speed at which you can proceed to a less formal level of address. There are some pitfalls the name game presents for business travelers that can be easily avoided.

CHINESE NAMES

Most Chinese names have either two or three characters, each of which represents a sound. As in most of the rest of Asia, the Chinese give their surname first followed by other given names. For example, in the name, Wang Tai Hoi, Wang is the surname. The Chinese realize that most Westerners don't understand their naming system, so they try and leave obvious clues to the proper order in business correspondence. While keeping the traditional name order, many Chinese will indicate their surname by using capital letters or underlining it. Thus Wang Tai Hoi may display his name in a letter as WANG Tai Hoi or Wang Tai Hoi, with Wang underlined. Only on very, very rare occasions would a Chinese name be "reversed," i.e., with the surname placed last, purely as a courtesy and a concession to English or American style.

A Chinese surname is often passed down through the father, but Chinese women always retain their family name even after marriage. Women normally put their husband's surname first, then follow it with their own names. For example, if Miss Zhao Ling Kit married Mr. Wang Tai Hoi, she would be known as Mrs. Wang Zhao Ling Kit where Wang is the husband's surname and Zhao is her maiden surname. However, in a short form of address she would be known as Mrs. Wang. It is becoming more common for many Chinese women not to use their husband's surname at all in business. In that case, despite being married to Mr. Wang, Zhao Ling Kit would be known as Ms. Zhao. One can easily understand why it is often imperative to inquire how a person would prefer to be addressed.

CULTURE CAUTION: The populations of the Sino-Asian cultures of Hong Kong, Taiwan and Singapore will often adopt English given-names or initials for use during international travel. This is less a reference to a colonial past than a sign of international business savvy.

VIETNAMESE NAMES

In Vietnam the surname is given first, followed by the middle and given names. A person is normally addressed by their given name and a title. These informal (as opposed to professional) titles are based on the relative ages of the people involved in a conversation. The same Nguyen Thanh Chinh could be addressed as Anh Chinh (older brother Chinh), Ong Ching (grandfather or the senior Chinh), or Em Chinh (younger brother Chinh) depending on the age or status of the speaker. Similar designations exist for women (Chi, Ba, Em).

JAPANESE NAMES

Traditionally the family name, or *myoji*, came first in Japan, but that practice is now mostly reserved for historical figures. Today, the most common practice is to put the name in western order—given name first and family name last. Thus, Sokichi Abe would be Mr. Abe to Westerners. Like the Chinese, some Japanese will capitalize or underline their surname in correspondence with foreigners to help them avoid a mistake. Where Japanese names become interesting for foreigners is in the use of suffixes as forms of address. The suffixes indicate honor and status. If you do not use a suffix, it indicates that the person you are addressing is either a close friend or someone you consider inferior to you because of age or social status. Among the most common suffixes:

San: The most common (honorific) title in Japan, it is the Western equivalent of courtesy titles such as Mr., Mrs. or Miss. Thus, Sokichi Abe would be Abe San, which means, simply, Mr. Abe.

Sama: More honorific than San, it is often used in written correspondence, including business letters.

Dono: Even more honorific than Sama, it is sometimes used in letters, but almost never used in conversation anymore.

Sensei: Means "born before" and is usually used when addressing a teacher, instructor or mentor. A student would use the term when addressing a university professor. Professor Abe would be Abe Sensei.

Senshu: The Japanese equivalent of superstar, it is a title reserved for great sports players. For example, the great Japanese baseball player Suharato Oh would be Oh Senshu. Sumo wrestlers have their own suffix—Zeki.

Kun and *Chan*: Used to address a friend of the same age or someone of equal or inferior status. It is used with first or given names. Parents often use it as a diminutive for their children. Kun is for males and Chan for females. Thus, Sokichi Abe's parents might have referred to him as Sokichi Kun and his sister Miho as Miho Chan.

KOREAN NAMES

Again, the surname comes first, followed by the given names (or name). Most Korean have two given names, like Roh Tah Woo or Kim Young Sam. In the Korean culture the use of personal or given names for address is usually restricted to members of the same family and close friends. Courtesy titles are coming into greater use when it comes to international business but generally it is OK to addresses a Korean colleague by his/her surname only. Married women do not take their husband's name, so you are liable to hear Mr. Roh introduce his wife as Mrs. Kim—her maiden name.

RUSSIAN NAMES

When it comes to dealing with foreign businesspeople, Russians, regardless of whether they are dealing with an overseas visitor or a local businessperson, give a high priority to formalism. Often in initial encounters Russians (it is also common on the Indian subcontinent) will address you using your business title, such as Company Director Smith or Company Treasurer Jones. You should do likewise. Though it may sound awkward, the use of titles (Director-General Koslov) is the accepted norm. If in doubt refer to the business card you have been given. To address a Russian by his or her first name is an insult.

Russian names are listed in the same order as in the West: first name (*imya*), middle name (*otchestvo*) and last name (*familiya*). The quirk here is that the Russian middle name is a patronymic—a name derived from the first name of one's father. Take the name Mikhail Sergievich Gorbachev. The first name is Mikhail (the Russian version of Michael) and the last name is Gorbachev. The middle name Sergievich means quite literally the "son of Sergie." Russian women add the letter "a" (the female ending) to the end of their last name and their patronymic. For example: Raisa Gorbachev (Mikhail's wife) is known in Russian as Raisa Maximova Gorbacheva—the feminine "a" added to her last name as well as her patronymic Maximova or "daughter of Maximov." Once Russians move beyond the initial formal stage of a relationship, they use the first name and patronymic as a less formal method of address.

SPANISH NAMES

In most Hispanic cultures (Argentina being one major exception to this rule) people will have two surnames, one taken from their father and one from their mother. Only the father's surname, which is listed first, is commonly used when addressing someone. Those unfamiliar with the Latin construction often wrongly believe the paternal surname to be a middle name. Take the name Julio Cortez Garcia. He would be Señor Cortez, with Cortez being his paternal surname and Garcia his maternal surname. Say Señor Cortez met and married Rosa Perez Carrera. She would become Mrs. Rosa Perez de Cortez. Their, child whom they named Pablo would be Pablo Cortez Perez, taking the surname of the father and the surname of the mother. Pablo's "last name" is Cortez, from his paternal surname.

In many Spanish-speaking countries, it is becoming fairly common to connect the paternal and maternal surnames with a hyphen and use it as a last name, e.g., Cortez-Perez. There are several options when it comes to addressing married females. Once married, Rosa Perez Carrera could be addressed as Señora Rosa Perez Cortez, Señora de Cortez (literally, wife of Cortez) or La Señora.

In this example, Rosa Cortez should never be referred to as Mrs. Julio Cortez—a common form of address for married women in North America. Like the Russians, many Latin cultures diminutivize first names. Thus, Francisco becomes Paco and Guadalupe becomes Lupe. Visitors should avoid such diminutives unless invited to use them.

INDIAN NAMES

Hindus generally do not have family names and instead use the father's initial first with their given name. Thus, the name V. Naipal really means Naipal, son of Vijay. He would be referred to as Mr. Naipal. The same name structure is true for females. But if P. Samateer—a female—marries V. Naipal, she will be known as Mrs. Samateer Naipal. One other note: When dealing with Westerners, Hindus with extraordinarily long names might shorten them for convenience. Thus, S. Ramsanlati might shorten his name to Mr. Ramsan.

ARABIC NAMES

In Arabic, an individual is addressed by his or her first name and any title they possess. A Dr. Abdul bin al-Qazar would be addressed as Dr. Abdul. The word "bin" means "son of" and may be present any number of times in a name as it often represents genealogy. Another common name structure is Abd, followed by an attribute of God. Thus Dr. Abd Al Qazar al-Haj would be Dr. Abd Al-Qazar. Many will take the title Haj if they have completed a trip to Mecca, the holiest shrine in Islam.

A WORD ABOUT THE NAME GAME

It is indeed a verbal jungle out there and the best way to avoid a costly name mistake is to do your homework in advance. Learn a culture's naming system and practice the names of your contacts before you arrive. If you are unsure of the correct pronunciation or word order ask the local consulate or a university language school or a local translation service for their advice. When it comes to meeting strangers, it is important to concentrate on the name as you are being introduced. Stop thinking about what you are going to say and listen instead to the introduction. Repeat the name immediately in conversation or as you prepare to shake hands. Look at the person's face to create an association with the name. To hear the name repeated, you can ask how it is spelled or how it is pronounced. When leaving, even after a brief conversation, use the name in your good-bye.

Face-to-Face Greetings

Once you have a handle on the naming structure of a culture, the next area of importance is the physical greeting you can expect from a foreign colleague—and what type of greeting they can expect to receive from you. Not everyone appreciates the back-slapping, death-grip handshake Americans are famous for. On the other hand, Americans may deem the traditional reserve of the Japanese greeting (a bow) as an indication of aloofness and mistrust. It is really up to the visitor to adapt and, in this case, when in Rome doing what the Romans do is the best course.

TO EACH HIS OWN

Each culture has its own form of acceptable greeting behavior, usually based on the level of formality found within the society. The rules of social distance etiquette vary by culture. Africans, for example, are far less structured in their greetings than Europeans. Expect a warm physical greeting, an extended handshake or a hand on the shoulder in most African cultures. Also expect to be asked how your trip was and how your family is doing. The tradition of long greetings stems from the time when Africans once walked miles to visit neighboring villages on social calls. The arrival and a gushing greeting was considered the least a villager could do for a traveler. Don't be impatient with such a long drawn-out exchange and don't hurry things along. Rather, get into the spirit and appreciate that the person you came to see is prepared to take the time to sincerely inquire about your welfare.

In Argentina, greetings are usually effusive with plenty of hugging and kissing, not unlike the French *faire la bise* (kiss on both checks). This is even the case in business meetings, unless they are of a highly formal nature. In Argentina, men kiss women, women kiss women, but men do not kiss men. By contrast the Chinese way of greeting shuns the physical. It is generally a nod or a slight bow. However, when dealing with individuals from cultures where more direct physical contact is the norm, e.g., a handshake, the Chinese will adapt and shake hands. Don't interpret a soft handshake or lack of eye contact as a sign of weakness or lack of aggression. It simply means that your Chinese colleague is not overly used to physical contact when greeting a stranger.

SPACE ADVENTURES

In Islamic cultures, special care should be taken when greeting a member of the opposite sex. A non-Islamic woman doing business in such a culture can determine the method of greeting. It is up to her to decide whether to offer her hand during an introduction. Don't be surprised though if it is taken reluctantly. After all, physical contact between the sexes is limited (and the amount varies greatly by the degree of Islamic influence in the culture). For men, the rules are different when greeting an Islamic female. Rule number one is never greet a woman with a kiss. Also, you should never offer your hand to a woman first. Rather, wait to see if she offers hers to you. If she does, it is acceptable to shake it. Otherwise, a verbal greeting will suffice.

Finally, each culture has its own rules on space. For example, the Australians, the Argentinians, and most Asians will move in very close during an introduction and almost be right in the face of the person they are meeting. North Americans and many Europeans will feel uncomfortable with this invasion of "private space" and consider it an aggressive gesture. It is not. It is important to realize that crowding is simply a cultural norm. In most Arabic cultures, men will literally grab the arm or shoulder of a colleague to emphasize a point.

Business Card Etiquette

One of the first impressions you will make on a foreign colleague is through your business card, and in many cultures, especially in Asia, the exchange of business cards is a meaningful ritual rather than a casual informality. This is especially true in Japan, where the business card exchange is as formal as it gets anywhere in the world.

Today, it is more a necessity than a courtesy to have your card translated into the local language of the country you are visiting. Bilingual cards are the norm, with one side printed in your home language and the other side in the foreign language in which you are dealing. If you are using a one-sided card, always hand your card to a colleague with the printed face up. If it is a bilingual card, be sure that the side using the local language is face up. Never fling a card across the table or onto a desk. It is the height of bad manners or *nyetkulturny* (devoid of culture) as the Russians would say. Asians consider it an extraordinarily rude gesture.

THE PRIVILEGES OF RANK

If presenting to a multitude of foreign contacts at once, give your card to the highest-ranking individual or leader of the delegation first. This is a sign of respect and avoids embarrassing the lesser-ranking members of the delegation who may even refuse your card if the head honcho has not yet received one. In most Asian cultures, presenting a card with two hands conveys respect and an appreciation of the importance of the ritual. It is best to hold the card by the two upper corners when making the presentation. Likewise, you should receive a business card with both hands. Once you have it in hand, take time to read it—not merely a glance but a deliberate study. Often this is an ideal time to repeat the person's name, which will help you connect the face to the name.

In Japan and in many other Asian cultures it is insulting to put the card directly in your pocket, wallet or card case without giving it sufficient study time. In Japan it is best to lay the card in front of you on the table, especially during the first meeting. This is a sign of great respect. (One exception to this rule is in Korea, where it is considered odd behavior to stare at the card or venerate it by placing it on the table. There it is OK to have a glance and place it in your pocket for later reference.) While you may write on your own card, it is considered rude and disrespectful to write on someone else's. Treat the card with respect. Ideally, carry a small pocket cardholder or case.

In the Islamic world the left hand is considered unclean. Even in many non-Islamic areas of Africa and Asia, the tradition has evolved of using the right hand in preference over the left. So when presenting or receiving a business card use the right hand.

In Europe and North America, business cards are far less formalized and are used merely to keep track of who's who during a hectic meeting schedule. If you come to sell in these societies, your hosts will be concentrating on your product, not your business card.

The Rules of the Card Game

- It's not only polite to have your card translated into the local language it is now considered a must. Make it work for you.

- Always present your card with the printed side up or, in the case of bilingual cards, with the local-language side showing.

- Wait to be introduced before presenting your business card.

- Present the cards one at a time in the order of the hierarchy of the delegation.

- Content: include your name and business title. In some cultures it is common to include your academic degrees as well.

- Business titles can be confusing and often do not translate exactly. If your title is one that is not internationally common, such as Chief Learning Officer, consider using a translation that avoids the literal and rather portrays your status and job in words or concepts that may be more familiar to your host. Don't inflate job titles. Also make sure to check the translation. You don't want Vice President of Sales to come out as President of Vice Selling.

- Well-known or trademarked acronyms (such as IBM) need not be translated nor do words included in logos.

- Take plenty of cards. It can be highly embarrassing to run out of them and in some cultures it would be an insult.

- Many executives carry two sets of cards. One set is used purely for introductions and has no direct contact information. The other is used for more serious encounters and includes detailed contact information.

- Always treat your colleagues' cards with respect.

Conversational Taboos

Small talk is often what makes the business world go round but it can also present a minefield that can blow up a relationship at the start. The best way to avoid this pitfall is to steer the conversation away from some basic taboos such as politics, religion, race and negative history and toward less volatile subjects such as sports, family, food or travel experiences. If your host insists on discussing a controversial subject, it is important to listen well and remain open-minded. Often it is best to simply let the person vent their feelings.

In many cultures where emotions run high (Russians, for one, are noted for their long-windedness and penchant for emotional debate), one way to avoid an escalation of the verbal confrontation over a controversial subject is to let the long-windedness act in your favor. Don't interrupt their diatribe but rather let them exhaust themselves in emotion and historical explanation and rationale. When they are finished you will find that they feel a lot less strongly than they did when the disagreement started and may be willing to compromise, or at least see some value in your point.

Before you visit a new culture or country, it is wise to have some knowledge of its history. Not only will it help to put much of what you learn in context, it can also help you avoid serious gaffes about the history of a nation. Bringing up the purges of Soviet dictator Joseph Stalin and other negative aspects of that era will most likely make a Russian highly defensive. Discussing the claims of Holocaust survivors with a Swiss business colleague can only lead to trouble. Dredging up the less than savory or controversial past is not a way to impress a business colleague or further a potentially lucrative business relationship.

The Importance of Socializing

In most cultures the business day hardly ends at 5 P.M. In fact, in many cultures outside of North America, sundown signals the start of "serious" relationship-building time—essential to the successful completion of business. The social occasion is often more important than the formal business meeting earlier in the day when it comes to closing a deal. It's not so much that actual details of the business at hand will be discussed but rather relationships will be reinforced.

Many cultures, however, are less subtle about the course of their business meals. In the United States, it is not considered rude to deal with specifics of the deal at mealtime. American attitudes towards mixing business with pleasure are linked to their belief that you "take care of business" before you have the right to relax. After all, the power breakfast is not meant to be a social occasion; it is a way of squeezing a few more hours of precious time out of the working day.

WORK HARD, PLAY HARD

Regardless of the country you are in, it is essential to accept any invitation to meet outside of business hours. Pleading jetlag, lack of hunger, illness or alcoholic abstinence can be insulting to a host and is more often than not taken as a sign of smugness and superiority. Deprived of this relationship-building time, it would be difficult to imagine business moving ahead at all in certain cultures.

Of course, meal times vary in different cultures. Do your homework and learn the times when everyone eats and plan accordingly. In many Latin cultures (almost all of Latin America, Italy and Spain) as well as the Middle East, lunch is the main meal of the day—and the meal where business relationships can be cemented. Tanking up at the breakfast buffet may leave you stuffed for lunchtime just when you need to be impressing your foreign colleagues over a seven-course luncheon. Plan ahead. Eat a light breakfast instead—and remember that supper in countries where lunch is king is often very late in the evening and also a very light meal.

DINING TREPIDATIONS

If you travel, sooner or later you will be faced with the choice of trying some exotic dish that may on the surface sound or look repulsive. Most businesspeople have a story connected with the first time they tried dog in Korea or sheep's eyes in Saudi Arabia or hot dogs covered in chili in the United States or hippo steaks in South Africa. Remember, rejection of such food is tantamount to rejection of your host's culture and country. Sometimes there is simply no way out and it is necessary to "take one for the team," as the Americans would say. One way to cope is to simply remain ignorant. Don't ask too many questions about what you are eating—simply try and enjoy it. If a food looks absolutely awful to you, try swallowing very small bites quickly—you probably won't even taste it. The revulsion people feel about certain foods is probably 95 percent mental. Crocodile does indeed taste like chicken—and often so do many other strange meats. And who knows, if you can get over your own culturally generated mental picture of what you are eating, you may even like the taste.

Social Drinking Protocol

In many cultures alcohol remains a great facilitator, the lubricant that loosens up the relationship and greases the social skids on the way to a successful business deal. While American business meals have moved towards a complete shunning of alcohol, most of the rest of the world still enjoys a tipple during lunch and at after-hours meetings in connection with business.

In many countries, such as Russia and South Korea, the ability to consume (or at least attempt to consume) great quantities of alcohol in short periods is still considered a measure of an individual's manhood—or womanhood to a lesser extent. In several Asian cultures, especially China, and in Russia, formal toasts are still the norm (never propose a toast before the host—it is the height of *nyetkulturny*). Always be prepared with something cheery or witty to say. Avoid the profound phrase or statement or an attempt at a double entendre. Keep the language simple, and avoid subtle messages. This is supposed to be a joyous occasion, not a stage for hidden social comment.

Perhaps the best-known drinking culture in the world is Russia. Of course, no Russian meal is complete without vodka, which is big business in the country. The white spirit alone accounts for 5 percent of all retail sales in Russia. And yes, it is true that an open bottle must be consumed. But this has less to do with some deep-rooted Russian tradition than it does with the unavailability of screw tops and re-sealable bottles.

BARRIER BREAKDOWN

In many Asian cultures, as in Russia, it is almost impossible to avoid consuming large amounts of booze. In such rigid hierarchal cultures as Korea and Japan, alcohol helps to break down the strict social barrier between classes and allows for a hint of informality to creep in. It is traditional for host and guest to take turns filling each other's cups and encouraging each other to gulp it down.

For someone who does not imbibe (except for religious reasons) it can be rather tricky escaping the ritual of the social drink. Though loathe to admit it, individuals in cultures where heavy drinking is acceptable probably don't entirely trust someone who is abstemious. They don't like doing business with strangers and social drinking is part of relationship building.

If you disapprove of alcohol keep it to yourself. Displaying a superior attitude about sobriety can be a relationship killer. Of course, nursing one drink throughout the evening is one way you may be able to escape but more expert subterfuge is often necessary. More than one businessperson has been known to feign drunkenness after just one or two drinks to avoid the real thing. One British banking executive recalls how he repeatedly outfoxed his Russian colleagues by simply substituting water for vodka, drinking one shot of liquor for every three or four consumed by his Russian hosts without ever missing a toast or appearing to be a non-participant. The switch became easier—there was less danger of being found out—as the night dragged on.

When it comes to social drinking, there are some different rules for women. These are discussed in a later chapter.

CULTURE CAUTION: If you are a large man you will find that when you travel to Asia you will be challenged to drinking contests by hosts and strangers alike. Korea and Vietnam are particularly competitive in this area. It is a slippery slope and it is usually best to decline the invitation or let your opponent win. You have nothing to gain if you win except a painful hangover, and much to lose.

Global Dress Codes

Realize it or not, you communicate through what you wear, your hairstyle, the polish of your shoes and even the look of your fingernails. Clothes may not make the man—or the woman—but the reality is that how you look goes a long way in leaving a great first impression. Dressing the part of the successful businessperson is critical. While you may want to show style, being too flamboyant or cutting-edge may actually be a distraction. Clothes should serve as a gentle backdrop to your personality and mission. Outlandish hairstyles, excessive makeup, mountains of jewelry or a strong scent of perfume or cologne may cloud your image as a professional and send the wrong signal to your foreign colleague.

Although in most cultures, the wealthy tend to be show-offs when it comes to clothes and jewelry, if you are visiting on business don't try to match them caret for caret or fur for fur. Visitors are better off exhibiting quiet good taste. There is one exception to this rule: an expensive watch is usually noticed and is considered a subtle symbol of success and prosperity in just about every culture doing international business.

KEEPING IT SIMPLE

With the advent of the global village and the internationalization of business, the room to be inventive in business dress and toleration for local custom has diminished. While international business travelers are not yet wearing the same "uniform," as such, there has been a clear tendency toward a more international standard of dress for both men and women. A well-fitted dark suit—usually blue, gray, or black—is appropriate for almost all formal business situations and most social occasions, including evenings out at restaurants or the theater. Even at more casual social affairs, being dressed smartly pays dividends. The rule of thumb: when in doubt, overdress for the occasion.

For global business travelers heading to more tropical climes such as Africa or the Middle East, the same dress code still applies in most places: that is, a conservative and preferably tropical weight suit. A light-colored dress shirt—the best color is white—and a tie are standard. Though most such cultures are not fanatical about it, long-sleeve shirts are preferred. Short sleeves are OK for after work casual meetings.

For women—remember, you are still dealing in a mostly male-dominated world—skirts and dresses are more the norm than pants in most every part of the world outside of North America. For women, power dressing, as the Americans like to call it, won't gain any points at the negotiating table in most places. It may in fact make it harder to break down the stereotype of businesswomen as pretenders to male power.

CULTURE CAUTION: Although most of what is considered "standard business attire" is Western in style, some cultures will encourage visitors to wear local dress. Hot weather nations such as those of sub-Saharan Africa and Southeast Asia are very accommodating in this area.

COLOR COUNTS

If you assume that a dark conservative suit has the least chance to offend, you are probably right. But danger lurks in the fashion accessories that men and woman can choose. The most clear and present danger is in the actual color of the accessory—the tie or the scarf you choose. Cultures attribute different characteristics to different colors. For example, while most of the world sees the sun as being yellow, in Japan it is clearly red. The red sun is an important national symbol which appears on the national flag. When Japanese children paint the sun they paint it red and find it odd that children in the West think the sun is yellow.

The color of your accessories can actually insult a foreign host or, if done correctly, can add to a positive impression. For example, in China the color red is the traditional color for weddings and is considered good luck, so a red tie is a positive omen. However, a woman wearing a white scarf might earn sympathetic looks. The color white is the traditional Chinese color symbolizing mourning.

A businessman visiting Saudi Arabia recalls how his choice of a bright green tie drew favorable remarks from several local colleagues. Green is the color of Islam. However, the visitor had no intent to honor that religion, rather he had chosen a green tie because it was St. Patrick's Day and he wished to show off his Irish roots. Initially, he simply couldn't figure out why Saudi Arabians would care so much about an Irish holiday. Only after he became more familiar with the region did he discover the real reason his green tie earned him compliments. It's probably a good thing the businessman did not wear his green tie in the Czech Republic where green is the symbol for poison and toxic materials.

Some International Styles

Countries and cultures often pride themselves on their fashion sense and boast of individual styles. Indeed, what is perfectly acceptable dress in one country may be far too casual or out of place in another. However, even in the most casual of countries, Israel, there is a growing acceptance of the "international business uniform," dark suit and smart tie. When in doubt, overdress. You can always dump the tie and go casual.

THE UNITED STATES: CONFUSING AT TIMES

You can't judge a book by its cover here. It is often impossible to tell just whom you are dealing with based solely on dress. Waiters wear tuxedos and Silicon Valley technology wizards worth millions wear shorts and T-shirts to the office. A saleswoman in a department store is more apt to be better dressed than the female executive in charge of the store itself. For business outside of Silicon Valley and Hollywood, visitors are best advised to wear conservative suits and ties and women stylish but conservative skirts or pantsuits. Extremes of fashion are generally not appreciated outside of the fashion and music industries. Dress on the East and West coasts tend to be a touch more racy than in the Midwest or South.

FRANCE: STYLE AND QUALITY

The French, as would be expected, have a genuine appreciation of fine workmanship, expensive materials, originality, harmony and style. Middle managers may not own a lot of clothes but what they do own is of the highest quality. French businessmen prefer the "uniform" but will accessorize their dark suits with colorful ties or carry a designer briefcase. They never loosen their ties or roll up their sleeves. That would be unstylish. Local businesswomen are chic. Painted nails and high heel shoes should not be mistaken as a sign that they lack business acumen. For foreigners, it is a real challenge dressing to French style standards. The best advice is don't try to match the French on style points. Just make sure what you wear is crisp, conservative and of high quality. The French do not tolerate a lack of *soigner*—that is, putting care and thought into your appearance.

RUSSIA: IT'S THE SHOES

Russians have high expectations of foreigners when it comes to clothes, especially business attire. They judge others quickly by what they wear—and one of the first things they notice are shoes. Russians have a thing for shoes—they are status symbols. You may notice that one of the first places a Russian will glance during your first meeting is at your feet. (This is one of those Soviet-era habits that die hard. In the "bad old days" shoes were *defitsitny*—goods that were chronically in short supply—and those that were available were rather frumpy and tended to fall apart when they got wet. Good shoes were imported and those who had access to these valued imports were deemed to have some status within the community.) Fashion tastes are very different here than in Europe or the

United States. High fashion for Russian women tends to be rather flashy, very high heels, tight dresses, pounds of makeup and biggish hair. Russians themselves are new to wealth and tend to overdress, even for business. Showy jewelry, expensive watches and accessories are common items, meant to impress a visitor.

SOUTH AFRICA: FRUMPISHLY ELEGANT

It is safe to say that South Africa is not one of the fashion meccas of the world. Style is defined by simple, if sometimes frumpish, elegance and is more Western and more American than it is African. When doing business long-sleeved shirts are preferred over short-sleeved ones which are more casual. In this male-dominated culture, businesswomen still rarely wear trousers.

BRAZIL: A CASUAL ELEGANCE

Like the French, Brazilians are obsessed with style, but tend to dress more casually than the French. In many organizations, ties are optional for senior management but the amount of formality varies by region with cities such as Rio de Janeiro being more casual than Brasília, the seat of government. Still, foreign visitors should play it safe and dress conservatively unless absolutely sure that ties are optional.

SAUDI ARABIA AND OTHER ISLAMIC STATES: MODESTY OVER COMFORT

Despite heat, it is modesty over comfort for both the locals and the foreign visitor. At least on the initial meeting, it is appropriate for visiting males to wear the international business "uniform"—dark suit and tie. Don't worry about being uncomfortable—everything is air conditioned. While Western women are not expected to dress in the traditional black chador, they are expected to keep their arms, legs and ankles covered. Long skirts are the most appropriate, with sleeves at elbow length or longer and necklines that are high. Leave the backless and sleeveless dresses at home. The shorts Western men wear in hot weather bear a strong resemblance to the undergarments Arab males wear under the *galabayyas* or flowing caftans. So foreign males who dare to wear shorts in public in many Arab countries actually look to locals like they are walking around in their underwear.

ISRAEL: STILL HIGHLY CASUAL BUT...

Until recently, formal dress for an Israeli man meant a clean shirt and new jeans. But in a country where neckties were once shunned because they signified class differences in an egalitarian society, things have changed. Israelis no longer snicker at suit-and-tie-clad businesspeople. Still, this is a country with no real dress code. When conducting business, dress comfortably and more casually than you would back home—but don't overdo it.

INDIA: BRITISH ROOTS

Business dress in India is surprisingly formal, harking back to its days under British rule. Conservative is good here. One obvious tip for foreigners. Don't wear or carry leather. A leather belt or briefcase can be insulting. To a large portion of the population, the cow is sacred.

Most Japanese executives will have a high-quality but rather boring wardrobe. Conservative suits, white shirts and unexciting neckties are the order of the day for men. Smart skirts without any flashy accessorizing is best for women. Remember, this is a society that values group harmony over individualism. The Japanese are fashion conscious but more about quality than trendy styles. This shows up in business dress in expensive hand tailoring and expensive but rather tame accessories. Details should be given careful attention, including belts, shoes, collars, briefcase and wallet. The Japanese are offended by scruffy rumpled dress and during the summer months Japanese executives will actually shower and change clothes two or three times in one day. They expect visitors to match them in appearance. Visiting businesswomen should wear conservative business dress, with jewelry and perfume at a minimum.

Dining Etiquette Rules

Though each culture has its own peculiarities when it comes to dining customs, the following list of basic dining etiquette tips is valid for all cultures. The list is a mix of accepted universal custom and common sense. The way you behave at a meal will have an impact on the impression business colleagues have of you.

- Place your napkin on your lap only after everyone has been seated. Be discreet, do not open the napkin with a mid-air snap or flourish but rather open it below table level and place it on your lap. If you must leave in mid-course, place your napkin on the chair or to the left of your plate. Never, never place it on your plate. When the meal is concluded place the finished napkin to the right of your plate.

- Never begin eating until everyone has been served, unless invited to do so by the hosts.

- Forearms are OK on the table but elbows are not. In some cultures, particularly in Asia, it is considered rude to put your hands beneath table level.

- It is common in Europe, Asia, and Africa for diners to keep the same flatware throughout a meal. It is acceptable to wipe them off with a piece of bread.

- Do not point or gesticulate with your knife (or any other implement for that matter) while engaged in conversation at table. It is considered the height of rudeness and bad breeding.

- In Europe and Africa, the salad is served after the main course. In America it is served at the start of a meal.

- In most European and Middle Eastern cultures, coffee will be served after dessert and, in the case of Europe, after the cheese course which concludes the meal. In the United States, cheese is often served as an hors d'oeuvre.

- When it comes to formal toasts, follow the lead of the hosts. In many Asian cultures only counterparts of equal stature may toast each other.

- Always taste your food before adding any seasonings, including salt. It is rude to season without tasting and may actually reflect negatively on your character by implying that you are prone to making hasty decisions before checking out the facts.

WHEN DINING AT SOMEONE'S HOME

- If you arrive before most guests and are seated, rise when introduced to guests—both male and female—for the first time.

- In most cultures it is rude to arrive empty-handed. Although lavish gifts are usually not expected, flowers for the hostess are the best bet. Some cultures, especially the French, find a gift of wine slightly *déclassé*.

- Eat what is on your plate and praise the host/hostess. In most cultures leaving food uneaten is rude and considered a poor reflection on the host.

- If at a home where servants or hired staff are serving the meal, you should be courteous, but don't be overly friendly to or engage the house servants in conversation. Not only will your host feel uncomfortable but so will the hired help.

- When in doubt follow your the manners your own culture prescribes—and look confident doing it.

- In most Asian cultures it is appropriate to leave one's shoes at the door. Follow the lead of your host but never insist on keeping shoes on. Be sure you wear a clean pair of socks without holes.

CHOPSTICKS: A SPECIAL CASE

Asian dining is subject to the same rules of common sense as anywhere else in the world, but there are a few basic do's and don'ts when it comes to handling chopsticks. Among them:

- It is considered rude to wave your chopsticks around as you decide which dish to sample next.

- Never stick your chopsticks into food such as rice and let them stand upright. Sticking chopsticks into a bowl of rice is reminiscent of incense sticks at a funeral.

- It is bad manners to use chopsticks like a fork to spear your food with the tips.

- Avoid pulling or dragging dishes toward you with your chopsticks. Pick up the dishes in your hand instead.

- When the meal is finished replace your chopsticks on the chopstick rest just as you found them when the meal began.

- Not all Asian cultures use chopsticks (e.g., Thailand, Philippines) and asking for them in such situations would be considered an insult.

- If you are from the West, your hosts may find your ability to use chopsticks fascinating and they may comment upon it. This bit of quaintness can seem patronizing, but it should be taken as a compliment regarding your cultural acumen.

Checklist: Preparing for a Visit

Whether you are traveling to a new culture for business or hosting a visiting delegation from another country, there are some basic issues you need to address in advance to ensure a relatively smooth, trouble-free interaction. Among them:

- NAME Get it straight. Practice any troublesome names beforehand and learn the word order of names.

- THE GREETING When greeting your colleagues, will they expect physical contact, a hug, a hardy handshake or will they shun the physical? If women are in the delegation, determine if physical contact during a greeting is acceptable.

- FOOD If visiting a new culture, learn the meal times and which meal is considered the main one of the day and plan accordingly. If hosting a reception or a dinner, be aware of foods that might offend guests (e.g., don't offer pork to a Moslem or beef to a Hindu). Seek out local help in preparing a banquet.

- DINNER SEATING If hosting a meal, remember that some cultures demand that the most senior member of the delegation be given a place of honor at the table. Make a seating plan accordingly.

- CLOTHING TABOOS Think twice about any article of clothing that may offend. Don't wear leather in India. Regardless of whether you are home or away, women should dress modestly if dealing with individuals from an Islamic culture. No bare arms or short skirts.

- COLORS Remember, colors have different meanings in different cultures. White may be a festive color in the West but in China it symbolizes mourning. Purple symbolizes sadness in Thailand, suffering in Taiwan, but wealth in Nigeria.

Some Cultural Quirks

WHAT THE BUSINESS TRAVELER CAN EXPECT IN SOME CULTURES

UNITED STATES

- While most of the rest of the world finds interruptions rude, Americans will often interrupt each other and finish one another's sentence.

- Many Americans believe the number 13 to be unlucky. Often buildings will go from the 12th to the 14th floor, skipping the number 13 entirely.

- Business communication and negotiation are often informal and even when formal, they will be less so than in most other cultures.

- Americans are notoriously blunt and prefer to speak their minds. They have no concept of "face" (see Chapter 13 for a discussion of this concept). When they disagree, they say so—a fact which often causes embarrassment to individuals from cultures where such bluntness is not appreciated.

- Americans are very health conscious. Never smoke without asking permission. It is not only rude, but probably illegal to smoke in most public buildings.

MEXICO

- In Mexican business circles, the idea of nepotism is accepted and criticism of it is taken as an insult.

- Mid-day rest periods (*siestas*) are still quite common, even for executives. Business may be conducted later into the evening to make up for this rest period.

ARGENTINA

- Argentinians are heavily into psychoanalysis and the country boasts one of the highest ratios of mental health professionals to general population in the world. Specialized clinics have been established by many industries, businesses and trade unions as an integral part of the regular employee benefits package.

- Manners in Argentina are more formal than in the rest of Latin American. Like the British, they shun informality and casualness which can leave a bad first impression.

- The Argentine view of time is more like that of Europeans and North Americans than that of any other Latin Americans. The *mañana* attitude is uncommon in Argentina.

SAUDI ARABIA

- Be careful what you wish for—you might just get it. When you openly admire a possession of a Saudi host, he just might feel obligated to give it to you—even if it is something he treasures. So go easy on the compliments.

- Don't ask specifically after one's wife or daughters; it shows disrespect. Rather, ask about the family or the children.

- It is impolite to point the sole of your shoe at someone you are addressing.

- As in all Islamic cultures, use your right hand for everything even if you are left-handed. The left hand is considered unclean. It is reserved for toilet functions.

GERMANY

- Privacy is important and Germans will expect you to knock before opening an office door.

- Of all Europeans, Germans put the greatest value on their personal space and do not like being crowded. A distance of more than two feet (60 cm) is expected when conversing among non-familiars.

- It is rude to shake someone's hand with your other hand in your pocket. It is considered disrespectful.

CHINA

- Avoid the number four, which is highly inauspicious because it sounds like the word *si,* which means death. Chinese buildings often do not have a fourth floor.

- Red ink should never be used to address a letter. It is too heavily associated with the destructiveness of fire, although red for wrapping paper or stationery is associated with special occasions.

- The Chinese are impressed by status. Presenting letters of introduction from well-known business leaders, overseas Chinese, or former government officials who have dealt with China is an excellent way of showing that you are both a person of high standing and that you mean business.

- Avoid appearing arrogant or over-confident. Confucian beliefs condemn this type of behavior.

FRANCE

- Don't smile unless the French do. They find it phony and childish behavior and prefer to offer an empty stare. If you smile at a Frenchman, he'll think you are mocking him. If you smile at Frenchwoman, you are flirting with her.

- Don't point. To indicate someone or something, use your entire hand with palm open.

JAPAN

- Respect of hierarchy is important. If you are hosting a visiting Japanese delegation and putting them up in a hotel, make sure the most senior executives are put on higher floors than junior executives.

- Blowing your nose in public is considered highly offensive. A cloth handkerchief is considered uncouth; better to use disposable tissues.

- Only children eat while walking outside in public.

RUSSIA

- Russians are incredibly superstitious. Though they may joke about their beliefs, most, when pressed, will admit to paying them credence. Coupled with these superstitions is a surprisingly firm faith in "old wives' tales" that take on an aura of truth even in the highest levels of society. One such example: Following the 1986 Chernobyl nuclear disaster in Ukraine, word spread that red wine could prevent and cure radiation sickness. So great was the local hysteria, the Soviet government marked the region for additional red wine supplies in lieu of apparently much more sophisticated medical treatments. There were few complaints and red wine virtually became a prescription drug.

- Monday is considered a bad day to start a journey or a business venture. Don't be surprised if Monday morning business meetings are hard to schedule.

- If you leave something behind in Russia that means you are destined to return.

INDIA

- As a matter of pride, government officials insist on referring to the city of Bombay as Mumbai, the original pronunciation. However, many in the business community prefer calling the city by its old name. In your communications with government officials, refer to the city as Mumbai.

- India celebrates its ethnic diversity. One example: India rupee notes have their denominations written in 13 languages: Hindi, English, Urdu, Bengali, Tamil, Gujarati, Marathi, Telugu, Bihari, Punjabi, Rajasthani, Kannarese, and Malayalam.

CHAPTER 6

Communicating Across Cultures

THE MOST IMMUTABLE BARRIER IN NATURE IS BETWEEN

ONE MAN'S THOUGHT AND ANOTHER'S.

— WILLIAM JAMES

DOING BUSINESS INTERNATIONALLY means that you will come into increasing contact with individuals who speak different languages and live in different cultures. Even the most simple form of communication will become a challenge. Knowing that cultural differences exist is only step one of the process. Learning to deal with these differences and perhaps turn them to your advantage can make the difference between a successful and unsuccessful international business deal. There are more than 6,200 different languages in the world today. Merely knowing the language, though, is still not enough to be able to effectively communicate. You must have some understanding of thought patterns, values, societal norms and of how individuals from different cultures process information to be an effective communicator.

High Road, Low Road

For example, as mentioned in Chapter 2, cultures usually fall into high-context or low-context ones when it comes to listening and information processing. Individuals from low-context cultures, such as the United States and Germany, are much more precise in their communication, providing mountains of detail, and assume a relatively low level of shared knowledge with the individual to whom they are communicating. Meanwhile, high-context cultures are the exact opposite. Communication tends to be imprecise. In high-context cultures (Asia, Latin America), personal encounters and efforts at building a relationship are essential before business can begin. Also, you must establish if a culture is task-oriented or relationship-oriented. Knowing the thought processes of your potential business partner will allow you to choose the communication method and strategy that maximizes your business opportunity.

Two important rules of thumb to remember when attempting to communicate cross-culturally: (1) Don't be overconfident. You should always assume there are differences in the way information is received and processed. Do not take thought processes for granted, even if someone speaks the same language as yourself; it is dangerous to assume that they think the same way or hold the same values. (An example: the Argentinians and the Spanish. Though they speak the same language their approach to business and the level of formality expected in communication is very different.) (2) Use uncomplicated descriptive language to explain your position. Using visual aids and being clear and concise in written materials can play an important role in ensuring better understanding.

Responsibilities

Regardless of the cultures that the speaker and the listener originate from, both have certain responsibilities to each other in cross-cultural situations to ensure a maximum of understanding and a minimum of potentially disastrous miscommunication. The communicator must ensure that the verbal message and any non-verbal means of communication are consistent with each other. The communicator should convey information accurately and concisely in descriptive language and should ask for feedback from the listener to verify that the message was received properly. Give the listener ample time and opportunity to ask questions—and make sure you are confident enough not to be personally challenged by questions.

The person receiving the communication should be an active listener who concentrates on the message being communicated. The individual should answer and respond at the appropriate time and ask for clarification or further explanation if there is any doubt about the tone or content of the message. It is better to ask questions and ask for the message to be repeated than to walk away not fully understanding it or making wrong assumptions about ambiguous content.

Who Speaks What

When it comes to the number of native speakers, English is only the fourth most-spoken language in the world after Mandarin, Hindi and Spanish. Yet when it comes to the number of people throughout the world who can speak and understand English, it becomes the second most common language on the planet, after Mandarin. In fact, you only need to learn six of the more than 6,200 languages (Mandarin, English, Hindi, Spanish, Russian and Arabic) known to man to able to communicate with more than half the people on Earth.

The Global Business Language

The vast number of people who can speak or understand English would alone make for a good argument as to why the language is considered the lingua franca of international business and international telecommunications, as well as the Internet. (No less than 80 percent of all the information on the Internet is in English. It is the United States that dominates the world of computers and the English language that dominates the Internet.) While the proliferation of English in business, at least in this century, owes much to the economic might of the United States, it was the spread of British colonialism, the mixture of empire and commerce, that many scholars believe is the root of English as the world language of commerce. In the same period as the zenith of the British empire, the international importance of other European languages, especially French, declined. But there are other factors that argue for the use of English as the global business language. English is remarkable for its diversity, its propensity to change and be changed. This has resulted in a variety of forms of English, as well as a diversity of cultural contexts within which English is used in daily life. Also, the English language has grown up in contact with many others making it a hybrid language that can rapidly evolve to meet new cultural and communicative needs.

Perhaps the most important reason that English is considered the global business language has to do with the overall wealth of the world's English speakers. Researchers at Georgetown University in the United States have estimated that English speakers alone count for 33 percent of the world's gross national product. Japanese speakers account for 9 percent, German speakers, 8 percent, and French speakers, 6 percent. English has become the world's business language because its speakers are the best in the world at doing business—at least measured by overall wealth.

LINGUA FRANCA, LINGUA ENGLA

Much to the chagrin of purists in different cultures, the globalization of world economies has forced businesspeople to search for some form of a common tongue. Of course, it would be foolish for any businessperson to assume that their counterpart, regardless of their country of origin, is apt to speak English when it comes to business, but it is more likely to be so than any other language. English already shares the languages curriculum in Europe with French, German, and Spanish and the same is true in most schools worldwide. The use of English as a teaching medium has permitted rapid internationalization of higher education and adult training.

As English continues to flourish in the role as the global language of business, proficiency in the English language will open the door to the new international skilled job market and likely become one of the mechanisms for dividing the world's "haves" from the "have-nots." The ability to speak English will be a prerequisite for any serious businessperson wishing to perform in the global marketplace.

Despite its adoption as a common language for business, there are vast differences in the way English is spoken throughout the world. So great are the differences that one could consider them almost as separate "dialects" of the same language. In Hong Kong, for example, one international management consulting firm has identified at least ten different dialects of English in use—from American and British English to Chinese English to Hong Kong English. In extreme cases, speakers from different parts of the world may not even understand one another despite speaking what on the surface looks like a common language—English.

English: Similar Differences

If anybody should be able to communicate across cultures, you would think the Americans and the British would. After all, they share a common heritage and language—English. But, alas, put a British businessman in a room with an American executive and the danger of miscommunication and misunderstanding is high. Consider these potential problems in opposing interpretations of the same word.

- BOMB In the United States this means that something is a massive failure: "The project was a bomb." But in Britain if you said, "The project went a bomb," you would be saying it was a huge success.

- TABLE In the United States if you say you have decided to table the proposal, it means that you are going to put it aside, perhaps indefinitely. However, in Britain, to table a proposal means to bring it up for consideration and ultimately a decision.

A couple of other problem areas: In Britain when you call someone a sod, you are not referring to them as a piece of turf, but rather as someone dumb or unreliable. And finally, when the subject of schools arises, the confusion sets in. In Britain a "public school" is what Americans call a "private school." In America a "public school" is what the British call a state or government school.

So, if two similar cultures linked by a common language can experience fundamental communications problems, consider just how difficult it can be to get the more subtle aspects of a message across to someone from a culture that has not only a totally different language but also a completely different philosophy, method of processing information and listening context. This is an important reason to test understanding frequently in meetings with individuals who may speak not only a completely different language but simply another version of your own native tongue.

Adaptable English

In cultures that are unaccustomed to the jargon of global business, English nomenclature for business terms has been adapted for local use. The French have spent considerable time trying to stamp out "Franglais"—the irritating adaptation of English words into French vocabulary (le weekend, le jumbo jet). However, in many other languages, English adaptations have filled a gap, especially in business. For example, as Russia marches toward a market economy, English words have entered the Russian language, mostly through the back door of phonics, to fill the gap. A few examples:

- Biznesmeny (biz-ness-MYEN-nee): Those engaged in Western-style commerce, or, as the Russians would say, bizness. The word also carries a connotation of wealth and worldly sophistication as well as the negative one of "schemer."

- Buckcy (BUCK-see): What biznesmeny pursue—money. Derived from "bucks," American slang for dollars or cash.

- Griny (gree-NEE): Green, the color of buckcy. In particular, it means the U.S. dollar.

- Franchaizy (fran CHAIS-ee): Those involved in one of Russians hottest trends, franchising.

- Komissioner (co-mi-shen-ER): No, not an important officeholder but rather someone, usually a salesperson, who works on a commission—a very new concept in Russia.

- Konsultant (con-sul-TANT): A business consultant—an unheard-of profession in the former Soviet Union but now one of the quickest ways for the old communists with connections to cash in on the new market economy.

The Subtleties of Speech

Individuals from low-context cultures (such as the United States), where the meaning of words is king, have few problems saying "no" to a deal. When they say, "No, I am not interested," they simply say "No" and move on. They leave little room for doubt or interpretation. However, in the majority of the world's cultures (Asia, Africa, the Middle East) individuals place great value on "face" (for a detailed discussion of the concept of "face", see Chapter 13 on cross-cultural negotiations). The loss of face means the disruption of group harmony, bringing shame to the business organization or losing one's own reputation or credibility.

In high-context cultures (such as Japan, China, Kenya, Saudi Arabia), individuals find it extremely difficult to give a direct "no" answer. They may mean "no," but they will almost never say it bluntly. One of the key reasons behind the inability to say "no" directly is the desire for African, Arabic or Asian businesspeople to preserve personal relationships—the lifeblood of business in most high-context cultures. They fear the relationship may be permanently damaged if they give a blunt negative answer. In Asian cultures, where group harmony must be preserved at all costs, it is essential to avoid any act or word that might damage this harmony.

Individuals in these cultures are highly inventive when it comes to giving a negative answer to a question, a request or a proposal without ever saying the word "no." If you are not attuned to these subtleties they are easy to miss. Here are some typical replies heard in African, Asian and Arabic cultures that may not sound like a "no" but more than likely mean "no":

- I have to think about it.
- Yes, it sounds interesting but there may be some difficulties.
- I need to check with my superiors.
- I will do my best, but I cannot promise.
- This may take time.
- I am excited but it sounds complicated.

CULTURE CAUTION: Remember that the context of a business situation is usually dominated by the buyers. The sellers, no matter whether host or guest (Western or Eastern), bear the responsibility for getting their point across.

Avoiding the Pitfalls of Slang

The quickest way to confuse a business colleague who speaks another language or is relying on an interpreter to communicate is to make use of slang and local idioms. An idiom is an expression unique to a given language and often to a given geographical region. Usually it is impossible to figure out the meaning of an idiomatic expression from the words used to form the expression. Most non-Spaniards, for example, wouldn't have a clue what to do if they were told by a Spanish colleague to *vete a freir esparragos* which literally means to "go fry asparagus" or, as the Americans would say, "go fly a kite." The expression in both languages carries the connotation of being told to "get lost." Similarly, if a British businessperson said someone has "met their Waterloo" most Asian businesspeople would not know it meant defeat. But if a Japanese executive were to refer to *Odawara hyojo* (the council of Odawara) few non-Japanese would know the term is slang for a long drawn-out and futile negotiation. (The idiom refers to a centuries-old Japanese warlord council that debated so long on how to defend the castle of Odawara that by the time the decision was made the enemy had overrun the fort.)

A SPORTING CHANCE

While the Americans are probably most guilty of using sports terminology as slang in business negotiations, they are not the only nationality prone to this common error. An American telling a visiting Russian businessman that his company must gather its "team players" (general sports idiom for people who work together) and "step up to the plate" (a baseball expression that means take responsibility) and devise a "game plan" (an American football expression that means a strategic plan) to jockey itself into position (a horseracing term meaning to put yourself in a good spot) to close the deal or else risk "striking out" (baseball talk for failure) will probably leave both the businessman and his translator "out in left field" (baseball expression meaning clueless). Avoid sports idioms in all languages. They are the most overused type of idiom in the world and they usually mean very little to anyone unfamiliar with the culture—or the sport!

International Idioms

All cultures have idiomatic expressions that are unique in meaning, but there are some expressions, while not quite the same in a literal translation, that can be figured out by comparing it to idioms in your own language. Often with a little common sense the business traveler can figure out their basic meaning. It can even make for an interesting game. Some examples:

ITALIAN	TRANSLATION	ENGLISH EQUIVALENT
Nudo come un verme	Naked as a worm	Naked as a jaybird
Pigliare due piccioni con una fava	Catch two pigeons with one bean	Kill two birds with one stone
Tandare a singhiozzo	To go by hiccups	Moving by fits and starts

FRENCH	TRANSLATION	ENGLISH EQUIVALENT
C'est du Chinois	It's Chinese to me	It's Greek to me
Epargne ta salive	Save your saliva	Don't waste you breath
Revenons à nos moutons	Let's return to our sheep	Let's get back to the subject

SPANISH	TRANSLATION	ENGLISH EQUIVALENT-
Poner el grito en el cielo	To scream at the sky	To hit the ceiling
Estar vivo y coleando	Alive and wagging your tail	Alive and kicking
Vete a freir esparragos	Go fry asparagus	Go fly a kite

A Special Note on Japanese Idioms

No mention of idioms and slang would be complete without a mention of their use in the Japanese language, which employs colorful images and graphic detail to capture a point. Some examples of Japanese idioms that business travelers may encounter:

- *Ate-uma*: Similar in meaning to the American phrase "a stalking horse," it refers to a male horse that is used to excite a mare in preparation for mating with a stallion. In business it means a dummy proposal or a preliminary negotiating point that is used to determine what the other side is really thinking.

- *Daikoku bashira*: This refers to the main pillar of a building that supports the roof. In business terms it means the individual who is the glue that holds a company or a working team together. Basically, it means a pillar of strength.

- *Gaden insui*: This literally means "to bring water into your own rice paddy" and refers to a businessperson who tries to manipulate all aspects of a discussion to their own advantage or credit. A rough English equivalent would be to "toot your own horn."

- *Tsuru no hitokoe*: When a flock of cranes are feeding there is always one crane who stands watch. When that crane gives the signal, the flock departs in unison, no questions asked. In every Japanese company there is always a tsuru no hitokoe—the one executive whose word is law.

- *Gaku Batsu*: This is the Japanese version of the "old boys network" and refers to people, usually within the same company that have all graduated from the same university.

Telephone Etiquette

The telephone has been around for decades and is a key tool in international business, yet few people ever think about how they use it and what the reaction to one's telephone manner may be on the other end of the line. There is a cultural disconnect when communicating by telephone and to ignore the basic communication differences that exist between cultures just because you are talking on the phone is a mistake. One British businessman says that during international calls he always tries to visualize not only the person he is talking to but the physical circumstances of the location as well. "When I am speaking to a colleague in Paris, I visualize tree-lined Parisian streets and it reminds me to be a little more genteel and more conscious of my manners than if I was speaking to a guy in New York," he says.

SO NEAR, YET SO FAR

It is important to remember that the phone is often the first significant personal contact you have with an overseas colleague. Depending on your telephone manners, it can be used to build your image and a potential personal relationship or it can get things off to a poor start. Be patient if there is a language barrier and retain a sense a humor. A British advertising executive recalls how she was telephoning an ad agency in Nairobi, Kenya and encountered trouble understanding the heavily accented English of the Kenyan receptionist. "We just didn't connect well. She kept asking for my name and I kept saying 'Fiona, Fiona'. Finally I spelled it out 'F for Freddy, I for India. Anyway about an hour later I received a return call from an agency executive who asked for Freddy. Obviously the receptionist took down F for Freddy as my first name. Fortunately the call came through on my direct line. Once we got connected we both had a good laugh and the relationship got off to a good start."

BASIC RULES OF INTERNATIONAL TELEPHONE COMMUNICATION

- Even before you pick up the phone, know the time of the locale you are calling. Nothing worse than rousting a colleague out of bed for a non-urgent matter just because you are ignorant of international time differences.

- Remember to be sensitive to the customs and ways of the person and culture you are calling. Treat the conversation as if you were meeting in person—on their turf. One London investment banker says he even bows when calling a colleague in Japan. He swears it makes a difference.

- Always try and use uncomplicated language. Because you cannot see facial expressions or read body language over the phone, it is hard to judge how well your message is being understood. The simpler the language the less chance of misunderstanding.

- Don't hurry the pace of your speech. Talk slowly and distinctly.

- Be prepared with what you want to say. Write a script or keep notes about important points you want to touch upon. Clearly state the reason and purpose of your call. Be enthusiastic.

- Smile, just as you would if you were meeting in person. It can make your voice sound upbeat and pleasant.

- Concentrate when you listen and never interrupt someone on the other line. Often people will allow themselves to be distracted while on the phone. When dealing in a cross-cultural situation, be cognizant that the slightest distraction can cause you to misunderstand the subtleties of the message. Be aware of time delays in satellite connections.

- When dealing with secretaries or message takers it is important in some cultures to remind them to get a pencil and paper and to write the message down. Be sure to ask them to repeat the message and the contact numbers you have given. More than one international business deal has been squashed because a caller has assumed that the message taker on the other line clearly understood instructions.

- Should a phone conversation start to turn sour, it is important to remain diplomatic and not risk ending a relationship on the telephone. Show an eagerness to resolve the problem or conflict. You will not have an opportunity to put the damage right with a friendly gesture or a drink after work as you would if you were dealing with someone in person.

- Try and return calls in the same business day. If international time differences make that impossible then return the call the next day at the latest. Failure to return a call is downright rude.

When connecting on the telephone, your voice is all you have. Make it work for you. Be confident and purposeful without being arrogant. And remember, a telephone call can be just as important as a face-to-face meeting, especially if you are building a new relationship. Be prepared just as you would for a personal meeting. If you are not feeling up to the challenge, then take more time to prepare.

SPEAKERPHONES

If you want to put a conversation on a speakerphone, make sure you ask the caller first if it is permissible and be sure to identify any other individuals by name and position if necessary who may be participating in the conversation or who are in the room.

VIDEO-CONFERENCING

As a way to control travel costs and increase the frequency of contact, many international companies are increasingly using the option of video-conferencing. While still not as personal as face-to-face contact, it is a good compromise between the faceless phone call, e-mail or fax and the in-person visit. It also allows for each side to get a limited read on a speaker's body language. For this reason, it is important for the speaker to make sure the message and the body language are consistent in tone. Often, those not directly involved as a speaker may forget that what they do or how they react can be seen on the other end. It is surprising just how many off-color remarks or bored gestures are conveyed by the camera to people on the other side—all without the sender even being aware he or she is on camera.

VOICE MAIL AND ANSWERING MACHINES

Yes, sometimes it can be annoying to be put through to someone's voice mail or an answering machine. But when leaving a message don't show your annoyance or frustration. It can be counterproductive. Some tips on handling voice mail:

- Be prepared with a clear, brief, and purposeful message. Use a written script if necessary.

- The ideal voicemail or answering machine message is less than 30 seconds long.

- Always give the time and day you called.

- Give your name and number both at the beginning of the message and at the end. If talking internationally remember to give your city and country code unless it is obvious and repeat all numbers slowly.

- Be positive and upbeat in your sign-off.

CHAPTER 7

Non-Verbal Communication

HE KNEW THE PRECISE PSYCHOLOGICAL MOMENT WHEN

TO SAY NOTHING. — OSCAR WILDE

IT'S OFTEN NOT WHAT you say that counts but what you don't say. A wink, a subtle hand gesture, a scratch of the chin can all be signals that punctuate the spoken word. Whether you realize it or not, you are constantly communicating your feelings, your reactions and your state of mind without ever uttering a word. Your general appearance is one form of non-verbal communication. So is your posture, your facial expressions, the amount of eye contact you achieve, the hand gestures you use and the amount of physical contact you employ. Even the silence with which you greet a proposal—the so-called pregnant pause—is a form of non-verbal communication. This type of communication serves as a complement to the spoken word and can often be your only first-hand knowledge of a foreign colleague who speaks a language you don't understand.

Researchers have shown that the words a person speaks may be far less important than the body language used when delivering the verbal message. They estimate that less than 10 percent of the whole message understood by an audience is the actual content, some 30 percent is attributed to the pitch and tenor of a person's voice and 60 percent to other forms of non-verbal communication from body language to facial expressions to hand gestures.

If a person is giving off negative signals through body language such as shaking their head from side to side, even if they are uttering a positive statement, listeners are more apt to cast the incident in the negative, recalling the negative body language rather than the positive verbal message. Few businesspeople take the time to read these non-verbal clues or to control them. Making non-verbal communication work on your behalf can provide a big advantage in the realm of cross-cultural communication.

Cultural Nuance

Understanding non-verbal communication is a true art—mainly because it varies so significantly from culture to culture. One's culture determines how close we stand when talking with another, or how much eye contact we demand. Culture also determines what non-verbal signs we use to express anger or hatred or trust or approval. Don't underestimate the cultural differences in the interpretation of non-verbal forms of communication. What is a gesture of joy in one culture may be considered a rude insult in another.

Consider the case of one British businessman in Iran. After months of doing the right thing—building relationships with Iranian colleagues, respecting the influence of Islam on negotiations and avoiding any potentially explosive political small talk—the executive was elated once a formal contract was signed. He signed the papers and turned to give his Persian colleagues a big thumbs up. Almost immediately there was a gasp and one Iranian executive left the room. The British executive didn't have a clue as to what was going on—and his Iranian hosts were too embarrassed to tell him.

The explanation was really quite simple. While the thumbs-up gesture means "good, great, well-played" in Britain, in the Persian culture it is a sign of discontent and borders on the obscene. "I don't think I was ever more embarrassed in my life. I felt like a child who yells out a vulgar curse word without having any clue as to what it means," the executive says. "My colleagues accepted my plea of ignorance but the relationship was damaged. It wasn't that they thought I had truly meant the gesture as interpreted in their culture but rather that I was totally ignorant of it. I just never suspected there was anything wrong with it."

The lesson here is simple. Communicating effectively across cultures requires more than understanding the written and spoken language. It involves a basic knowledge of the acceptable non-verbal forms of communication within a culture as well. In this case experience is probably the best teacher.

Non-Verbal Communication Types

While even in spoken communication there is enormous room for ambiguity, body language is even more inexact and one needs to be careful interpreting it. A grin, a nod, a wink, a frown does not always have some sort of profound meaning—though in certain cultures such facial expressions can be highly revealing. The key to understanding the meaning behind facial expressions and body movements is not in the individual expressions or movements themselves, but rather in the transition from one body movement to another.

Take an individual who when you begin a discussion is, literally, sitting on the edge of their seat. That gesture in and of itself is meaningless because that is how they are comfortable and like to listen—leaning forward on the edge of their seat. Then, after thirty minutes of talks, that same individual begins leaning forward even more. That would indicate an active interest. But say the same person begins leaning back in their chair after 30 minutes—that would indicate a loss of interest.

LEARN TO LOOK

Getting a meaningful read on an individual's body language takes concentration and keen powers of observation. But there is no denying the payoff. The most effective method of reading body language is a two-step process. First, observe the individual's mannerisms during the initial part of a discussion when tension is at its lowest and the subject is apt to be the most friendly. Then, as the talks continue, you can note any sudden changes in behavior or posture. Remember, the key to understanding body language is not the gesture itself but rather the transition from one posture to another.

But researchers warn against being overly captivated by the myths of body language. Reading body language is not a foolproof method of judging a person's true intentions and sincerity. This would mean that one of the main reasons spoken language was invented was to help humans deceive each other and cover up the truth of non-verbal communication—that is hardly a reasonable assumption.

Basic Body Linguistics

DRESS AND APPEARANCE

There is one form of non-verbal communication that you can maintain a great deal of control over—your physical appearance. As mentioned earlier in this book, clothes may not make the man—or the woman—but the reality is that how you look goes a long way in making that first impression. A rumpled look, an unshaven face, perhaps too short a skirt or too high a heel, can leave someone with a negative impression or at least signal that you are unprepared and not a businessperson to be taken seriously.

The purpose of clothing has changed much since humans first donned animal skins for cover. Today, clothes are considered an expression of the individual and a way to identify a person as a member of a certain class or profession (a businessman in a suit, a doctor in a lab coat). Dressing to fit the part is essential. It may not be fair but it is a reality.

EYE CONTACT

The eyes are said to be the window to the soul—and they can reveal the deeper meaning behind the spoken word. But the amount of proper eye contact varies greatly from culture to culture. For example, Americans take direct eye contact as a sign of honesty and sincerity. It shows interest and attentiveness while a lack of eye contact or shifty eyes is taken as a sign of untruthfulness.

Now compare this to the French attitude. Eye contact is considered a statement of equality and is too personal a gesture to use with strangers in a social setting. However, in business meetings, the French will demand at least some direct eye contact. To refuse to meet someone's eyes is an unfriendly gesture. Finally, compare this to the attitude in Japan where they believe that the less eye contact, the higher the level of esteem. To divert one's eyes from a business colleague is a sign of respect and reverence.

FACIAL EXPRESSIONS

Researchers estimate that the human face is capable of creating in excess of a quarter of a million different expressions. Emotions such as happiness and sadness are not easily hidden by facial expressions in most cultures. The ability to produce the proper expression at the proper time can be a powerful way to re-enforce the spoken word. But even the most basic of facial expressions, the smile, can mean different things in different cultures.

For example, Americans consider the smile a highly positive sign—a signal of a warming relationship. However, while Americans are quick to smile, the French are wary of smiles and laughter, especially among strangers. The French smile only when there is an explicit reason. A French human resources magazine went so far as to list 13 different types of smiles and their meaning, from weak and cowardly to mocking. Americans may throw smiles around quite nonchalantly but to the French smiling can be serious business. Compare these two attitudes to Japan where the smile has little place in business negotiations. Usually the only smiles you do see are at the successful conclusion of a contact. A Japanese executive is likely to interpret a smile before then as a sign of lack of seriousness— or even as a gesture of mockery.

PERSONAL SPACE

In some cultures individuals regard space as personal territory and detest the invasion of their turf. The formal term for the amount of space around us or between us and others is *proxemics*. This, too, can be a form of non-verbal communication. How closely people position themselves to one another during a discussion can communicate what type of relationship exists between them. For example, researchers have determined the proxemics found in American culture:

0-18 inches is intimate space reserved for family and close friends
18 inches to 4 feet is personal space used in most interpersonal interactions
4-12 feet is social-consultative space used in more formal interactions

Of course, Asian and Arabic cultures are minimalist when it comes to proxemics. In these cultures, there is little regard for personal space, and judging the warmth or type of relationship by the amount of space allocated to you by individuals would lead to false conclusions. For businesspeople used to a wide swath of personal space, it is important to hold your ground and not back away when encountering an individual from a culture where space is less important. To back away in these circumstances would be offensive and rude and can lead to a comical "chase" as one person backs away while the other steps forward to close the distance.

POSTURE

Straight, erect posture, shoulders back, head held high are generally considered the attributes of an individual who is confident, energetic and self-assured. But posture can also be an indication of the existence of communication barriers. Generally, a relaxed posture, a comfortable seating position, uncrossed arms, and lack of stiffness indicate openness with no communication obstacles. On the other hand, abrupt movements, shifting seating positions, crossed arms or legs may signal defiance, disinterest or an unwillingness to listen. Generally in most cultures:

- Slumped posture means low spirits or can signal defeat or disinterest. (In Confucian cultures it denotes a lack of internal harmony.)

- Leaning forward shows openness and interest.

- Leaning backwards or away from the speaker indicates a defensive posture or disinterest.

- Crossed arms or crossed legs signals a defensive position.

- Uncrossed arms shows a willingness to listen.

SILENCE

The act of remaining silent is far from a passive action. However, in different cultures it can mean very different things—or, in the case of Asian cultures, it may mean nothing at all. American, German, French and Arabic executives take a silent reaction to be a negative one. Likewise, when businesspeople from these cultures show no reaction to a proposal or presentation, it should be taken as a negative. However, in Asian cultures silence is not equated with failure or a negative attitude. Rather it simply means that executives are taking time to digest the information and put it into context. The same is true in Scandinavian countries where more thought is given to a reaction following a presentation or discussion than in other European cultures. While such silences may seem awkward to some, it would be wrong to expect an immediate reaction of any depth or meaning in cultures where silence is not thought of as a negative.

GESTURES

Hand and body gestures are often used to emphasize a point and add meaning to the spoken word. When used properly they can be a powerful force in capturing the attention of an audience. But the reverse is also true. You can undermine your message by subconsciously using gestures that send negative signals. As a listener, watching out for the hand movements or body gestures employed by a speaker can give an interesting insight into the true attitude behind the words. Again, the meaning of some gestures varies greatly according to culture. For example, the OK sign, with thumb and index finger forming an "O" and the remaining three fingers slightly raised, means everything is fine and going well to an American. However, to the French the gesture means exactly the opposite—that a proposal is absolutely worthless, a zero. To the Japanese, it has no positive or negative connotation at all but rather is a commonly used symbol for money. The reason: the "O" formed by the thumb and index finger suggests the shape of a coin.

POSITIVE VERSUS NEGATIVE BODY LANGUAGE

Across all cultures, there are some basic gestures and movements that do have a common meaning. Figuring them out is not brain surgery. Some examples of positive body language and gestures:

- THE NOD A fairly rapid almost subconscious nodding of the head signals agreement with what the speaker is saying. It can be a useful signal given by a listener to encourage a speaker and build enthusiasm. Of course, a slower series of head bobs may mean your audience is literally nodding off to sleep.

- MOVING CLOSER, LEANING FORWARD This is an almost uncontrollable action on the behalf of listeners when they are really interested in a subject. It also means that you have overcome fundamental resistance and barriers to communication that existed have been overcome. If you bring people to the edge of their seats, you have them hooked.

■ PLENTY OF HAND MOVEMENT, PALMS OPEN The more the hands move, the more open and involved a speaker is with the audience.

■ NOTE TAKING This generally shows a heightened amount of interest and a seriousness about listening. This is more true in North America than in other cultures, though. (Americans almost always attend meetings and presentations armed with notepad and pen.) However, in some cultures (Germany is one example), taking notes is the job of a secretary and not an executive. To take notes would demean your status.

Researchers agree that negative body language is much less reliable as an indicator of mood or interest than positive body language. The listener may simply be sitting in an uncomfortable chair, suffering from an extreme of temperature (too hot in the room or too cold) or may be nursing a hangover from the previous night's social fling. Regardless, some basic gestures and movements that may have negative connotations include:

■ WITHDRAWAL, LEANING AWAY FROM THE SPEAKER As would be expected this means the opposite of leaning closer to a speaker. It is perhaps one of the strongest and uncontrollable negative signals a listener can send.

■ FOLDED ARMS An act of defiance indicating that you need to overcome obstacles or skepticism before hoping to reach the listener.

■ HANDS ON FACE This is a signal that an audience may be listening to what you have to say but may not wholly agree with it. Holding one's chin while resting the elbow on the table usually means the listener is bored. (In Asia, it can also indicate unhappiness.)

■ SHIFTING POSITIONS Again, if not due to a listener's physical discomfort, it indicates boredom, disagreement and perhaps impatience with the content or length of the presentation.

■ THE YAWN Self-explanatory. You have lost your audience. Cut out the detail and put more energy into the discussion.

■ WANDERING EYES Eyes darting around the room, open stares, flipping through printed handouts, checking a wristwatch are all indicators of a lack of interest and attention. If you see this toward the end of a presentation, wrap it up in a hurry.

Reading Reactions in Different Cultures

Successfully reading body language and the meaning of gestures in different cultures is truly a subtle art form. The following examples taken from four distinct cultures from four continents show just how diverse a meaning body language can have.

READING THE AMERICANS

Directness is a highly valued trait in the United States. Because they are a very animated people and not averse to letting others know how they feel, Americans can be relatively easy to read. And often they expect you to pick up on their non-verbal signals. When they are restless or bored, they fidget. When they are impatient they drum their fingers on the table. When they are ready to leave they look at their watches. Even when they attempt being discreet, it is difficult for them to hide their true feelings. Their body language is usually a giveaway.

For Americans the handshake is a vital test of their opponent—the firmer the better. Direct eye contact is taken as a sign of honesty and sincerity. To avoid it is to run the risk of being thought of as lying, distorting the truth or covering something up. Raised voices and animated gestures do not necessarily indicate anger. They may reflect enthusiasm and excitement. Americans will tell you when they are angry. Uncertainty or reluctance to agree are often indicated by shrugging the shoulders or looking away. Pointing at someone to clarify meaning is normal but emphatic or repeated pointing usually indicates agitation or aggression.

Americans will sometimes emphasize a strongly held commitment, belief or position by banging on the table or suddenly standing up. Raising the eyebrows or a sudden pulling back of the head indicates surprise, disbelief or astonishment. Basically, with America executives, what you see is what you get. Deliberate deception is really not their style—and they probably couldn't hide it if they wanted to.

READING THE RUSSIANS

As in America, handshaking is serious business in Russia. The general rule of thumb is that should a Russian become demonstratively physical—bear hugs, death-grip handshakes, exuberant backslapping—your meeting went very well and the personal relationship that lies as the basis for business deals is well on the way to succeeding. On the other hand, a stone face and lack of warm contact is a clear indicator that something is amiss.

Russians do use body language and hand gestures rather than verbal communication to signify their excitement, approval or disapproval of an individual, an idea or even a business proposal. (A case in point is the late Nikita Khrushchev's shoe-banging episode at the United Nations in the 1960s. Russians do believe that physical gestures lend drama to simple communications and help to underscore the intensity of feeling.) While many Russian businesspeople will sit poker-faced during a presentation, they will provide subtle clues as to their feelings by using facial expressions and gestures. Winks and nods are good things if coming from your Russian counterparts.

While American businesspeople are apt to be all smiles from the start, Russians may be just the opposite. (It has been suggested that the chronically poor state of the country's dental health is the real reason behind the severe rationing of Russian smiles.) Here, the smile is highly valued and used only when needed. Should you look across the room and see your Russian counterparts with happy smiley faces, that is a very good sign. However, beware the grim face—it means you are not getting through. Try and maintain direct eye contact with your Russian counterpart, even if you are using an interpreter to discuss business. Looking away during a conversation is not only considered rude but it casts doubt on your sincerity. If a Russian avoids eye contact, then you are probably getting less than half the truth.

READING THE SOUTH AFRICANS

Because South Africans are generally so bubbly and talkative, silence says a lot. They are polite as well and if you are boring them, they, unlike the Americans they admire, will suffer through in silence. When the questions stop, consider it time to go—you've lost your audience. South Africans often use hand gestures in conversation but it is impolite and seen as a personal challenge to point at someone with your index finger wagging. The amount of hand movements a South African generates while talking is a good indicator of the degree of passion that individual has for a particular topic or proposal. It is also considered rude to talk with your hands in your pockets.

South Africans use facial expressions to signal their interest or reactions to a speaker. It is a highly developed form of communication and a good indicator of whether or not you are hitting the mark. At a meeting South Africans will steal glances at one another or at the boss to judge a reaction. Because so much business is done on trust, eye contact is essential, especially in the white community. Black African businessmen seem less hung up on that and are more into physical contact. A warm handshake followed by an arm around the shoulder means you had a successful meeting.

"It is much easier to tell how things went after meeting with a black South African businessman. They are always polite, more so than the whites, but they also like to be more demonstrative physically in their approval," says one British businessman who has been in South Africa for over a decade. "After one particularly good meeting, my black South African counterpart walked me out to my car in the parking lot and for ten minutes never once took his arm off my shoulder. I knew then we had a deal."

South Africans like to be right and seem to appreciate positive re-enforcement. If you are listening to a South African, nod agreement. It is a highly positive gesture and if you do it in the appropriate places it will make the speaker much more at ease. It is also smart to express agreement verbally on occasion to reinforce the nods.

READING THE JAPANESE

The Japanese avoid strangers, shun physical contact, rarely smile, avoid eye contact and subject themselves to rather strict rules of public behavior, including a severe limit on emotional expression. The Japanese are taught virtually from birth to mask their feelings behind blank impassive faces. Even such non-verbal communication forms as dress and appearance are masked behind conservative clothes and a lack of individual style.

Of all global cultures, the Japanese are masters at non-disclosure and at masking emotions. They are indeed hard people to read. Learning to put a mask over one's true feelings and emotions is part of growing up in the Japanese culture where the expression of emotions, even through involuntary facial expressions and gestures, is improper behavior. (Remember, this is a culture that values group harmony and conformity and shuns individualism.) The Japanese have, in effect, the uncanny ability to alter whatever they feel "for public consumption."

Before they can be displayed in public, true feelings must be refined through the innumerable rules of social behavior and social roles that lie at the heart of Japanese society. Behavior that is permissible for public display is known as *tatemae*. Behaving in a tatemae manner supports the Japanese ideal of social harmony. Often, visitors remark about the emotionally blank faces of the Japanese or the feeling that what emotion is expressed appears insincere. This is because, under the rules of tatemae, the Japanese conjure up whatever facial expression the situation calls for and the visitor expects. Smiles, for example, are rationed and displayed at the expected time—at the end of a successful deal. To smile beforehand would violate the rules of tatemae. Also, a smile is sometimes a mask to hide displeasure.

The passive, expressionless face that masks the Japanese executive can be unnerving to visiting business executives, who mistake the passiveness for a negative or disinterested reaction. In fact, the expressionless face may be concealing nothing more sinister than a daydreaming executive thinking about the party after work. However, because the Japanese display such little emotion through gesture and expression, they are especially sensitive to any body language you might display—and in fact may exaggerate the meaning.

Gestures Around the World

As explained earlier, one person's positive gesture may be another person's insult. The world is full of non-verbal gestures that can mean the exact opposite in different cultures. Some examples of the type of gestures an international business traveler is likely to come across:

Everything is Great
• United States, Germany

Things are Good (Not Excellent)
• Mexico

Worthless (Zero)
• France, Most of Europe

Symbol for Money (coins)
• Japan

Vulgar Gesture
• Spain, Russia
• Paraguay, Brazil, Uruguay

Threat of Bodily Harm
• Tunisia

THE OK SIGN

The "OK" sign, when the thumb and index finger form a circle, means "everything is great," in the United States and Germany. In Mexico it means things are just good, not excellent. In most other European countries as well as in Argentina it means something is worthless—an absolute zero. In Japan it is a symbol for money, usually coinage. In Spain, Russia, Paraguay, Brazil and Uruguay it is considered an vulgar gesture. In Tunisia it conveys a threat of bodily harm.

<u>Approval</u>
• United States
• Great Britain
• Russia

<u>Highly Offensive</u>
• Iran

<u>Rude</u>
• Australia

THUMBS UP

It signals approval in the United States, Britain and Russia. However, in Iran it basically means "screw you." It is also considered a rude gesture in Australia.

<u>Disapproval</u>
• United States
• Canada

<u>Rude</u>
• Greece

THUMBS DOWN

In the United States and Canada it shows disapproval. In Greece it is considered a rude sign and is often used by motorists to signal their anger over someone's crazy driving.

Obscene Gesture
· Pakistan

If Raised in Air — Obscene
· Lebanon

CLOSED FIST

An obscene gesture in Pakistan, if raised in the air it is an obscene gesture in Lebanon.

Victory
· Great Britain
· United States
· Most of World

Peace
· United States (from the 1960s era)

THE V SIGN

In Britain and many other parts of the world, the signal for victory, is to make a V sign with your middle and index fingers. It also signals the number "two" in Bulgaria and in the United States also means victory. Survivors of the hippie era of the 1960s in America would interpret it as a "peace sign."

<u>Offensive Gesture</u>
- Great Britain
- South AFrica

TO HELL WITH YOU

An offensive gesture in England and South Africa is the V for victory sign done with your palm facing yourself and thrust upward.

<u>Highly Offensive</u>
- United States
- Most of Europe
- Many Parts of World

THE FINGER

In the United States, most of Europe, and many other parts of the world this is a highly offensive gesture.

Highly Rude
- Central America
- Turkey

THE FIG
This sign is made when the hand is in a fist and the thumb protrudes upward between the index and middle fingers. It is a phallic symbol and considered highly rude in Central American countries and Turkey.

Shaking Head Left to Right
- United States — No
- Most of World — No
- Bulgaria — Yes
- Saudi Arabia — Yes
- Malaysia — Yes

Nodding Head Up and Down
- United States — Yes
- Most of World — Yes
- Bulgaria — No

NODDING/SHAKING HEAD LEFT TO RIGHT
In most cultures, nodding one's head up and down signals agreement or means "yes" and from side-to-side means "no." However, in Bulgaria it's just the opposite. Nodding your head up and down means "no." To signal "yes" in Bulgaria, Saudi Arabia and Malaysia, shake your head back and forth.

Encouragement / Sympathy
• United States

Offensive
• Thailand

PAT ON THE SHOULDER

In the United States it is a sign of encouragement, a signal that a job has been well done or a way to express sympathy. In Thailand it is considered offensive, the action an adult takes to scold a child.

Surprise
• United States

Hello or General Greeting
• Philippines
• Most of World

RAISED EYEBROWS

In America, this gesture signals surprise. In the Philippines, a quick lifting of the eyebrows is a non-verbal signal meaning hello.

Romantic or Sexual Connotation
• Paraguay

Everything is OK
• United States

Impolite Gesture
• France
• Australia

WINKING

In Paraguay it carries romantic or sexual connotations. In the United States it is a sign of a joke or a way to indicate everything is OK. In France and Australia it is considered impolite.

Disbelief
• United States

Boredom
• Hong Kong

BLINKING

In the United States it can be a sign of disbelief. In Hong Kong conspicuous blinking by a listener is a sign of boredom.

Person is Crazy
- North America
- Europe
- Germany (expecially)

I'm Thinking About It
- Africa
- Peru
- Argentina

TAPPING YOUR TEMPLE WITH YOUR FINGER

In North America and most of Europe it means someone is crazy. In most of Africa, Argentina and Peru it is a slight delaying tactic and means "I'm thinking about it." In the Netherlands and Germany, if you want to signal that someone is crazy, you tap your forehead with your finger. In Germany, you can be sued for making such a gesture. (It is considered a form of slander.)

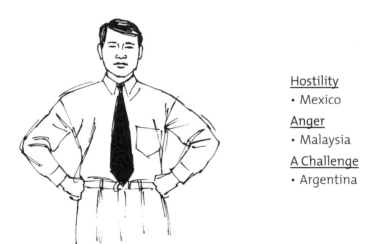

Hostility
- Mexico

Anger
- Malaysia

A Challenge
- Argentina

HANDS ON HIPS

In Mexico it signals hostility, in Malaysia it shows anger, in the United States impatience, and in Argentina it indicates a challenge.

Rude and Suggestive
• Argentina

SLAPPING THE INSIDE OF THIGHS

In Argentina it is an extremely rude and suggestive gesture when done by a male in relation to a female.

Enjoyed a Meal
• Brazil

Sign of Humility
• India

PINCH OF THE EARLOBE

In Brazil it is a signal that you have enjoyed a meal. In India it is a sign of humility—an admission that you are wrong.

<u>I Don't Know</u>
• Portugal

<u>Dull or Boring</u>
• France

<u>Get Lost</u>
• Italy

CHIN FLICK

The chin flick—the act of brushing your fingers (palm inward) off the bottom of your chin and away from your face—signals "I don't know" in Portugal. To do the same gesture, but using the thumb would mean that something no longer exists, or has died. In France flicking the fingers across one's check means dull or boring. In Italy it means a rather strong version of "get lost."

<u>Rude</u>
• All Europe
• Japan
• China

HANDS IN POCKET(S)

Everywhere in Europe it is rude to talk with your hands in your pocket. It is something only a guilty child would do. In Japan and China, it is rude to stand with your hands thrust into your pockets.

Extremely Rude
• China
• Japan

Bad Upbringing
• France

NOSE BLOWING

The Chinese and the Japanese find blowing your nose in public extremely rude. In France, sneezing in public is OK but blowing your nose in public is the height of bad upbringing.

Cheap or Stingy
• Colombia

Untrustworthy or Unreliable
• Netherlands

TAPPING THE INSIDE OF THE ELBOW WITH THE OPPOSITE HAND

In Colombia it means someone is cheap or stingy. In the Netherlands it means someone is untrustworthy or unreliable.

Boredom or Disapproval
- United States

Arrogance
- Finland

ARMS FOLDED

A sign of boredom or disapproval in the United States, in Finland it is a sign of arrogance.

Vulgar Guesture
- France

SNAPPING THE FINGERS OF BOTH HANDS

A vulgar gesture in France.

<u>Drunk</u>
• France

<u>Deal is No Good (it stinks)</u>
• United States

FORMING A CIRCLE WITH YOUR THUMB AND FOREFINGER AND PLACING IT OVER YOUR NOSE (PINCHING YOUR NOSE)

In France it is meant to indicate that a person is drunk. In the United States pinching your nose with thumb and forefinger means either the proposed deal is no good (it stinks) or the person proposing the deal has body odor. In the Netherlands, to signal that someone is cheap, you would rub your nose with your forefinger from the bridge in a downward motion.

<u>Talking too Much</u>
• France

PLAYING AN IMAGINARY FLUTE

Unique (mostly) to France, it means that "someone is talking too much" and is becoming annoying.

<u>Don't Know/Don't Care</u>
• Italy

<u>Reluctance to Agree</u>
• United States

<u>Ridiculous</u>
• France

SHOULDER SHRUG

In Italy it signals that you don't know or care about something. In America it signals a reluctance to agree. In France it means something is ridiculous.

<u>Highly Offensive</u>
• Thailand
• Myanmar (Burma)
• Middle East
• Islamic States of the former USSR

SHOWING THE SOLE OF YOUR FOOT OR SHOE

It is extremely offensive to show the sole of your foot or shoe to someone. This is because the sole of the foot is the lowest part of the body and something which is usually dirty and soiled. This is especially true in many Middle Eastern countries and the Islamic states of the former Soviet Union. In Myanmar the feet are considered unclean in general and it is rude to show the soles of your feet or even raise them by placing them on a desk or a chair.

Highly Offensive
• Italy
• Most of Europe

THE "ITALIAN SALUTE"

In Italy, most of Europe, and many other parts of the world this is a highly offensive gesture roughly equivalent to "The Finger" in the USA.

The Secret of the Handshake

Outside of Asia, the handshake is the most common and most meaningful physical contact you will have with a business colleague. Of course, not everyone shakes hands alike and not all variations are deliberate. Still, analyzing a colleague's handshake after the fact may provide some clues into his or her character and intentions. This is, by nature, a rather inexact science. Some handshake basics:

■ A handshake in which an individual grips firmly but not too firmly, pumps your hand once or twice and looks you straight in the eye can signify an individual who is confident, sees you as an equal and intends an honest, up-front negotiation or discussion. If a person continues to hold onto your hand for longer than expected, he or she may be attempting to show sincerity.

■ If while shaking your hand an individual tries to guide you into a room or towards a seat, it may indicate that that individual likes to be in control and insists on having his or her way. It can signal difficult talks if things do not go their way. In many Asian nations, however, such an action should be seen as a sign of respect and friendship, not a power play.

■ If someone grips your hand and then twists their hand so it is on the top, the signal is that of a competitive person who is saying that, although you may be starting out as equals, he or she will win in the end.

■ Most people have been the victim of a handshake where an individual attempts to crush your hand in a vice-like grip. This is an indication of a person who is competitive and plans to win at all costs but associates physical strength with acuity. Their bark (or, in this case, their handshake) is often much worse than their bite.

- When offered by a Westerner, the limp handshake that resembles grabbing hold of a dead fish usually indicates someone with low energy and a lack of enthusiasm and confidence. In Asia such a handshake is common and is an indicator of equality, not deference. Some Southeast Asian societies will actually use their other hand to support their handshaking wrist. This is a sign of respect not weakness.

Written Communication

IT IS A LUXURY TO BE UNDERSTOOD.

— RALPH WALDO EMERSON

SURPRISINGLY, THE CAVE DWELLERS that inhabited the earth millennia ago had a simple solution when it came to the challenge of communicating in written form across cultures. They used pictographs—carved or drawn pictures describing a simple concept or event. No words, no alphabet, no chance of lost subtleties and confused meanings. Gradually, over the years, the pictures became symbols, and the symbols became "letters" to represent sounds. The Egyptians used hieroglyphics—a combination of pictographs, ideographs and phonograms—and later became the first to use pictures to represent sound in addition to ideas and objects.

Of course, writing tools have changed over time with sharp-edged rocks and charcoal giving way to pen and ink and finally to typewriters and computers. Today, despite all the talk of a paperless society, our main source of formal communication remains the written word—on paper. (Why else would the U.S. postal service deliver 200 billion pieces of mail a year?) And as business becomes more global, the challenge of communicating in written form across cultures is an everyday event.

Writing Rights and Wrongs

The key to clear cross-cultural written communication is to use plain language, familiar words and short, clear declarative sentences. The less cluttered the writing and the less complicated the thought expressed, the easier it is to translate. The goal of business writing is to express your meaning and business points clearly and without confusion or unnecessary amplification. Be authoritative. You are looking to inspire confidence in your personal abilities, your company and your product or service. Unlike a face-to-face negotiation, you will not be around to clarify ambiguous points for the reader. When your letter is read, you have no control over the reader's pacing or pronunciation. Punctuation may be ignored—and you aren't there to say "Hey, I didn't mean it that way."

Though it may not necessarily be the case, most people equate writing ability with thinking ability. Muddled, unclear and imprecise written communication leaves the impression that the writer is also a muddled, imprecise thinker. In business communications you cannot afford to be misunderstood or misinterpreted. The danger of that happening rises exponentially when dealing across cultures.

Know Your Audience

As when communicating verbally, it is essential when preparing written documents to know the composition of your audience. Remember, low-context cultures put great value on detail, precision, statistics and well thought-out and clear arguments. The more detail you provide for a low-context audience, the better. A high-context culture, on the other hand, will tend to look for something in the business letter that reveals an individual's personality. Details such as the quality of the paper stock, its size and color, the choice of printing fonts, the ink color and the company letterhead design are the written equivalent of "non-verbal" forms of communication. In high-context cultures the medium is the message. How a written presentation looks can be just as important as its content in such cultures.

When dealing across cultures, especially with an individual whose primary language may be different from yours, the more visual aids in the form of graphics and charts that you can provide the lesser the chance of a misunderstanding. A smart, elegant and professional layout, even of a simple business letter, is important when it comes to creating a favorable first impression.

Directions, Please

It may be obvious, but not every culture reads and writes the same way. Like English, Arabic and Hebrew are written horizontally—but from right to left. Japanese can be written either horizontally or vertically. When written vertically, the columns read from right to left, that is, the opposite direction to written English. When written horizontally the lines and the pages of books normally proceed from left to right, as in English. It is surprising how few people realize or remember the differences in reading and writing practices.

One global executive recalls presenting a Japanese colleague with his company's latest full-color brochure detailing the company's history and its products. "The cover was an absolute knockout. We were all very proud of that. A lot of sweat and tears went into the design. Well, I presented the brochure to my Japanese colleague. I remember he fingered it for a few minutes and then flipped it over. He actually began thumbing through it from the back end toward the front. Well, the back was simply a blank white page. We never thought of it. We lost the impact of our great front cover and ended up giving Japanese partners a brochure that to them seemed to have a blank white front cover. It was a good lesson."

The company now produces full color front and back covers for Asian clients.

International English Choices

English may be the international language of commerce—but which English? American English? British English? Australian English? Indian English? Documents written by native English speakers tend to be written in their own native brand of English—and tend to be overwritten and flowery. Comfortable in the language, they tend to overdo it and generally ignore how the reader on the other end, who may speak an entirely different brand of English or another language completely, will interpret it. Oddly, non-native English speakers often write the clearest and most concise English-language documents. The reason: they use an international or simplified brand of the language.

A South African exporter recalls receiving three different proposals (all in English) from three prospective partners—a South Korean, a Frenchman and an American. "It was extraordinary, but both the South Korean and French proposals were so much easier to understand. They were straightforward and to the point. The American proposal was so full of adjectives and complicated sentences, it was like I was reading another language. It was odd but the proposal from the native English speaker was the hardest to understand." What is international English? It is English that avoids contractions, catch phrases, sports clichés and puns. It is more formal than spoken English and uses simple sentences to convey ideas.

Jargon Can Help

As in oral communications, jargon and slang should generally be avoided unless you are 100 percent certain that the person you are communicating with uses and understands the specialized vocabulary. Sometimes jargon can actually make for more accurate communication. But this is true only if there is a common understanding of the terms. (Think of two computer programmers exchanging written correspondence. Obviously jargon and highly technical terms are appropriate. The same could not be said of an executive proposing a joint-venture in consumer goods with an emerging market entrepreneur.)

However, many executives in virtually every culture are guilty of overusing jargon. Too often executives believe that a puffy formal prose style mixed with a smattering of buzzwords, jargon and specialized terminology makes for good business writing, that it shows the writer's intimate knowledge of a subject. Somehow, they believe that using such terms as "enclosed herewith" sounds more professional and more businesslike. Well, it doesn't. It confuses the issue and clouds the number one goal—clear communication of an idea. The rule of thumb: If jargon does the job because your audience will easily understand its meaning, use it. If there is any doubt at all—avoid it.

Business Writing Tips

- Keep your written communications focused and on target. Don't ramble.

- The number one aim is to communicate an idea—not to tell a story or impress a colleague with a shower of words. To communicate effectively you need to be a model of clear and precise thought.

- Be brief. Ask any professional writer and they will tell you that one of the most creative skills they possess is knowing what to leave out.

- Use the active voice. It cuts down on wordiness.

- Write first, correct later. Complete a first draft before stopping for corrections and editing. Delaying to find the exact word on first draft may result in lost ideas. Get thoughts down on paper first; improve and edit later on.

- Using many adjectives and adverbs is not the same as being creative. Too often business writers use unnecessary adjectives and adverbs that clutter the text and hide the idea they are attempting to communicate. Being creative does not mean being wordy.

- Clichés should be avoided whenever possible. The worst business writing is usually full of them.

- Find a colleague who will be critical—and specific. How many times have you heard someone say, "Not bad, but it still needs some work"? What does that mean to the writer? Ask for specific examples, specific criticism and avoid generalities. If asked to edit or read over someone's work, don't be vague. Tell them exactly what you think does not work.

- A formal tone is better than informal. Business communication is generally meant to be formal. One common error is when the writer uses the first name of a colleague in the salutation and then signs the letter with his or her full name. If you are familiar enough with someone to use their first name, then you may use your first name when signing off. Of course, in cultures that value a more formal approach to business dealings, this could be a serious error. Unless 100 percent certain of the relationship, use full names in the salutation and when signing off.

Questions To Ask Yourself

Once you have completed and edited your letter or communication ask yourself these questions. They will ensure that your communication will accomplish your intended goal.

- Does my writing give the impression I want? Is it too informal? Too wordy?

- Have I included any nonessential ideas or words that detract from the main points?

- Does the company letter and envelope give the proper impression? What will someone from another culture think?

- Do I have the address correct? Have I spelled all the names correctly and used proper titles when appropriate?

While Westerners can become fanatical about producing perfect documents, some cultures are not as obsessed with typographical errors. Take the Chinese, for example. They have been known to deliberately leave typographical mistakes in magazines and books so that readers who find them may feel superior.

The Translation Process

You've slaved over a document, crafted each word to ensure brevity and clarity. You're convinced you've made your essential points. In other words, all that is left to be done is to have the document translated and sent overseas. This perception is optimistic but wrong. Sending out a document to a professional translation service is just the start of a critical process—not the end. Too often the process is almost an afterthought. It is at the translation stage where serious errors crop up.

Remember, you want your business partner to read and understand exactly what you wrote—not what some translator thinks you meant. It is too important to leave to chance but it is amazing just how many professional business concerns treat this task as a nuisance, trying to rush the process through and get the document, including translation errors and important meaning changes, out the door.

Getting the Job Done

Translation should be more than simply changing the words of one language into another. Professional translators need to be sensitive to the expectations of your target audience and its culture. Some tips on getting the job done properly:

- Seek out the advice of colleagues for recommendations concerning professional translation services. The quality and skill levels of both translation agencies and individuals vary considerably.

- Ask for client references and then check those references thoroughly.

- Ask to see samples of completed projects—as well as assurances that projects will be completed on time.

- Ask if the individual or agency will translate a test document for you. If you are unsure of the quality ask another agency or individual to back-translate the test.

- Some agencies and individuals specialize in certain technical and industrial areas of translation. If you are in a highly technical field, seek out the specialists.

- Once you have settled on a professional translator, it is important to work closely with the individual doing the work. They need to be briefed about the audience, the tone and the purpose of the document to be translated.

- Let the translator know the exact purpose of the document. Is it an introductory document? A final proposal that calls for immediate action? The purpose and tone you seek can make a difference in the selection of words used in the translation.

- Clearly explain any technical terms to be used. Make sure the translator understands the concept. If necessary provide the translator with a glossary of terms to be used.

- If the project is a lengthy one, check on the work in progress. Don't wait for the end to check on quality; it may be too late then.

- Allow ample time for the project. A rushed translation will lead to errors.

- Consider having the document translated back into the original language, even if this will add time to the project. If there is no one in your firm to check the translation, consider going to another agency or individual. Back-translation will ensure that the tone and purpose are correctly presented.

■ When dealing with marketing materials or brochures, back-translation should be built into process time. The extra cost of back-translation can save money if such materials need to be reprinted because of translation errors.

■ If the document you are having translated is a brochure or report that involves a desktop layout, re-layout the document once it is translated. Translated materials will most likely not fit properly into an existing document layout.

Does Size Matter?

When dealing across cultures, size does matter—at least in paper stock. Whenever practical, marketing materials, sales brochures, catalogs and other printed materials should be produced on paper sizes normally used in that country. The reason: file folders and ring binders used in other countries may not easily accommodate material printed on different-sized paper and, thus, have less of a chance of being saved for reference and more of a chance of being thrown away. Also, if a company truly wants to appear global, it needs to meet global standards. Using materials that are not conducive for use by the targeted market may even be interpreted as a sign of arrogance—or, worse yet, ignorance.

"I know that paper size really does matter to customers," says the British representative of an U.S.-based business research organization. "It speaks right to the credibility of the research material we provide. If it is on A4 paper (ISO) it is perceived as being more global and aimed specifically at a non-U.S. market. When European customers see reports on U.S.-sized paper, they immediately dismiss it as being U.S.-oriented and probably of little use. Besides they can't file them properly. They can't put them in binders. It simply is not customer friendly to produce materials for Europe on U.S. paper stock."

Internet Translation

While language may be the last great barrier to direct communication in a globalized economy, computer boffins have developed what many thought might be impossible—software that can translate into foreign languages. While the idea is noble, the results so far are less than perfect. Most experts believe that machine translation will probably never exceed 85 percent in accuracy. At present the websites available probably score much lower.

Still, for the businessperson interested in instantaneous translations, where comprehension is important but exact syntax and style are not critical, the machine translations available on the web should suit fine. It is ideal for pre-trip research and can give one the gist for things like e-mail and simple documents. The software will typically translate documents into draft-quality language. Exact grammar and word order may be non-standard and stylistic convention may be lost. The Windows-based programs work with different Web browsers and can translate Web pages between English and most European languages.

Quite simply, don't expect the translations provided by machines to match those done by professional human translators. The software and websites clearly state that the translations provided by the machine should not be used for things like legal documents or contracts. It is easy to see why.

International FAX

The fax machine is probably the most often-used communication device for international business—even more so than the telephone. While e-mail is slowly catching up with the fax, nothing is more efficient for transmitting documents, cutting costs and defying time-zone differences. As more and more countries begin to recognize faxes and facsimile signatures as legal documents, the fax has become the best friend of the global businessperson. Here are some tips for proper usage:

- Limit the number of pages you fax. Usually anything over 20 pages is excessive.

- Treat a fax like a business letter.

- To see what your presentation and company letterhead will look like when it arrives overseas, try faxing samples of your material to yourself first. If it looks bad, re-format.

- Always include a cover letter stating the total number of pages, the date (written out to avoid confusion internationally), whom it is to be sent to, whom it is from, as well as your telephone and fax number in case there are problems with the transmission. Even include your e-mail address in case they want to switch media.

- Remember, many companies turn their fax machines off overnight, so be aware of the time of day of your fax destination.

- Don't assume your fax arrived. Paper runs out, faxes get stuck in mailrooms or lost. If urgent, follow up the fax with a telephone call confirming its arrival.

- Send "hard copies" (regular paper) via mail when important documents are involved.

- In many emerging markets, faxing can be very expensive. Do not assume you will get a fax response.

- If you are faxing contracts, check the local law in the target market to see if facsimile contracts are binding.

International E-mail

With the globalization of the Internet, e-mail has become, to some extent, the business letter of the 1990s. Communicating via e-mail should be viewed no differently than communicating in writing on company letterhead or fax. (In fact many firms have developed a standard e-mail letterhead to give communications a more formal look and feel.) There are some obvious advantages to international e-mail. There are no long-distance international telephone bills, no express courier expenses, no waiting for paper correspondence to cross the globe and no need to wait up until midnight to telephone a colleague on the other side of the globe. Also, if dealing in a compatible time zone, the recipient can ask questions immediately. Just as in any other form of written or oral communication, it is important to remember cultural sensitivities when e-mailing internationally.

There are some obvious disadvantages as well. Unlike a telephone conversation, e-mail does not allow for many personality traits of the individual sender to filter through. Often, people will act out of a sense of urgency and reply to e-mail without proper thought or composure. E-mail tends to become almost like conversational speech, sometimes sloppy and often informal and ambiguous. Using e-mail as an international tool of business requires self-control. Finally, it is easy for a receiver of e-mail to misread the tone of a note. This can lead to angry exchanges and misunderstandings.

PROPER INTERNATIONAL E-MAIL ETIQUETTE

- Be formal. For some reason, it is always tempting to slip into a casual and informal chat mode when using e-mail. Of course, such informality is appropriate in some circumstances, such as exchanges with in-house work colleagues. However, when using e-mail internationally treat it as a formal business correspondence. Use full names and titles in addresses. In international e-mail always err on the side of formality until familiarity is established.

- Always put something in the subject area. E-mail without a subject is often rejected or treated as junk mail. Make sure the subject is brief but revealing and to the point. Don't try and be cute. If a subject area is vague, the e-mail may not be read in a timely fashion—or worse, not read at all.

- Keep messages short—but not to the point that meaning is lost or can be confused. Most e-mail is either written in such shorthand that it may be meaningless to the uninitiated or so long-winded that the key point or points are buried.

- Run a spell check and read the message over several times for clarity. Sloppy e-mail reflects poorly on the senders and their companies.

- Develop a standard sign-off (e-mail signature). Use your full name, title and return e-mail address in case the communication somehow gets separated from the header. Also, it is smart to provide proper international telephone dialing codes and contact information when sending e-mails overseas.

- Dates and Time. When sending an international e-mail that includes dates and times, be sure to write out the date in full to avoid confusion. When putting a time, make sure you clearly state what time zone your are using.

- When e-mailing to a different culture be aware of the rank and position of the receiver. Even if e-mail tone begins to shift to something less formal it is still important to provide senior officials in cultures like Japan and China with the amount of respect they expect. This holds even in the electronic universe.

- Humor. Just as informal written correspondence, humor does not translate well across cultures. Different cultures have different perceptions of what is funny or appropriate.

- Currency amounts. When using currency figures, be sure to clearly state which currency you are dealing in and try and use both currencies—the one of the sender and the one of the receiver.

- Know who is receiving your e-mail. Do not simply hit the "reply all" button unless you know exactly who is receiving the return message.

- Remember, nothing is private when dealing with e-mail. Messages can easily be accessed by others and company administrators have the ability to access messages even in personal mailboxes.

- Take care with attachments. Using attachments is risky business internationally because of the plethora of software programs in use. Unless you are sure the receiver and sender systems are entirely compatible, do not use an attachment. Often attachments simply cannot be opened because of software incompatibility. Rather try and keep the whole letter in the body of the message.

- Don't confuse the receiver of your e-mail by sending the same message through multiple mediums, like fax or post, unless you clearly specify that you are doing so.

- Be patient before re-transmitting the same message or sending a follow-up message. Sometimes your e-mail will arrive during the receiver's off-work hours, or while they are out of town on business or vacation. Some e-mail programs now include an automatic answering function that will advise the sender that you are out of the office until a certain date. If you have one, use it. It relieves the anxiety of the sender.

- Use self-control. Think before responding and take time to compose a thoughtful message. If angry wait a day before responding.

CULTURE CAUTION: Be aware that some large corporations do not accept e-mail into their system unless your return address has been cleared in advance by their "gatekeeper." As protection against computer viruses, this security measure may apply to attachments.

International Postal Addresses

Finding and interpreting international postal addresses may be one of the most baffling and challenging aspects of overseas correspondence. Each nation, each culture has its own quirks for postal addresses. There is no rule of thumb for Asian addresses or African addresses or European addresses. The only way to be certain is to ask. One thing is for sure: all those numbers in the address mean something to someone. Remember, getting the person's name correct is essential. In some countries it is mandatory to print the address in the local language to ensure delivery.

CHAPTER 9

Cultural Landmines for Women

ONCE MADE EQUAL TO MAN, WOMAN BECOMES HIS

SUPERIOR. — SOCRATES

THOUGH WOMEN IN MANY cultures have made tremendous gains in business in the past 30 years, the reality is the world of international business is still mostly run by men. The "old boys network"—that bastion of male domination that invented the global business system—continues as the status quo in world business. From Bangkok to Berlin, males remain the main authority figures. Men promote men, men give other men the plum assignments, the promotions, the key responsibilities. Why? Because men feel more comfortable with men. They drink together, golf together, swap stories together. Basically, men can talk with other men with few inhibitions. Regardless of your view, the reality is there and women have to deal with it. But those men who still insist on stereotyping women as the weaker, less capable sex, had better look over their shoulders—someone is gaining on them. Women may not yet run the show when it comes to international business, but their impact is being increasingly felt across virtually all cultures.

Business Challenges

The unfortunate reality in most cultures is that women in the business world are not yet taken seriously. In Asia, Africa, Latin America, many parts of Europe and even pockets of the United States, visiting businesswomen can expect to run into a condescending attitude at one time or another. Unlike a male, don't expect rank or title to automatically gain respect for you if you are a woman. Expect to be tested. At times, remarks, including sexual innuendo, will be aimed at provoking a reaction or simply for shock value. A thick skin is required, at least in the initial phase. Take the remarks, including compliments about appearance, in stride and move on to the next point. A lecture in political correctness or female equality can be counterproductive. It may also demonstrate your lack of cultural research.

UNDERSTANDING THE MOTIVATION

A key to coping effectively is to remember that in most Islamic, Asian and African cultures, few men have ever had the experience of working or socializing with women as equals or as colleagues. They are on highly unfamiliar ground. Adopting a tolerant and understanding attitude will help you earn their respect.

One the most prevalent myths about foreign businesswomen entering a new culture is that the men of that culture will treat her just the same way as they treat local women. That is false almost 100 percent of the time. Even in a country like Saudi Arabia, where strict conservative religious views forbid most interactions among unmarried members of the opposite sex, a visiting businesswoman from another culture will be afforded the same status as a visiting businessman. Local male counterparts are most likely to be interested in your product or proposed business deal.

With the globalization of business, savvy businessmen from male-dominated cultures are smart enough to realize that the rest of the world does not follow their gender norms and they had better adapt if they wish to deal internationally. They are perfectly aware that women may occupy radically different social, cultural, legal and economic positions in their home country and generally they are prepared to work with whomever they must to conclude a deal. In more conservative cultures, foreign businesswomen are often treated as something akin to being neuter—neither male nor female but some sort of third sex.

Strategies for Coping

Coping in male-dominated business cultures requires patience, tact and toughness. In many cultures, the woman will be tested, her credentials questioned and her authority challenged. The confident professional businesswoman will invariably pass the test if she demonstrates early on that intimidation will not work. It is essential to establish your rank and authority early in a relationship. Men not used to dealing with a foreign female business colleague will often look for any excuse to discount her or force her into a gender stereotype they are more familiar with.

The female leader of a business team should make it clear that she is in charge by ensuring that her name appears at the top of the team list. It's OK to flaunt your title and authority. She can ensure that her status is honored by instructing team members to defer to her when questions are directed to others that would normally be asked of a man in her position. Be conscious of seating arrangements. In many Asian cultures, the leader of the delegation will be expected to occupy a specific place at the negotiating or dinner table. You are the leader; it is your seat. Take it. If you don't do so your status and authority will be called into question. Some simple coping strategies:

- **DO YOUR HOMEWORK** Know what the status of women is in the local culture. This will help you better understand the roots of an odd behavior. Also know what is expected of you as a business professional.

- **ANTICIPATE PROBLEMS** In many cultures don't expect to be treated as an equal— at least on first meeting. Often, women must work exceptionally hard at winning the same respect as male colleagues. It may not be fair but in some cultures it is the rule of the game.

- **ALWAYS DRESS AND ACT PROFESSIONALLY** You will be under exceptional scrutiny and you do not want to give off any non-verbal signs that can be mistaken as anything but professional business conduct and appearance.

- **BE TOLERANT AND UNDERSTANDING** Accept compliments about your appearance in the spirit they were intended. Don't become defensive about your gender.

- **MAINTAIN YOUR SENSE OF HUMOR** Business travel is stressful enough without dealing with gender issues as well. Learn to laugh at yourself. It relieves stress.

- **PREPARE YOUR TEAM IN ADVANCE** If you are the leader of a team, prepare your team in advance for gender shock. Ensure they show support. The fact that a women is heading the delegation should be treated in a matter-of-fact fashion, without any indication that this is anything but routine.

- **AGE IS A FACTOR** Look out for generational differences and be ready to adjust. The globalization of business has brought more enlightened attitudes to younger business executives from traditionally male-dominated societies. Just because you were treated one way by a member of an older generation, it doesn't mean you will meet the same behavior from a younger generation member. You would be surprised how these sudden shifts in treatment can throw you off balance or off guard. Losing concentration could lead to a poor business deal.

Women in Global Business

NORTH AMERICA/UNITED STATES

From a global gender perspective, the United States is probably the easiest country for a woman to do business. Generally, women are seen to have earned their rank and are accepted as equals based on experience and credentials. The cultural sensitivities forced on males by federal anti-discrimination laws and the strong women's movement has had a real impact. When it comes to dealing with an international businessperson, gender plays a minimal role—provided the businessperson has earned their position. Proving one's worth as a visiting businessperson is still important but a woman will not necessarily find herself at a special disadvantage.

While the rest of the world may view the United States as a bastion of female equality in business, American women know that things are far from perfect. Even in the United States, the concept of "equal pay for equal work" still lags. In 1996, the average pay for women in all professions was still only 73 percent of the pay of white males. While not great, it is still an improvement on 1970 when the figure was just 58 percent. In top corporate management, females are still hitting the glass ceiling. The 1997 Fortune 500's list of America's largest companies included only two women CEOs and among the Fortune 1000 companies there are a total of only seven. Financial World magazine's listing of the top 100 money earners on Wall Street in 1997 included no women.

Despite these statistics of inequality, there is no denying another set of statistics that clearly indicate women do play a highly significant role in American business and, by extension, on the world stage. Consider these statistics compiled by womens' organizations and the U.S. government:

- Women now outnumber men in institutions of higher learning. Between 1975 and 1991 women's enrollment in higher education increased from 45 percent to 55 percent.

- There are nearly 8 million women-owned businesses in the United States as of 1996, generating nearly $2.3 trillion in sales.

- Women-owned businesses employ one out of every four U.S. company workers— a total of 18.5 million employees.

- The top growth industries for women-owned businesses between 1987 and 1996 are: construction; wholesale trade; transportation/communications; agribusiness; and manufacturing.

- Women entrepreneurs are taking their firms into the global marketplace at the same rate as all U.S. business owners. As of 1992, 13% of women-owned firms were involved in international trade.

Canada is somewhat of a strange mix of European and American attitudes when it comes to females in business. But a visiting businesswoman will find it relatively easy to operate in both English- and French-speaking sections of Canada and is unlikely to meet any significant gender bias that would hinder professional performance.

MIDDLE EAST

Compared to most other cultures, women in the Middle East have made relatively fewer inroads into the business community. The Middle East as a whole has the lowest rate of female employment in the world—just nine percent. The one exception is Israel where over half of the women are employed and females make up about a quarter of all middle and top management positions.

While Islamic countries do place restrictions on the activities of women, there are some exceptions. For example, Turkey, which is officially secular but is predominantly Moslem, has almost as many women executives as men. In Egypt, women have risen to senior management positions and own large international companies. Perhaps one of the most repeated myths about business in the Middle East is that women have been totally shut out of international trade. It simply isn't true for all countries. If you arrive in the Middle East expecting never to deal with a woman in business, you will eventually be proved wrong.

By the same token, being an expatriate businesswoman in the Middle East presents special challenges because of cultural attitudes. Remember, though, that local males will not treat you the same way as they treat local females. A visiting businesswoman has special status and while still subject to some basic local tenets concerning modesty, dress and social interaction, obstacles can be overcome. If you act professionally, respect local traditions, and have a product, skill or service that is in demand, you will, as a female, be accepted in any country in the Middle East.

ASIA

Traditionally the roles of men—ruler, protector, breadwinner—and women —wife, homemaker, child-raiser—have been clearly defined in many Asian cultures (Taiwan, Singapore, Hong Kong—cultures that have strong family business traditions are exceptions where women do play key roles in business). Few females sought to break the mold. Male dominance begins with birth. Asian cultures have always valued male offspring more than female. (Consider China where the government's one-child policy has led to an increase in infanticide with parents sometimes killing the first born if it is a female.)

In Asia it has always been the man who is out in the world while the woman stays at home. While women have made some inroads against this stereotyping, there remains a long way to go. Female business successes have concentrated in certain professions and business sectors considered by Asian males to be "female occupations"—advertising and public relations, fashion and design, consumer products and cosmetics.

Because of the propensity to maintain group harmony in most Asian cultures, Asian males faced with working with a visiting businesswoman will try extremely hard to swallow their traditional attitudes and get along. They will already feel pressure because you are a foreigner but by-and-large they can deal with that. The fact that you are both a foreigner and a woman creates an enormous amount of pressure on them to do the right thing. The visiting female professional should remember that Asian males are working without guidelines in this respect and behavior may sometimes seem erratic, awkward or even condescending.

Don't interpret small acts of courtesy or chivalry, such as opening doors, or allowing you into the elevator first, as sexist. They are just trying to be kind to a visitor and to navigate correctly in uncharted waters. (If you have any doubt that their behavior is special, take a trip on the Tokyo subway system and observe how men treat Japanese women there. Elbows fly and women, like men, are pushed aside if a male spots an open seat.)

LATIN AMERICA

In most Latin American cultures, women are loved and respected. Beauty and elegance are treasured values in women—but basically their place is in the home, not in the boardroom.

Much is made of the macho attitude of Latin American males toward women, but when it comes to business, visiting female professionals will generally find themselves treated well. There will be no condescending attitudes at the negotiating table—although life may be a little different after hours or out in the street. Unlike Asia and the Middle East where the female executive is relatively rare, women have entered the Latin American business world in appreciable numbers. In many Latin American nations, the traditions of family-run businesses and the existence of matriarchal business dynasties and family structures has meant that women have long played important roles in big business.

Today, women hold 25 percent of all management positions in Latin America and the Caribbean. The percentage of women in the business population has continued to rise, especially in urban areas, where they accounted for 45 percent of the workforce in 1995. A total of 70 percent of women with university or technical degrees are working outside of the home. However, like just about everywhere else, their wages lag behind those of men. Throughout Latin America female wages trail male wages in all jobs by between 10 and 40 percent, depending on position and profession.

EUROPE

When it comes to women in business, most of Europe is not as liberated as people think. Attitudes towards women vary greatly on a country-by-country basis but the overall tone of the continent is one of male domination. A 1997 report by Eurostat, the statistical agency of the European Union, showed that in Europe, too, female wages are well behind male wages across the board. Female wages as a percentage of male wages are 84 percent in Sweden, 73 percent in France and Spain, and just over 64 percent in the United Kingdom. This includes both full- and part-time workers but excludes overtime. Women managers, however, are worse off compared with male managers. In the UK they receive two-thirds the pay of male counterparts. Even in Sweden, which is nearest to equality, it's only 80 percent.

But there are increasing signs that female participation in the professions will increase in the future. Twenty years ago women were in the minority in higher education in every EU Member State. But the average is now 103 women to every 100 men. Females outnumber men in this field in over half the European countries. Bulgaria (153), Iceland (136) and Portugal (131) boast the highest ratios. However, in Germany there are still only 77 women to every 100 men, with 89 in the Netherlands and 92 in Austria—three countries that have highly conservative attitudes when it comes to women in business.

Visiting businesswomen will generally find a highly professional atmosphere. Whatever gender bias European males have will most likely be kept hidden. But because most European countries (outside of the southern countries) are low-context cultures that demand great detail and precision in business, it is important that businesswomen arrive well prepared. Where a visiting businessman may be afforded a break if not totally prepared, the same break will probably not be extended to a woman. Her lack of knowledge will be blamed not on her individual lack of preparation but on her gender. Prepare for business and for added scrutiny.

EASTERN EUROPE/RUSSIA

Forget all the gibberish about gender equality boasted by the former communist constitutions of eastern and central Europe and the Soviet Union. While women did have some mandated political representation and access to higher education, the emergence of capitalism has wiped out many of these artificially mandated gains. Finding female executives in these countries is akin to finding a needle in a haystack. In the former communist states of eastern and central Europe, the rule of thumb is fairly simple: if a management job comes open it is reserved for a man. First, because a man is by tradition the family breadwinner and second, because the woman's true place is in the home. As a general rule when the employment situation becomes tight, the woman is sent back to her family regardless of her qualifications or performance.

When it comes to the treatment of visiting businesswomen, you can expect a gracious welcome but expect to be tested from day one on your knowledge and to be quizzed about your educational and professional background. Eastern European males would rather be dealing with another male, but you will be tolerated, if not totally accepted, as "one of the boys."

AFRICA

To a large extent in Africa, the term businesswoman is an oxymoron. This is still a male-dominated continent—females are to be seen and not heard. Women are conspicuously absent as hero figures in African history mainly because much of its history—and its heroes—is based on armed struggles, from the colonial days to the guerrilla wars of the anti-apartheid movement to the bloody civil wars in Rwanda and Burundi. The politics and the business of settling Africa was simply a man's game.

Women have made some very modest gains in both politics and business in recent years. The obstacles to progress are threefold. Traditional African culture has always relegated women to second-rate status, responsible for home and family and absent from the power structure. Polygamy in the rural areas is common but only men (polygyny) can have multiple spouses. And finally, education for African females was often an afterthought as it was difficult enough to find resources to educate the males. As independence swept through the continent in the late 1950s and 1960s, the notion of black economic empowerment really meant male empowerment with men assuming the power roles in business and government. The age of gender enlightenment is still a generation or two away.

Even in South Africa, probably the most progressive country gender-wise on the continent, women's rights are few. A poll by Johannesburg's *Business Day* newspaper found that 53 percent of women believe that gender prejudice in the private sector remains unchecked. Women comprise just 2 percent of board members within South Africa's top 1,000 companies. Women now make up 41 percent of the country's workforce, but they still receive on average just 50 percent of the pay of males.

Social Grace Under Fire

This may be the trickiest part of international business for any female to handle. The successful conclusion of business in relationship-driven cultures such as Latin America and Asia depends heavily on personal contact—most often outside an office setting. The business meal and the after-hours business drinking play key roles in reinforcing personal and business relationships. Regardless of the culture, women should always plan to attend business dinners. Joining in the after-dinner festivities should be considered optional and left up to your best judgement. However, in some cultures, such as Japan, it is understood that women will not be joining in, since the activities will often be very male and sometimes sex oriented (the hostess bar). While you may miss out on some valuable relationship building time (you should use the dinner to accomplish this), you will not miss out on any serious business discussions. The after-hours foray is meant for pleasure and to get to know someone better. Always try to establish the itinerary beforehand so you can judge if the after-hours entertainment is suitable.

MAINTAINING STATURE

Often, there is a natural urge to want to be accepted as "one of the boys." In most cultures men and women do have clearly defined roles and no matter how hard you try you never will be thought of as such. And, besides, you really don't want to be. Your role as a professional businesswoman bestows a certain status. Enjoy it and accept it. Don't try to out-male the males.

One word of warning: if you do attend such a fete while overseas be aware that a night of welcoming toasts and countless drinks can drive the level of sexual innuendo to a maximum. Take off-hand remarks about your appearance in stride and move onto the next point. If someone oversteps the bounds of decency, give a stern but brief rebuff but avoid a public lecture in political correctness. If worse comes to worst, make a polite excuse about being overtired and leave the party. You will not be penalized the next day. One advantage that a foreign businesswoman has over her male counterpart is that women are generally not expected to match the males drink for drink. In fact, given the stereotypical views of women in Latin America, Asia and Europe, matching a man drink for drink would be the totally wrong thing to do.

CULTURE CAUTION: Like other aspects of business, this particular social dynamic is a function of which side of the business deal is in a buying position and which in selling. As is true in most cases, buyers need tolerate less than sellers when it comes to uncomfortable social situations.

THE DUTIES OF HOSTING

There are some basic do's and don'ts if you are acting as host to a visiting business delegation on your home turf. (Note that all but the second recommendation can apply to male hosts as well as female.)

- Entertaining after hours is greatly appreciated and in some cases expected. Though ideally the activities should include yourself, catering to the activities that counterparts might enjoy may win you more friends. Try and learn some of the likes and dislikes of your guests in advance.

- Make sure that the spouses and children of counterparts are well situated and secure during the after-hours entertaining.

- Asian, African, Latin American and some European males are generally uncomfortable with women paying the bill. Either arrange to settle the account in advance or discreetly excuse yourself and pay the bill away from the table and out of sight of your guests.

- Order last. This will let the restaurant staff know you are the host of the meal and that the staff should defer to you. Remember, it is important to reinforce your authority.

■ As the host it is your job to initiate the eating and drinking. Propose a toast or simply begin eating. In Asia, make sure that your guests are served in order of rank.

Gift-Giving Problems

Basically the same rules apply for women as they do for men when it comes to international gift-giving rituals (see Chapter 10) with one major exception. Often it is not a bad idea for a visiting businesswoman to include gifts for the spouse and children of a business contact. While the same action by a visiting male might be found offensive in some cultures, especially in Islamic countries, such a gesture by a female would be appreciated while underscoring the nature of the gifts you are giving—a token of appreciation for a business colleague. In some cultures a female giving a gift to a male can be embarrassing for the recipient or, worse yet, be misconstrued as something other than a business gesture. Including the wife and kids eases the tension and clarifies the message.

Sexual Harassment

Sexual harassment occurs everywhere, just more frequently in some cultures than others. In most of the world outside of North America and Europe, there is as yet little legal recourse. In international business it is virtually impossible not to hear conversations and witness actions that are discriminatory against women. In many cultures, for instance, it is the norm for an executive to ask a female member of his team to serve tea or coffee. In many parts of Asia where the concept of family is central, a foreign businesswoman will be asked personal questions about marital status and children. In this latter case, the same questions will be asked of foreign males.

Foreign businesswomen are certainly not immune to sexual harassment in international business. Of course, any physical coercion is totally unacceptable, but what about verbal harassment? How should you react? First, remember to keep a cultural perspective. The remark you found obnoxious may actually have been just a fumbled compliment. You must weigh the outcomes. Is it really worth jeopardizing a business deal because of one jerk? Will you be hurting your career or the chance of future overseas assignments? Will any action be taken? Remember, the act you consider harassing will and should be judged not in your home country context but in the context of the country in which you are doing business. (One course of action to consider: take the harasser aside and give a private but stern rebuke or, alternatively, take another member of that delegation aside and mention the behavior that is bothering you and see if it can be stopped.)

Dress Codes

You know it's not fair. Men can get away with wearing the same suit several days in a row but you need to change outfits daily—maybe even twice in the same day if a business dinner is included. Women have not agreed upon an international business uniform as men have (the dark suit, white shirt and stripped tie). To be on the safe side, and if you want to be taken seriously, dress conservatively but not severely. While pants are acceptable in many cultures, the only country where you can be sure of full acceptance is in the United States. How you look is important in reinforcing your professional credentials. So here is a semblance of an international dress code for women:

- Dress conservatively and tastefully. That generally means wear a dress or skirt with a blouse. Avoid pants.

- Choose restrained shades of darker colors.

- Keep jewelry and perfume to a minimum. Many cultures wear little or no perfume. In Japan, many men claim to be allergic to Western perfumes.

- Sensible but smart shoes are best. If you are a tall woman, be conscious of your height. Don't wear high heels if you will end up towering over your foreign male counterparts. In many cultures men are very sensitive about it. In Japan and other Asian cultures, it can be a distraction and actually hurt your chances of building relationships. The men will simply be intimidated.

- Adopt a conservative hairstyle.

- In hotter climates wear natural fibers that breathe, which will make you more comfortable. Short sleeves are OK but backless or sleeveless garments should be left home.

ISLAMIC CULTURES

Of course, modesty is the watchword here. Conservative Western-style dress (except for shorts) is appropriate in most areas. However, in more traditional societies such as Saudi Arabia and Iran, attire for women should be highly conservative. Dresses or blouses should be long sleeved and loose fitting. Dress length should be at a minimum below the knee—longer is better. In most Islamic countries, it is not necessary for a visiting businesswoman to don a veil, or chador.

Two countries with the strictest dress codes for women are Saudi Arabia and Iran. Saudi religious police energetically enforce a highly conservative interpretation of Islamic dress codes, and may rebuke or harass women (foreigners included) who do not cover their heads or whose clothing is too revealing. In more conservative areas of these countries, there have been incidents of local citizens stoning, accosting, or chasing foreigners for perceived dress code violations.

International Networks

When it comes to international business, global networks, organizations and associations for female professionals and executives abound. Women working together to advance and promote women have made a difference and eased the way for women in what essentially remains a man's world. Some examples of global women's networks:

- THE INTERNATIONAL ALLIANCE (TIA) is an umbrella organization made up of over 30 women's business organizations and networks representing 10,000 women around the world. Individuals who don't have a network affiliation, or who want to provide additional support to the organization, may also join as Alliance Associates. Through its activities and conferences, TIA fosters an environment that assists women in reaching their potential and enables them to contribute significantly in business, the professions, academia, government and not-for-profit sectors.

E-mail: info@t-i-a.com

- ADVANCING WOMEN is an international directory of information for women in the workplace with excellent links to global workplace sites and networks on the Internet.

  Internet Address: http://www.advancingwomen.com/

- ORGANIZATION OF WOMEN IN INTERNATIONAL TRADE (OWIT), a U.S.-based non-profit professional organization, is designed to promote women doing business in international trade by providing networking and educational opportunities. Members include women and men doing business in all facets of international trade, including finance, public relations, government, freight forwarding, international law, agriculture, sales and marketing, import/export, logistics, and transportation.

  Internet Address: http://www.owit.org

- WOMEN IN TECHNOLOGY INTERNATIONAL (WITI), founded in 1989, this U.S.-based organization is a rapidly growing association of more than 6,000 members, 95 percent of whom are professional women working in technology organizations. WITI is dedicated to increasing the number of women in executive roles by helping them become more financially independent and technology-literate and by encouraging young women to choose careers in science and technology.

  Internet Address: http://www.witi.org/Center/Offices/About/

  E-mail: info@witi.org

- WOMEN'S INSTITUTE OF MANAGEMENT (WIMNET) is a businesswomen's on-line network which provides database search facilities via the Internet to businesswomen around the globe. Headquartered in Kuala Lumpur, Malaysia, it enables networking and the identification of potential business partners. Initially, the database concentrated on businesswomen and women executives based in Malaysia. Now the scope has expanded to include women worldwide, as well as potential women executives and entrepreneurs.

  Internet Address: http://www.jaring.my/wimnet/

- CANASIAN BUSINESSWOMEN'S NETWORK: This Canada-based organization acts as a link between individual businesswomen and businesswomen's associations in both Canada and Asia through the Association of Southeast Asian Nations (ASEAN), introducing them to new business opportunities. The countries where the network operates presently are: Canada, Singapore, Thailand, Malaysia, Indonesia, Philippines and Vietnam.

  E-mail: cabninfo@apfc.apfnet.org

Gift Giving

GIVING IS THE BUSINESS OF THE RICH. — GOETHE

GIFT GIVING IS one of the oldest social traditions known to man. While one rarely hears about the positives of gift giving, history is strewn with the negative impact of the process. The defenders of Troy in 1200 BC are still smarting from the wooden gift horse left behind by the Greeks. (The phrase "beware of Greeks bearing gifts" obviously doesn't apply anymore in a literal sense to the world of international business.) In cultures that are high-context and relationship-driven (as opposed to low-context, task-driven cultures) business is built upon personal relationships and gifts are an integral part of those relationships. Perhaps with the exception of Japan, where gift giving is ingrained in the national culture, the importance of gift giving is probably overrated in most other parts of the world. Still, giving an inappropriate gift or one that is culturally insensitive can cause serious harm to a business relationship—more harm than not giving any gift at all.

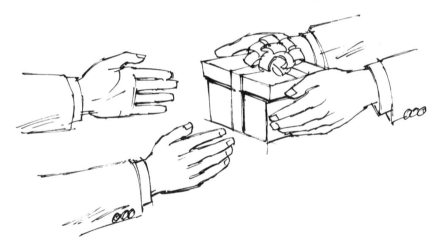

Gift or Bribe?

Gifts should never replace the basics of good business practices and etiquette. They are a supplement to, not a substitute for, a sound business proposition. Of course, a gift should never take on the appearance of a bribe, even in countries where such practices are commonplace. A gift is just that—a freely given token that shows appreciation or respect. A bribe—well, that is part of the mandatory cost of doing business in some places in the world.

Some basic questions to consider if planning to give gifts internationally:

- Who are the appropriate people that should receive gifts? Is there someone you must give a gift to?

- What is an appropriate gift and what might be considered culturally insensitive?

- When should you give the gift? At first meeting? At the conclusion of a contract?

- And, finally, how should you present the gift?

International gift giving can become a cultural minefield. The taboos vary from culture to culture. To give the proper gift one must understand the culture of the receiver.

The Value of Gift Giving

Giving the appropriate gift in a timely fashion not only cements personal relationships in some cultures but it can truly enhance a company or personal image. The right gift conveys respect to the individual and by the same token can convey a company and personal image of global sophistication, even power. In relationship-driven cultures, the gift reflects the company image and intentions and gives a potential partner insight into how both you and your company think and are likely to act in the future. Still the main purpose of any gift should be to please and honor the recipient. If you keep that in mind, you will never produce a gift that can be inappropriate or, worse, insulting.

Consider the case of General Motors Corp. which was involved in a titanic struggle with several other major auto manufacturers to secure a partnership with Shanghai Automotive Industrial to make cars in China. GM spared no expense, hiring local consultants and Chinese-speaking American employees to make sure the company did "everything right" to impress the Chinese with their cultural sensitivity and understanding of Chinese business customs. When General Motors gave Chinese officials expensive gifts from the New York jewelers, Tiffany's, the company replaced their signature white ribbons with red ones. The reason: In China red means good luck and white signifies sorrow or death. The Chinese were obviously impressed—not only with the cultural sensitivity of GM—but with the company's final business proposal as well. Still, showing its awareness of Chinese traditions didn't hurt. Through the thoughtfulness of the ribbon switch, GM presented itself as an internationally savvy company prepared to work in the framework of local cultural and business sensitivities. It came across as a class act and—who knows for sure—maybe white ribbons would have been a deal killer.

STAY OFF OF THE OFFENSIVE

One basic rule of thumb in international gift giving: ideally, any gift you present should be manufactured in your home country. Take special care to make sure that the gift is not manufactured in a country or region that may cause insult to the recipient (for example: it would be insulting, even in this age of near-peace and enlightenment, to give a Saudi Arabian colleague a gift manufactured in Israel). A British mining executive recalls how in the early 1980s, he happily presented a token of his company's affections to a group of Zambian mining officials during a business trip to that southern African country. "We had a stock of very expensive pen and pencil sets made up with our company logo. It was just a small token, you know, something to break the ice," the executive says. "Well, I gave out dozens of these sets and basically I didn't hear much about it—very few "thank yous" even. Later one of the Zambian officials cornered me at a reception and asked if I knew where the pen and pencil sets had been manufactured. I said I hadn't a clue. He told me, they had been made in South Africa—a country which Zambia at the time had no diplomatic relationship with because of apartheid. I could have died. How could we, as a company, have been so culturally insensitive? It was an insult to them." The executive says the deal eventually fizzled. Though he doubts it was only because of the pen and pencil set incident alone, he is sure it gave both him and his company a negative image. It certainly did contribute to the ultimate failure of the project.

Another point that should be remembered: Gifts with company logos should be used as small tokens only, not as a major sign of appreciation. Even when logos are used they should only be placed on gifts of the highest quality and the best taste. Remember, even the smallest gift reflects your company's image and personality. Keep the logo small so that it doesn't look as though the gift is nothing more than a company advertisement.

Where Gift Giving Matters

When it comes to the importance and expectations of gift giving, Japan is clearly in a class by itself. In other Asian cultures, because of the importance of personal relationships (high-context, relationship-driven cultures), gift giving is still important but not on the scale of that of Japan. In cultures such as China, Taiwan, Hong Kong and Singapore, it is now often considered more appropriate for a visitor to host an expensive and formal dinner or banquet, rather than to give expensive material gifts. The key here is reciprocity. If your foreign host decides to throw a banquet in your honor while visiting, it would be expected and appropriate to return the favor—during that visit. The following list will help you judge the relative importance of gift giving in each culture. The list refers to gift giving as a business practice. When invited to someone's home for a social occasion, regardless of the culture, it is always appropriate to bring some sort of gift for the host or hostess.

- Highly Important in Business: Japan, China

- Important But Not Fatal to Business: Asia/Pacific Rim, the Middle East, Africa.

- Somewhat Important, More as a Courtesy: Latin America, Eastern Europe/ Russia.

- Not Important Or Expected in Business: The United States, Canada, Australia, most of Western Europe.

Successful Gift Giving

Gift giving does not have to be a complicated process. With the proper research, an eye to cultural sensitivities and planning for the presentation, the chances of a cultural faux pas are greatly diminished. As mentioned previously, success can be assured if you provide the answers to such fundamental questions as who should be getting a gift? What is a culturally appropriate gift? And how and when should the gift be presented? Also don't be afraid to flaunt brand names. Well-known global brands such as Gucci, Dior, and Mont Blanc add value in most parts of the world and reflect favorably on the giver.

DO YOUR HOMEWORK

Taking time to do some research on the gift-giving traditions and expectations of a particular culture is fundamental to success. What can make you stand out further is to find a culturally appropriate gift that also takes note of the individual recipient's personal likes and interests. One particularly well-organized sales executive keeps personal files on international clients, detailing their likes, dislikes and hobbies as well as important dates (birthdays, promotions, etc.). Much of the information was gathered from personal observations such as taking note of the individual's office interior and whether there was a particular theme (one German customer seemed enthralled with the American West and cowboys). Also, personal conversations about hobbies and international travels were noted as well as personal habits (Is the individual a pipe smoker?). Also included in the file: information that helps him avoid any interpersonal faux pas. (One Swedish customer was a sworn teetotaler and thus a bottle of liquor or wine would have been inappropriate.) The information allowed the executive to give more personal gifts targeted directly at a customer's interests while avoiding any inappropriate gifts. He says he was immensely successful in building personal relationships through this process.

PRESENTATION PLANNING

The presentation can be just as important as the gift itself—and just as great a source of anxiety for the giver as choosing the right token. If you have done your homework, you will know if it is proper to give a gift at a first meeting (common in Russia) or at the conclusion of a successful deal (common in much of Latin America). As in the culinary sciences, the true success of gift giving is in the presentation. Some basics:

- A gift, regardless of its expense, should always be wrapped; failing to wrap a gift signifies an uncaring attitude and undermines the impact of the gift.

- In choosing the appropriate wrapping, be aware of any cultural color taboos (back to the Chinese aversion to white which symbolizes death). Also, the wrapping should be appropriate for the recipient. Wrapping an expensive pipe for a high-ranking executive of a construction company with a frilly bow makes the wrong impression.

- Always enclose a card with a personal comment with the gift. A business card, while not ideal, can work provided you include a personal note on the back.

■ Give the gift in a timely manner. Waiting till you return home from an overseas assignment may be too late. Delaying the presentation of a gift also diminishes its impact.

CULTURE CAUTION: A special gift sent after you return home will signify that you wish to remain in contact and are still thinking long-term about the business relationship. This can apply to regular holiday gifts over many years. Today's deal may not work out but there is always tomorrow.

The Etiquette of Receiving Gifts

Knowing how to appropriately receive a gift from a business colleague is not usually something a businessperson spends an inordinate amount of time thinking about. Still, it is an area where one can still offend. Always accept a gift gracefully, regardless of how you feel about the gift or the giver. Some basic do's and don'ts of receiving an international business gift:

■ It is considered rude in many cultures to unwrap or open a gift in the presence of the giver. In others, the giver may even request that you open it right away. When in doubt, ask the giver if they would like you to open it immediately.

■ It is best and safest to receive with two hands. (Use of the left hand in Islamic cultures and in some African cultures is offensive.)

■ In many Asian cultures, particularly in Japan, it is appropriate to politely show reluctance when accepting a gift. In China, a recipient may refuse a gift at the first, second or third offering so as not to appear overly greedy. Foreigners may wish to participate in this feigned humility, but it will not be expected.

■ In Buddhist cultures a gift is thought to benefit the giver, not the receiver. A simple thanks without great fanfare is appropriate.

■ Reciprocation is commonplace in gift giving. Make sure you reciprocate with equal value. Never outshine the host when offering gifts.

Refusing Gifts

Actually refusing a gift is fairly rare in international business circles. However, with the movement towards common global ethics standards, it is likely to become a little more common. It is important to distinguish between a proper gift of appreciation or respect, and a bribe masquerading as a gift. In American culture, it is perfectly acceptable to refuse a gift and, under certain circumstances, it is even mandatory. A Western executive is more likely to return a gift to a giver because it is considered too extravagant or might be misconstrued as a bribe.

Frequently in North American and European cultures, company policy states that an employee, regardless of rank, is not allowed to receive a gift of any size. As a courtesy to international colleagues, most companies and company executives will mention this up front to avoid any embarrassment to the giver. If you have any doubt about a counterpart's company policy towards gifts by all means ask—but do so discreetly. By the same token, any executive working for such a company should let a foreign colleague know as early as possible what the company gift policy is. Politely letting others know either beforehand or at the time the gift is offered that you appreciate the gesture but are prohibited by company policy from accepting is good manners and should never create hard feelings.

Refusing a gift in most Asian cultures is a tricky dance and runs a real risk of insulting and frustrating the giver if they are the host. If at all possible, accept it, even if you don't personally keep the gift but instead pass it on to a charity. Refusing a gift shows a lack of cultural sensitivity. Any company wishing to work on an international stage should make exceptions where the law permits for gift giving and receiving. Acting on a case-by-case basis and relying on the common sense and personal morals of employees is preferable to an outright ban on gift giving and receiving. Such a ban can be misconstrued as out-and-out rudeness in much of the world.

Gift-Giving Customs and Quirks

Perhaps there is no other aspect of international business that varies as much on a country-by-country and culture-by-culture basis as gift-giving traditions. Here is a look at some of the cultural quirks involved in gift giving in regions where it is a regular practice.

ASIA AND THE PACIFIC RIM

In most Asian cultures, gift giving remains an important aspect of the business relationship but failure to show up with tribute would not necessarily be a deal killer, especially if you are dealing with younger generations. Some cultural examples:

- The "Red Envelope" is used exclusively for monetary presents in Sino-Asian cultures, especially around the Lunar New Year and at weddings. While once having no negative connotation, the idea of the "Red Envelope" has now become synonymous with bribe-taking and bribe-giving.

- Four is considered an unlucky number.

- Asians prefer gift-wrapping that is bright in color (red and gold are best). The more elaborate the wrapping, the better.

- Generosity is appreciated and considered a sign of personal respect. Avoid presents that are grouped in four as this will bring bad luck to the receiver.

- In the Islamic cultures of Asia, always give or receive gifts with the right hand only.

THE MIDDLE EAST AND AFRICA

In most Arabic cultures gift giving is associated with the generosity and trustworthiness of a firm or individual. Being generous in the Middle East is an important trait and is tied closely to the tenets of Islam and the Koran, the Islamic Holy Book. But here at least the visitor is somewhat off the hook; according to custom, it is the Arab host that will normally be the first to present a gift. In this region of the world reciprocity is important. Giving a gift of lesser quality or expense than the one received is considered a personal slight, as is outdoing a host. Good gift ideas for this region of the world include: high-quality leather, silver, precious stones, crystal, and cashmere.

■ In Islamic cultures, gifts should never be accepted or presented with the left hand. When visiting the home of a Saudi colleague, men should not bring a gift especially for the hostess. It can be taken as an offense.

■ Compared to the Arabic cultures in the region, gifts in Israel are not as important. The attitude more resembles that found in North America: business is business; gifts are for holidays like Hanukkah.

■ South Africa is a mixture of business cultures and is best researched on a company-by-company basis.

LATIN AMERICA

Gift giving in this part of the world is much less ritualistic compared to Asia and the Middle East, but it still plays an important part in the social culture. Not presenting a colleague with a small token of appreciation at the conclusion of a business deal is considered rude—but not fatal to a business relationship. Most Latin American nations are high-context, relationship-driven cultures where gift giving underscores the value of business relations. Latin Americans simply appreciate and look favorably on individuals and companies that display thoughtfulness and generosity.

■ Gifts to women can easily be misconstrued as a flirtation. It should be made abundantly clear by content and presentation that no sexual innuendo is meant.

■ Avoid gifts that the receiver might feel compelled to wear or display unless very sure about his or her personal tastes.

Japan: Still a Very Special Case

When it comes to the rituals of gift giving, Japan is still a very special place. To the Japanese, the act of giving gifts is the basic way of communicating friendship, respect and appreciation. Gift giving is deeply rooted in the Japanese culture, dating back more than 400 years when the seasonal gift-giving customs of Ochugen (at mid-summer) and Oseibo (at year end) were established during the Edo Period (beginning in 1600). The idea of gift giving that arose at that time was closely tied to the Shinto concept of ancestor worship. Gifts were generally exchanged among family members and close relatives. This gradually extended to a greater social circle as well as business contacts.

Oseibo is considered the more important of the two gift-giving holidays and is traditionally the time when the Japanese present tokens of appreciation to individuals whose services or patronage the giver has received or benefited from during the previous year. Gift lists often include teachers, police and firefighters, doctors and important business contacts.

Today, according to retail industry figures, the average Japanese household buys gifts 26 times a year, spending more than US$60 each time. But, as in other Asian cultures active in the global economy, younger generations in Japan are no longer fanatical about following established traditions. Many have become more casual about the whole gift-giving scene and rituals. (The recession in the Japanese economy and increased exposure to Western business styles have caused many younger Japanese to rethink the cost, frequency and importance of gift exchanges.) The average number of gifts bought and their cost has actually decreased markedly in Japan in the mid-1990s.

BEHIND THE JAPANESE COMPULSION

Many travelers and sociologists will argue that when it comes to gift giving, the Japanese really have no choice. Giving gifts eases their conscience. The reason: *giri*, one of the fundamental social forces that guide Japanese public and business behavior. Giri is perhaps the most powerful of the social concepts that dictate interpersonal relationships in Japan. It is an unspoken social contract and debt that one incurs through interaction with others. The debt which weighs heavily on the Japanese conscience (and may not be terribly understandable to Westerners) is incurred in countless ways through even the most simple of human interactions. It seems to grow disproportionately when a foreigner is involved. Thus, when even the smallest kindness or favor is done for a Japanese person, that individual incurs a social debt which must be returned. This helps explain why, to many visiting businesspeople, the Japanese seem to go overboard with their expressions of thanks and seem compulsive about gift giving.

Actually the act of giving a gift is simply part of the process of giri—and partially relieves a Japanese individual of his or her personal debt to you. As mentioned previously, countries that fall under a Buddhist philosophy believe that the benefit of giving a gift goes not to the receiver but rather to the giver. It is all tied up with the concept of giri. The Japanese simply see the presentation of gifts as repayment for the obligations incurred through giri. You don't really have to do much to turn on the debt tap in the Japanese conscience. Just being civil or polite will place most Japanese under some level of giri obligation. Thus, one of the worst things you can do to a Japanese business colleague is to refuse to accept a gift or the offer of a favor. Such refusals mean their social debt to you cannot be paid off—a fact that will seriously bother your Japanese colleague and possibly even keep him or her awake at night because of shame.

TIPS ON GIFT GIVING IN JAPAN

Sure, the thought counts in Japan, but so does the value of the gift and the way it is presented. A poorly selected or culturally inappropriate gift or a botched presentation can end up doing more harm to a business relationship than giving no gift at all. Remember, at least in Japan—a high-context, relationship-driven culture par excellence, what you give and how you conduct the ritual and follow the established protocols will probably be interpreted as saying much more than it should about you as an individual and your company as a potential business partner.

- Don't give everyone the same gift. Individuals of higher rank should get (and they expect) better-quality gifts than their underlings. This is consistent with the culture's respect for rank and an individual's place in the social order. A failure to differentiate between rank could be viewed as an insult.

- By the same token, if meeting with a large group, do not use that time to present a gift to a single individual. It will embarrass the recipient and upset the treasured group harmony. Either present to everyone in the group or wait for a better moment.

- Gifts should always be wrapped and, as in China, never in white which connotes mourning and death. Also, the Japanese dislike surprises. Notify a Japanese colleague that you intend presenting him/her with a gift in advance.

- Regards of the value or extravagance of the gift, humility is important. Act as though the gift itself were "ho hum" and stress that you value the personal relationship, which the gift symbolizes.

- By the same token, it is acceptable to discreetly display the brand name of a gift. The Japanese know value, and there is no point in hiding the fact that the pen you gave is a Mont Blanc or the calling card case is a Gucci. Quality counts.

- The same rules for the ritual exchange of business cards apply to gift presentation. The most senior ranking executive comes first. Also, gifts should be presented (and accepted) with both hands. It is a sign of respect.

- Avoid giving any gift with a company logo. The Japanese view such gifts, regardless of the actual quality, as cheap promotional giveaways and an excuse for corporate advertising. Subtle is better.

- Remember, the Japanese view the number four as unlucky, so never present anyone with a set of four of anything.

- Gift giving is so ingrained in the culture that even extravagant gifts are never viewed as bribes. Bribes tend to take the form of services provided, rather than cash or material goods.

Culturally Incorrect Gifts

Is there truly anything that can be considered a safe gift internationally? The answer is probably no. Even something as innocent as flowers can blow up in your face if you give a culturally insensitive type (chrysanthemums in Belgium symbolize death, red roses in Germany symbolize a hot romantic interest) or the wrong color (in Japan, white flowers are symbols of death). A great deal of research should be done in advance of an overseas business trip to assure that your gifts are sending the right message. Chapter 19 of this book lists a wide variety of resources for garnering specific research on this topic.

CHAPTER 11

Humor Across Cultures

WIT IS THE SALT OF CONVERSATION, NOT THE FOOD.

— WILLIAM HAZLITT

DURING THE FIRST HALF of the twentieth century, psychologists believed that humor was a learned social trait. They theorized that somewhere on earth there existed groups or perhaps entire cultures whose people totally lacked a sense of humor. Of course, no such group has ever been found, leading psychologists to finally conclude that humor is indeed universal and pan-cultural. Every culture in the world—Chinese, American, German, Mongolian, Arabic—finds something to laugh at. However, what each chooses to laugh at will differ widely from culture to culture.

Humor vs. Laughter

The words "laughter" and "humor" are often used interchangeably and thus incorrectly. Humor is usually what causes laughter and is defined as "a perception that enables us to experience joy even when faced with adversity," and "the quality of being laughable or comical or a state of mind, mood, spirit." Laughter, on the other hand, is simply a physical motion of the facial and stomach muscles. It can be loud and happy, or low and devious. There are various types of laughter—many of which have little to do with anything humorous or funny. Researchers have noted that there is triumphant laughter—gloating over a defeated opponent and devilish laughter that comes about when someone sabotages an opponent or ensures a poor outcome. Fear, danger, surprise, stupidity, disrespect, frustration, and even suspense are all possible causes of laughter. Still, regardless of its source, laughter is a good thing and several studies have shown that it does have health benefits. Laughter relieves stress, reduces pain, and can generally help people gain a better perspective on life. Sometimes, if you are sure you know the culture and the make-up of your international partners well enough, it can even serve as an ice-breaker in business.

Humor and Culture

You can pore over economic data and read up on historical events to understand a country, its culture and its social issues. Another approach would be to listen to the jokes its people are telling. The prevalent topics of humor are more revealing about a country's mood than all the political and social commentary in the universe.

A modern-day example of where humor reveals the most deep-rooted concerns of a nation is Russia. In the late 1980's most of the jokes told on the street had to do with the oddities and failures of communism—and in particular the concept of social leveling where all shared the misery equally and none dared stand out from the crowd. Today, as the country battles its way through the early stages of robber baron-like capitalism and increasing social inequities, the humor centers now on the new Russian rich. An example: Ivan is driving his Mercedes at high speed outside of Moscow and smashes into a tree. The car is totally destroyed and Ivan is lying by the side of the road, moaning "Oh my Mercedes, my poor Mercedes." A peasant woman hears the moans and tells Ivan not to worry about his car. He should be more concerned about his left arm that has been torn off in the crash. Ivan pauses and looks to find that indeed his left arm is no longer attached. "Oh my Rolex, my poor Rolex," cries Ivan.

Humor in Business

There may be nothing more painful than to attend an international business conference and hear an interpreter announce something like: "The speaker is now telling a joke. When I finish interpreting it please laugh." Again, frames of reference and language are important. Word play and puns rarely work. Any joke that needs explaining—and virtually all of them do when told across cultures and in a language that needs to be interpreted—is not worth telling.

While Americans are fond of injecting humor into business dealings, it is the British that almost always insist on including some type of humor in negotiations and presentations. Of course, not all cultures believe it is appropriate to mix business with humor. While Germans are most willing to joke in bars and restaurants with business colleagues after hours, they find that humor in formal business negotiations has no place. They believe it shows disrespect toward the visitor and can create confusion and be a distraction when trying to concentrate on the smallest of details regarding the deal. (This is related to their coming from a low-context culture in which precision and great detail is expected.) The Japanese, too, see no need to inject humor into business affairs—too much is at stake. The Chinese feel the same way. The influence of Confucius and Buddhism, which demand sincerity and politeness, eliminates for the Chinese and Japanese much of what many Westerners find funny—that is, sarcasm and parody.

What To Do If Offended

Most people tell jokes that offend out of ignorance, rather than with a vicious intent. If you find yourself in a situation where the humor offends you, it is probably best not to storm off or make a scene. It is certainly important to stand on your principles but in an international business setting one should do it very discreetly. A good plan of action is to take the person aside and explain why in your culture such a joke is not considered funny. You will probably be doing the person a favor and you actually may save the joke teller from future embarrassment. Victims of hurtful jokes have a responsibility to give feedback that can change behavior rather than just get angry.

CULTURE CAUTION: While it is certainly useful to let your counterparts know what does and does not offend you, it is not the central purpose of your business trip. Minutia such as insulting jokes can usually be allowed to pass without comment—especially when you are a visitor intent on selling a product. Make sure your attempt at correcting an uncomfortable situation does not do more harm than good.

National and International Humor

Does each country have its own brand of national humor? To some extent, each culture has something different that tickles the collective funny bone. Sarcasm and exaggeration are particularly American brands of humor. The Japanese enjoy word play and puns, as well as sometimes violent slapstick comedy. The British appreciate parody, especially in the political arena. Kenyans, too, find visual slapstick funny—as well as word play in local dialects. Indians find humor in sometimes subtle, sometimes profound parables that in few other cultures would raise a chuckle. The Chinese find riddles and proverbs humorous. In the end it is the culture that dictates what individuals from different countries find funny. Unless you really understand your audience and what tickles their funny bone, you run a high risk of embarrassment by introducing humor into business or even social occasions.

While there may not be a single brand of humor that transcends all cultural barriers, researchers have noted a commonality in what makes people in different cultures laugh. A 1993 study published in the Journal of Marketing examined humor in advertising in four very different cultures: The United States, Germany, Thailand and South Korea. It found that in all four cultures, the vast majority of television ads contained humor or what the researchers termed "incongruent contrasts," that is, differences between what viewers expected to see and what they actually received. This difference, the incongruity is what makes something funny in most cultures. The "surprise" ending is pleasurable—it makes people laugh.

COMIC GLOBALIZATION

There may not be a global convergence of humor trends, but there are some international figures that do transcend their own culture to become the butt of jokes literally told around the world. Depending on a singular moment in time, the identity of the figure changes but often the basic joke remains the same. A German businessman recalls hearing this joke told in Hong Kong about Microsoft chairman Bill Gates—a global business icon of the 1990s. The joke: How does Bill Gates change a light bulb? The answer: He doesn't need to. He just calls a meeting and declares darkness the new international standard. This joke says as much about how Microsoft is viewed as it does about global business trends.

Cross-Cultural Meetings

DRIVE THY BUSINESS OR IT WILL DRIVE THEE.

— BENJAMIN FRANKLIN

TIME SPENT DOING business overseas can be expensive—and frustrating. Successfully arranging a business meeting in a country thousands of miles away should be considered your first small victory. This in itself can rapidly age even the most patient of entrepreneurs and international road warriors. Don't expect to be able to arrange meetings without a substantial amount of long-distance telephone and fax contact—much of it one way. Of course, any initial request for a face-to-face meeting should include as many specifics as possible about your company, your own qualifications (and those of any colleagues who will be attending the meeting) and an outline of what it is exactly that you are proposing. Most companies will consider your past experience in dealing in their region of the world a plus. References from other local companies you have dealt with or press clips (translated into the local language, of course) should be used since they help legitimize your firm's international or domestic standing.

Formal or Informal

Before contacting a potential international partner, it is best to determine such basics as whether their culture is a high-context one demanding full precise detail of proposals or a low-context one where less detail but a more personal level of communication is sought. You need to determine what level of formality will be expected of you in your approach.

FORMAL APPROACHES NEEDED	LESS FORMAL APPROACHES USED
Japan	United States
China	Australia
Russia	Canada
Germany	Nigeria
Argentina	Israel

If you determine that the country in which you wish to do business is relatively informal, then you can often eliminate the need for such practices as a formal letter of introduction from a third party or recommendation from a government trade mission. Instead, approach the firm directly in your initial communication. Of course, there are risks involved in deciding on a less formal approach and individual companies may demand higher levels of formality than expected. When in doubt seek out advice from local trade missions, embassies and chambers of commerce as to the best approach, even down to the individual company level.

Here are some general rules:

- Asian cultures demand higher levels of formality than most European cultures, which in turn are far more formal than the Americans, Australians and Africans.

- Age often plays a role in the level of formality demanded. Younger generations are normally less formal than older generations. This is especially true in Asian and Latin American societies.

- Smaller entrepreneurial firms are less formal than older established companies. Compare, for example, IBM—a suit-and-tie culture—with any of hundreds of Silicon Valley startups—jeans and T-shirts.

Making Arrangements

While the telephone is OK, written correspondence remains the most reliable form of communication. All written correspondence, including faxes, should be sent in both your native language and in the language of the country you are targeting. (E-mail is primarily done in English.) Do not simply rely on a telephone confirmation of a meeting—get it in writing. Also, be patient. Even with a fixer or go-between on the ground, actually getting a set time when all the officials of a company or companies you want to see will be available will take some doing.

Don't expect to throw together an overseas trip in a matter of days or even weeks (depending on how many meetings you wish to arrange). Often, executive secretaries and personal assistants, not wishing to disappoint the overseas businessperson, will suggest someone else to meet with in the corporation if their boss is not available. This can lead to a wasted trip. If you have firmly identified whom you should be meeting with, don't accept a substitute who is probably lower on the food chain and has no decision-making responsibilities or ownership in the proposed project or venture. Alter your schedule if necessary.

CULTURE CAUTION: Even the best laid plans tend to go awry. Meetings do often get canceled with little notice and on occasion the wrong people have been known to substitute. Losing your cool does not help but in most cultures even a modest show of indignation can lead to a re-scheduling. Once again, keep the purpose of your business trip in mind and be aware of the buyer-seller dynamic.

The Role of the Fixer

With the globalization of the marketplace, the importance of a formal letter of introduction as a way to court another firm or organization has diminished somewhat. It still remains important, however, in many cultures—especially with older, more traditional executives and companies. Unless you represent a company that is well known internationally, such as SONY or IBM, having a third-party set up either a written introduction or a first face-to-face meeting may be the most efficient route to go. In Japan, for example, it still is next to impossible to arrange a meeting with a senior executive of a big company without a formal third-party introduction. In some industries, such as investment banking (this even applies in more informal cultures), formal third-party introductions are still considered an essential first step.

Arranging for an introduction is not as complicated as it may sound, provided your company has a decent reputation, sound financing and a past record of honest business dealings. Your government's overseas trade mission, your bank, your auditors or accounting firm, and many business consultants specializing in international affairs can usually arrange for, at least, a written letter of introduction with a minimal amount of fuss. Tapping into a country's "old boys network" is not necessary. An introduction from a reputable third party—even if that party is not personally known to the company you are courting—is sufficient in almost all cases.

GET A FIX ON THE "FIXER"

If you decide to use a third-party consultant or "fixer" in a foreign country, it is essential that you carefully examine their credentials and reputation. Seek references that you can check. In many countries, especially those in the emerging market economies, individuals claiming to have influence or the ability to set your firm up with high echelons of government or private business, may be nothing more than hot air. Worse yet, they may conduct their business in unethical ways that can actually tarnish your company's reputation before you even start. Sometimes, such "consultants" may promise more than you are prepared to deliver. Because of the rapidly changing politics and business climate in such countries, a fixer claiming to know everyone in power one day, may not be able to beg a cup of coffee the next.

Preparing for the Meeting

There is no excuse for not having done your homework. A poorly conceived or explained proposal—one that has not been properly researched in the local marketplace—can ruin your credibility, even before the first round of drinks at a business dinner. A rudimentary knowledge of the country's history and geography is essential. The topics are certain to come up in most conversations sooner or later. Knowing what is expected of you or what you should expect from the meeting is essential.

In high-context, relationship-driven cultures the first meeting may be nothing more than drinks or dinner where your colleagues can get a feel for you personally. The first meeting may be about nothing more than establishing a personal rapport and determining if you are a person they can trust. Once this judgment is made, the nitty-gritty details can be dealt with in due course. If, for example, you are a Canadian company hosting a group of Italian businesspeople (Italy being a high-context, relationship-driven culture), it would be overwhelming to bombard them with facts, figures and overhead slides in the first meeting. They would feel more comfortable just getting to know their hosts, perhaps through small talk and an informal tour of your facilities. On the other hand, if the Canadians were hosting a group of German businesspeople, it would be fine to dive right into the facts and figures. In fact, you may find some impatience on behalf of the visitors if you do not.

THE AGENDA

It is best to agree on an agenda well before the first meeting takes place. Whether you are the host or the visitor, in order to frame the discussion and maintain some control, it is wise to be the first to propose a draft agenda (in writing). By all means ask your counterparts for their input, but try and maintain control of the main topics. It is polite and good business to let the hosts know the names and titles of those who will be attending the meeting. It is also important to let them know who is considered the head of the delegation. Inform them of any changes in your party. In many cultures, particularly in Asia, it is important that the head of your delegation matches the rank of the highest executive you expect to meet. Sending a junior executive to meet a company president is a breach of protocol and an insult in many cultures. Don't send too many people; it will overwhelm your hosts.

THE VENUE

If you are the host of a business meeting, the choice of venue and the level of accommodation and services (fax, Internet connections, telephones, secretarial) provided will have a direct impact on how you and your company are perceived. In high-context cultures such subtleties as the chairs, tables, air conditioning/heating, catering and toilet facilities are important and can have a positive or negative effect on the relationship. It is not unheard of in some cultures to deliberately try and make visitors feel uncomfortable in the meeting venue (uncomfortable chairs, high heat) in the hopes of gaining a negotiating edge. (The Chinese, Russians and the French have been know to do this.) Fortunately, this practice is becoming more rare.

In arranging meeting facilities you need to take subtle cultural tendencies into account. For example:

- Seating arrangements: Provide a clear and marked space for the head of the visiting delegation. In many cultures, the visiting delegation head expects a seat of honor; to not do so would be insulting.

- Beware of cultural color taboos: In some cultures white is far from a neutral color and is often associated with death and mourning.

- Be careful of floral decorations: If you decorate with flowers remember that different types of flowers have negative connotations in many cultures. For example, carnations are associated with death in France. The same is true of chrysanthemums in Japan and Belgium.

- Be conscious of food taboos: For example, don't serve pork to a visiting Moslem delegation from Syria.

THE ARRIVAL

Increase in distance traveled to conduct business on a global scale means that visiting businesspeople are often subject to jet lag—the physical and mental after-affects of traveling through several time zones. Jet lag is a very real phenomenon that can have an impact on even the most confident and eager traveler. Before beginning any meetings, it is wise to give yourself sufficient time to counter its effects. It is amazing how many international road warriors discount jet lag and how many bad deals and wrong impressions are made because it is ignored. Often the host company will meet visitors at the airport when they first arrive. Politely insist on some time to get settled in your hotel or accommodation before rushing off to your first meeting. An hour or two to compose your thoughts and get yourself acclimatized can make a big difference on the first impression you give.

PUNCTUALITY

No person in the history of business has ever been criticized for being punctual. Some cultures (German, Dutch, American) demand it. You gain no points for being fashionably late for a business meeting, regardless of the excuses you may offer. Always build in extra time to travel from your hotel to your meeting venue. And remember, the security at many offices these days resembles that of a bank— or a medium security prison. Don't be alarmed if asked to go through metal detectors or, if requested, to be frisked. Don't take it as an insult—it is, after all, for your safety as well.

INTRODUCTIONS AND GREETINGS

Every culture has a different approach or ritual for greetings and introductions. The Japanese bow with the lower status person bowing first, more deeply and more frequently. Americans will offer a handshake and often an extra pat or slap on the back. In India, the greeting is made with both hands together in a prayerful position held higher or lower to indicate the level of respect being shown. In the Middle East, men will often exchange kisses on the right check. The French will shake hands both on meeting someone and on leaving the room, as will most Latin Americans.

Introductions are usually done by seniority, which helps you target just whom you should be concentrating your efforts on to build a personal relationship. In Europe, the Middle East, and Africa you should always wait to be asked to sit down. Once seated, expect to be asked if you want coffee or tea. Again, it is a good idea to accept—it provides a break in the formality and allows for the start of personal conversation.

BUSINESS CARD RITUALS

Many cultures, especially the Japanese, put great stock in the exchange of business cards at the beginning of a meeting (see Chapter 5 for more details of business card protocols). Your cards should be in both your native language and in the local language. It is essential to include your title on the card. It is considered polite to study any card you have been handed and always have plenty of cards yourself. Everyone present at the meeting will expect to receive one. It should be clear with the introductions (and the advance exchange of faxes and letters) just who is in charge of the host party.

CONCLUDING THE MEETING

One rule that seems to cut across all cultures is to leave it to the hosts of the meeting to decide when it is concluded. This even applies when the visitors are also buyers or investors. If you are the host you will need to ask at the conclusion of your meeting if there are questions about any presentations or your company. (When in a sell mode, don't leave the follow-up in the hands of the foreign partner but rather tell them when you intend to make the next contact, even if they offer to get back to you first.)

Often, visitors will be escorted out of the meeting room. If the person you are meeting with should decide to escort you personally down to the outer lobby, take advantage of this time to hit on matters of personal substance such as sports, food, family or entertainment. This is truly prime relationship-building time outside of a formal atmosphere. Business deals can be won or lost on the time it takes to ride an elevator down twelve stories. Either party may take this opportunity to set up an after-hours meeting where business and socialization can mix.

Interpreters: Keys to Success

The importance and skills of the translator are oftentimes underrated. Consider the pressure they are under. A good interpreter must listen to your words and then instantaneously reproduce them without the benefit of a first draft to correct errors. This is far from a mechanical process. A good translator will be able to recognize and then incorporate all the non-verbal clues you use in your speech such as tone of voice, emotional expression and body language, including facial expressions. These non-verbal forms of communication are important elements of how your message is heard by the receiving party. A few things to watch for when using a translator:

▧ Does he or she use the proper tone and pitch of voice to get your message across?

▧ Does he or she use a soft voice when an angry response is given?

▧ Can the interpreter mirror the emotion of the speaker correctly?

Language-based misunderstandings are the bane of cross-cultural business. It is surprising how often in international business deals involving different languages that two parties agree to something that one or the other or perhaps both do not fully understand. When the contract is drawn up the subsequent battle over wording can wreck a relationship.

TEAM PLAYERS

Even if professional translators are being used, it is ideal to have a company employee on your team who has a solid understanding of the other language being used as well as the native culture of the other party. This person can act as a watchdog against possible language misunderstandings and may be able to clearly explain the cultural nuances of certain phrases and expressions that an interpreter does not have the time or inclination to do. Such a person can concentrate on the message being sent by the other side, looking out for such subtleties as body language and facial expressions that mean so much in high-context cultures. The added advantage of having such a person on your side is the ability to pick up some of the asides or comments from the other delegation which may be highly revealing of strategy or true intent.

INSIDE INFORMATION

If you are hosting a cross-cultural business meeting, consider using your own company employees as interpreters, if they have the basic skills. Employees will have complete knowledge of your company's goals and command of idioms, jargon and technical terms.

While you may want to try offering your company's employees as translators if you are the host, decline such an offer if you are the visitor. The role of the translator is simply too important and sensitive to be left to someone you neither know nor trust. Though they may be provided entirely in good faith, you can never know either their exact skill level or trust their neutrality for sure. Negotiating under a cloud of suspicion or mistrust rarely leads to a successful conclusion. Consider bringing your own translator; it is worth the expense. If you don't have an employee familiar with the native language or culture, hire a professional interpreter who you can at least be sure is neutral.

In many developing countries or those new to market economies, translators are a fairly elitist group—and many consider themselves underemployed or smarter than the two executives for whom they are translating. When employing a local interpreter, make it clear what their role is and that you need to know everything that is said. Editing by an interpreter can make or break negotiations. Most of the time you will be expected to supply your own interpreter and it is essential that you have someone you can trust and who has the technical expertise to translate in your field. There are agencies in the world's major cities that specialize in supplying interpreters in such highly technical areas as oil and gas exploration, computer hardware and software, and engineering. You simply cannot underestimate the value of a good and trusted interpreter.

SOME TIPS ON USING AND HIRING INTERPRETERS

- SCREENING IS IMPORTANT Interpreters need to be screened and tested to make certain that they fully understand technical language and idioms involved in your business. Make sure they also know the local dialect.

- GLOSSARY If the talks are of a highly specialized nature, consider providing the translator with a glossary of technical terms that he or she can refer to and study in advance.

- ESTABLISH GUIDELINES Before a meeting, plan with your interpreter the mechanics of how you will work, for example, how long you should speak before pausing for interpretation.

- DON'T EXHAUST YOUR INTERPRETER Stop every couple of sentences to allow for interpretation and limit each sentence to one main point. Don't begin another sentence before the interpreter has finished translating the previous one. Interpreters need a rest every two hours or so. Using an interpreter may stretch a meeting to three times its normal length, so be patient.

- POSITIONING An interpreter should never be seated at the head of the table or between you and your foreign associate. Never talk to the interpreter directly; rather look toward the person you are addressing. Speak slowly and clearly and avoid slang and idiomatic expressions.

- LISTEN INTENTLY Because the margin for error is great in translated negotiations, it is up to you to fully concentrate on all exchanges. As your counterpart speaks, study body language and facial expressions for any nuances. Focus on the counterpart, not the translator.

- TWO TRANSLATORS When each side has a translator of their own, the interpreters should only translate when their team is speaking. The translators should never interrupt each other or speak over each other.

■ NO PUBLIC REBUKES If you are unhappy with the speed or quality of the translation, do not rebuke your translator in public. This can be viewed by the other side as a sign of confusion or dissension on your team's part. If you need to be critical, do it in private.

■ REVIEW EACH SESSION After each session conduct a review with your translator. Quiz them about specific meanings, voice tone or any elements of strategy they may have picked up in the course of the meeting.

Guidelines for Successful Meetings

▨ Know your colleagues and their culture—what they expect from a first meeting and what you should expect from them.

▨ Agree on an agenda beforehand. It gives both sides time to prepare and ensures a smooth and productive meeting.

▨ It is polite and good business to let the hosts know the names and titles of those who will be attending the meeting. It is also important to let them know who is considered the head of delegation. Inform them of any changes in your party.

▨ Provide a comfortable venue and take time to work through any details to avoid violating basic cultural taboos about food, flowers or colors.

▨ Personalize whenever possible. Deals are built on trust and striking a personal chord will enhance your chances. This is especially important in high-context cultures and showing appreciation or curiosity about the local culture can ignite personal relationships. Casually mentioning that you would love to go to the local theater or see a rugby game might just get you an invitation. And that can turn into a real opportunity to establish a relationship with a potential business partner.

▨ If you are the host provide an information packet with meeting agendas, city and country maps, transportation guide and other non-business-related materials.

▨ If translation is going to be needed, try and supply your own—preferably a company employee, who shares your concerns and goals.

CHAPTER 13

Cross-Cultural Negotiations

NOTHING IS TO BE HAD FOR NOTHING. — EPICTETUS

THE ART OF NEGOTIATING is hard enough in your own country, dealing with colleagues who think like you, process information as you do, share a common set of values and speak the same language. Now consider a situation where there is little shared knowledge, few common values and a different language is spoken and you can readily see just how complicated negotiating international transactions can become. What is the likely outcome when the Japanese, who expect deference for rank, meet with the Americans who expect equality across the board? The chances of conflict, error and misunderstanding because of basic cultural differences are huge.

People from different cultures use different negotiating styles and approaches. They have different communications styles, different strategies for persuasion and a different set of protocols. Differences occur in the way a conflict is viewed, managed, and resolved. Still, as daunting as it may sound, the art of international negotiation boils down to this simple concept: the interaction of two sides pursuing one goal—profit—through divergent methods. Your plan should be to develop a negotiating plan that will minimize the potential of misunderstanding and conflict. You need to take cultural sensitivities into consideration in order to enhance the chances of reaching an agreement—and forming a business relationship—that will endure beyond the initial contract.

Zero Sum Thinkers

Negotiating is all about attitude. There are two basic approaches to how a final outcome is viewed. Some cultures view the negotiating process as a "win-win" situation—a process through which both sides gain. Other cultures adopt a zero sum mentality where someone's gain must always equal someone's loss. The sum of the net gain and net loss is always zero. Individuals from cultures that view negotiation through this "win-lose" prism see the process as a series of confrontational battles to be either won or lost. Individuals from the "win-win" perspective instead view negotiations as a collaborative effort seeking to maximize total gain. Confrontation, as this side sees it, is counterproductive. Trying to convince win-lose practitioners that a win-win strategy is possible is usually difficult. Sellers, of course, prefer to project a win-win approach while buyers tend towards the zero sum game.

CULTURE CAUTION: It is a common practice among some of the believers in the zero sum game to project a win-win facade in order to keep counterparts off balance. Be careful if counterparts continually talk of the importance of "long-term" or "harmonious" relationships.

The Concept of "Face"

Most international businesspeople would probably associate the concept of "face" with Asian and Middle Eastern cultures. The reality, however, is that "face" is a universal concept. It's just that other cultures call it something different. In the West, for example, it is self-respect, self-esteem or dignity. All individuals need it, and all individuals resent it when it is damaged by their own actions or those of others.

In many Asian cultures "face" is a deeply held value. Indeed, Confucian societies will go to extremes to avoid pointing out errors, faux pas, or indiscretions that would cause themselves or another to lose face—to be embarrassed—in front of a group. The value placed on saving and giving face is closely linked to the powerful theme of preservation of group harmony in Confucian societies as well as deep respect for the existing social order. To cause someone to lose face is seen as a challenge to their position within the hierarchy—and thus a threat to the group order. If an Asian loses face, which is equal to being socially discredited, he or she may no longer function effectively in the community. To lose face is shameful.

In Western cultures, the loss of face really means "personal" failure and is limited to the individual. In Asian and Middle Eastern cultures, however, loss of face is a group concept that brings shame not only to the individual but also to the company or organization he or she represents. Since most Asian cultures are collectivist with high risk-avoidance, saving face or giving face is the preferred way to resolve conflict and avoid embarrassing the parties involved. Giving face involves allowing someone enough room to maneuver, or, hiding your own reactions to give the other person a way to exit gracefully with their dignity intact.

Conflict Resolution

Collectivist cultures tend to avoid open conflict (most collectivist cultures are high risk-avoidance ones as well) while individualistic cultures meet confrontation head-on, often believing that confrontation is the quickest route to problem solving. In cross-cultural negotiations, conflict may be evident even before the two parties sit down to talk. The reason: the goals of the negotiations may be at odds with the task-driven, low risk-avoidance culture wanting to cut a deal at all costs and in a great hurry and the relationship-driven high risk-avoidance culture seeking to build a relationship first for future business transactions.

CULTURE CAUTION: Task-driven societies rely upon the rule of law to bind contracts. Collectivist cultures usually have very little codified commercial law and tend to rely on personal relationships to bind contracts.

Sociologists have identified five basic methods of conflict resolution which are found in various degrees in all cultures:

■ COMPROMISE: Nothing more than a willingness to "split the difference," this is an approach that is sometimes adopted by negotiators from cultures that are comfortable in a win-win situation. Most common selling mode.

- OBLIGING: Essentially the choice of those in weak positions who see making concessions as a way to resolve conflict.

- AVOIDANCE: The ostrich approach of burying your head in the sand and skipping past areas of conflict. Common in high risk-avoidance cultures, this approach can lead to vague contracts that become problematic when the details are tackled.

- INTEGRATION: An analytical approach that attempts to meld the priorities of the two opposing sides to reach agreement.

- DOMINATION: Common in individualistic cultures where negotiators are concerned only about winning. Those who take this approach tend to see negotiations as a zero sum game. Most common buying/investing mode.

Differences in Decision Making

When locked in negotiations it is important to take into consideration the differences in the decision-making process between cultures. In some cultures where power is decentralized (United States, Australia) decisions can be made quickly—and often by a single individual. However, in cultures with collectivist values (Japan, China), decisions are made by consensus and can take longer. (However, implementation of decisions is quicker in collectivists cultures as opposed to individualistic cultures that often demand the right to question the decision handed down.) Consider the examples of the United States and Japan where values and cultural influences play a major role in the decision-making process. The contrast begins with the basic objectives a business decision is meant to achieve. In Japan that objective is preservation of group harmony. In the United States it is usually maximum profit or operating efficiency.

CONSENSUS AND DECISIVENESS

Now consider a decision as to whether or not to buy out a competitor, say, in the steel-making industry. In Japan, where decision-making is decentralized, the process would be a bottom-up one. In the United States it is centralized and top-down. The Japanese will start with trying to define the question or problem, beginning with input from the lower ranks—the people who may be directly affected by the decision. From these lower groups, the decision is passed upwards or laterally until it eventually reaches senior management who are already aware of the consensus built from below. Keeping in mind that the Japanese objective is preservation of group harmony, the question would be framed as a decision to increase market share or simply grow revenue. One key consideration would be the impact on the company's current employees and those of the firm to be purchased. Once completed, the merger would go fairly smoothly because the consensus came from the bottom up and workers, not wishing to disturb group harmony, work hard to make it successful.

In the United States, senior management would begin the process, not by defining the problem, but rather by seeking a solution to the question of how to maximize profit from this acquisition. The route of the decision is purely top-down. Keeping in mind that the American objective is economic efficiency, the problem is framed as one of maximizing resources and return on capital. The decision would be objective and impersonal. If maximizing efficiency involves layoffs at both companies, so be it. The workers had no input on the decision and will question what is in it for them if they go along.

CULTURE CAUTION: The slump in the Japanese economy of the 1990s and the slowness of the economic response have caused the Japanese to re-evaluate their decision-making processes. Many Japanese companies and government officials have come to realize that they have much to learn from U.S. counterparts about making tough decisions in a timely fashion.

Cross-Cultural Negotiating Tips

The most critical phase for an international venture is the first negotiation and thus extensive preparation is critical. A learn-as-you-go approach can be deadly. Here are some negotiating preparation tips:

- It is essential to understand the importance of rank in the other country; to know who the decision makers are; to be familiar with the business style of the foreign company; and to know the issues well.

- Prioritize what is most important—your needs—and separate these points from those that are less important—your wants. This will allow you to focus on what is most important to you on the agenda.

- Consult recent history. What worked in the past for you or others in your company in specific negotiating circumstances may just work again.

- Develop a profile of your negotiating opponents.

- Are they task-driven or relationship-driven?

- How do they process information? Are they from a high-context or low-context culture? What are the important issues in their culture?

- What role does the concept of "face" play in your counterpart's culture?

- What are their time horizons?

- Is their communication style direct or indirect?

- Are they zero sum thinkers or is a win-win strategy possible?

- Is a formal agreement expected or more an agreement in principle?

- Know their decision-making process. Is it by consensus? Or is it individualistic? How risk-adverse is their culture?

- Develop an idea of the personal style of your main negotiating counterparts. Are they aggressive? Passive? Ego driven? Do they rely on intimidation? Stubborn, arrogant? Into brinkmanship? Is the individual competitive or cooperative? Talk with your team about what traits they observe.

Every negotiating team must enter with a clear goal of what they want out of the negotiations and a strategy for obtaining it. Understand the nature of agreements in the country, the significance of gestures, and negotiating etiquette.

- Because of the difficulties of cross-cultural communication it is essential that you present your arguments in a clear and uncomplicated manner. Use simple language.

- Prepare a list of potential positions the other side may take. This type of rehearsal will ensure that you won't be surprised and that you will have an alternate strategy for most possibilities.

- Be prepared to take advantage of your position if you are the buyer or investor. Conversely, recognize the relative strength of a selling position.

- Persuade, don't debate. A debate will not move you closer to your goals. Persuading the other side will.

- Allow the other side to make the first move. This way you can judge the level of the aspirations of the other side. If you open first you may end up giving more away than necessary.

- Be prepared to walk away from a deal. Often, no deal is better than a bad deal.

For a detailed discussion of negotiating tactics and strategies see "A Short Course in International Negotiating" by Jeffrey E. Curry, World Trade Press, 1999.

Contracts and Cultural Variables

Not everyone views the meaning of a written contract the same way. While Americans and Germans generally insist on intricate contracts (common in task-driven cultures) that are followed to the letter of the law, other cultures, such as Nigeria and China, with limited legal structures, will view contracts as more of a statement of intention rather than a formal binding obligation.

Always look for problems in the written documents stemming from any cross-cultural meeting or agreement. Translation can be imprecise and the whole sense or structure of a deal can be altered by the use or substitution of a single word in a written document. Documents and contracts should be provided in both languages (even if you use a common language to negotiate.) It is essential, though, that you have a member of your staff or a professional translator who is fluent in the other language compare the translations to ensure no ambiguity.

CULTURE CAUTION: International contracts are generally only valid and enforceable in the language of the country where the contract applies. Make sure your translated version is accurate.

CONTRACT VIEWS

A few examples of just how differently cultures approach the concept of the business contract:

- UNITED STATES U.S. contract law is probably the most complicated and exhaustive (as well as the most frequently used) body of legislation on earth. Contracts are long and generally cover every conceivable contingency.

- FRANCE Contracts tend to be rather long and involved—and they must be completely in French. Even commonly used foreign words such as Internet and computer cannot be substituted.

- GERMANY Contracts are even more detailed than in the United States. Once signed, they are strictly adhered to by the Germans—and they expect the same from you.

- EGYPT Contracts are regarded as guidelines for business relationships rather than as specific performance requirements. The content may be renegotiated, revised, and appended many times to reflect changing circumstances—usually on the Egyptian side.

- JAPAN Contracts are guidelines and any problems are arbitrated rather than litigated. Every contract will include a *jiji henko* clause that permits complete renegotiation if circumstances change. This is tied to the importance of giving face in Japanese culture, that is, allowing plenty of wriggle room for both sides to prevent an embarrassment.

- INDONESIA Like many Asian cultures, Indonesia views the contract as a set of guidelines. While the signing of a contract may be accompanied by great fanfare and celebration, don't assume its provisions will be met automatically. Continual monitoring and reminders are necessary. Look for "consultation fees"—a euphemism for bribes—to be built into most contracts.

- RUSSIA It is important to remember that even if you have a signed contract with a Russian firm, it may not be worth much. Russians have a different view of contracts than Westerners and see contracts as more a statement of intention rather than as a formal binding obligation with penalties. Russian business law, while improving, is still not sophisticated enough to deal with suits stemming from broken contracts.

- ARGENTINA Contracts are more a matter of personal honor than a company commitment. Appealing to the signer's personal honor is a more effective strategy than using lawyers. However, if the person who has signed a contract should change jobs, die or emigrate, you may have to renegotiate.

For a detailed discussion of the legalities and nuances of international contracts see "A Short Course in International Contracts" by Karla C. Shippey, World Trade Press, 1999.

Corporate Culture

GREAT BUSINESSES TURN ON A LITTLE PIN.

— GEORGE HERBERT

CORPORATE CULTURE IS THE GLUE, if you will, that holds an organization together. It incorporates an organization's values, its norms of behavior, its policies and its procedures. The most important influence on corporate culture is the national culture of the country in which the corporation is based. That may seem obvious, but there are other factors that also help to shape a corporation's culture—its views of and its interactions with the "outside world." The ownership structure of the company will go a long way in defining a corporate culture. For example, the culture of a family-owned firm is likely to be quite different from that of a publicly held company. Also, the industry that the corporation is part of will help shape its cultural values. For example, a high-tech computer software firm (a relatively young industry) is likely to have a much more informal and entrepreneurial culture than say that of an investment bank (a mature industry). And, likewise, an organization in a service industry will have a different culture than that of a manufacturing or mining company. Differences in the corporate culture of organizations in the same home culture and industry may still be profound—sometimes as profound as the differences between national cultures themselves.

Corporate-Culture Components

Like national culture, corporate culture has some basic components that make up the whole. While national cultural components include such things as language, religion, and humor, the components of corporate culture tend to be more utilitarian. No one single component can reveal the true internal make-up of a corporation but when they are taken as a whole, they present a clear picture of a company's values and goals. The key corporate cultural components are:

- THE SYSTEM OF REWARDS What type of employee behavior is appreciated and rewarded? Do risk takers move up in management ranks or does the corporation reward loyalty and long-term service instead?

- HIRING DECISIONS The type of individual a company hires says much about its culture. Is a company ready to grow and accept new ideas by hiring a diverse workforce or is it content to keep hiring the same type of individual to build a homogeneous workforce?

- MANAGEMENT STRUCTURE Does the corporation have a rigid hierarchical structure? Is it managed by an executive committee or a dominating chairman?

■ RISK-TAKING STRATEGY What is the corporation's view of risk? Does it encourage taking chances, trying new products and markets? Or is it content with well-established markets and products?

■ PHYSICAL SETTING Is the office an open plan that encourages communication and a sense of egalitarianism? Or are management offices segregated from the staff workplace? Is headquarters a monument to ownership or a functional working environment?

National Cultural Influences

As explained previously, Asians place a high value on concepts associated with social harmony, while Westerners put greater emphasis on individuals' rights and responsibilities. It is no surprise to find that Japanese corporations almost always place great emphasis on group harmony in their corporate cultures. They design a system that rewards conformity, hire staff that is relatively homogeneous and tend to shy away from risk-taking and the entrepreneurial spirit. By the same token, it should be no surprise that many American corporations are likely to hire an entrepreneurial type and reward risk. There is no escaping the fact that a national culture shapes corporate responsibilities, practices and traditions.

A pair of studies, one regarding six Asian nations completed in 1996 by Wirthlin Worldwide, and one regarding North America conducted in 1994 by David I. Hitchcock of the Center for Strategic and International Studies, revealed striking differences between the most cherished values of Asian and North American business executives. These studies underscore the point that national cultures do have paramount influence on the formation of corporate cultures.

IN ASIA THE TOP SEVEN VALUES LISTED BY EXECUTIVES WERE:

1. Hard work
2. Respect for learning
3. Honesty
4. Openness to new ideas
5. Accountability
6. Self-discipline
7. Self-reliance

THE TOP SEVEN NORTH AMERICAN (UNITED STATES AND CANADA) VALUES WERE:

1. Freedom of expression
2. Personal freedom
3. Self-reliance
4. Individual rights
5. Hard work
6. Personal achievement
7. Thinking for one's self

Cause and Effect

If you look at the traits emphasized by the business executives, you can begin to build a corporate culture—albeit a stereotype—of an Asian firm and a North American firm and to understand the differences in management technique and skills between Asian corporations and North American ones. In Asia, there is no mention of individual rights or any hint of reward for "thinking for one's self." Hence, the type of organizational structure that has emerged across Asia is one of a very hierarchical, bureaucratic corporation that values such intangibles as "respect for learning" and "honesty." By the same token, taking the values stressed by North American executives, you would expect to find corporations that are less structured and more entrepreneurial than Japanese ones—and, in general, that is very much the case. Remember, though, that within the same home culture, you still get vast differences in corporate culture. While IBM and Compaq may be in the same country and in the same industry, their corporate cultures in many ways are different.

One interesting footnote from these studies was that female Asian executives had a value profile that more closely resembled that of North American. Asian women focus more on independence and self-reliance while Asian men focus more on harmony and order. This difference may be due to the fact that women have been shut out of the "old boys' network" and have been forced to rely more on entrepreneurial skills than Asian males to succeed.

Profitable Corporate Culture

The concept of corporate culture is all well and good but does the concept have any measurable impact on a corporation's bottom line or on staff behavior? It certainly does, though the impact is difficult to quantify. Having a strong corporate culture provides a clear sense of identity for staff, clarifies behavior and expectations and usually makes decision making fairly easy because so much is already defined. People know where they stand and what is expected of them. However, a strong corporate culture also has a downside. Any corporation that has an entrenched culture will find change difficult. The inability to be flexible, to act quickly and to change rapidly are all competitive disadvantages in the global market economy. A weak corporate culture will simply have little influence on employee behavior.

When it comes to the bottom line, it is important for a corporation to have a culture of accountability. With a strong accountability culture, a corporation can avoid imposing a costly monitoring system which often hurts employee morale and diminishes productivity.

Finally, if you have a weak or mistrusting corporate culture, employees will vote "with their feet." In a tight labor market the bad workers will drive out the good and the situation gets even worse. A corporation will always need some type of controls but the goal is to have as few controls as possible—just enough to ensure that people don't violate the rules.

EMPLOYEE REACTIONS

In truth, measuring the positive or negative impact of a corporate culture on a company's bottom line remains an elusive goal. Most companies do not quantify the effects of corporate culture. According to a 1996 global survey of business executives in Australia, Canada, France, Germany, Holland, the United Kingdom and the United States done by the consultants Proudfoot PLC, only 38 percent of companies indicated that they measured the effects of their efforts to change corporate culture. Yet 86 percent claimed their culture change programs are successful. Methods of measurement included employee surveys (the most common practice overall), meetings, independent surveys and informal feedback. Despite the inability to measure impact, more than half of all executives surveyed (52 percent) felt that corporate culture contributes a great deal to the success of their companies. They just couldn't say how much with any great amount of certainty.

Views of Success

The main goal of any corporation is to be successful. But how you define success will, of course, have an impact on how you organize your business and its culture. Again, the influence of national culture and local expectations play a paramount role in determining the corporate view. Wirthlin Consulting's Worldwide Monitor finds what consumers in 13 countries view as success for a corporation. Most consumers said producing the very best products and services defined success (indicating their individualistic cultures). However, in Japan, the most notable attribute was caring about the country's social and environmental needs—a throwback to the culture's emphasis on the importance of the group over the individual. In Italy, if a company was well run and well managed, then it was thought to be successful—an indication of concern about that culture's history of chaotic politics and business management. In Mexico, a stable and profitable corporation was the benchmark of success. From these responses you can see the difficulties of attempting to set up a corporate culture that can effectively move across borders and meet the diverse needs of consumers in different countries.

The Ideal Corporate Culture

It would be impossible to give precise detail on what the perfect type of corporate culture should be for a global company. It depends so much on the cultures you are operating in, the subject industry and the basic cultural components. However, there are some basic traits:

- Any culture needs to develop a sense of accountability among staff and employees.

- It needs to be coherently transmitted across cultures. If it is too akin to the headquarters' culture, employees simply won't accept it.

- Think locally, act consistently. While flexibility is important, there must be a consistent application of principles across cultures.

- It must be attuned to the competitive requirements of the world market and be able to change to adapt to new market conditions.

The Concept of Corporate Citizenship

Is the business of business just business? While that statement may have been true years ago, in the era of globalization, it is flat-out wrong. Traditional economic views have traditionally identified corporate responsibilities as those which increase the corporation's profitability and productivity. The failing of this view was that it did not take into account the relationship between the firm's actions and the social setting in which it exists. It ignored the concept of "corporate citizenship" which is defined as the responsibility a corporation has to employees, shareholders, customers, suppliers and the community stakeholders where it conducts business and serves markets. At the minimum it entails observance of laws, regulations and accepted business practices where the corporation operates. The heart of corporate citizenship is building a relationship with the community. It's about paying attention to what is important to the communities in which the company does business, wants to do business, or needs to exist for business reasons. Businesses worldwide are rooted in the communities they serve. Healthy businesses depend upon healthy communities and vice versa. Corporate citizenship isn't just about signing on to the cause of the moment; it is the intersection of corporate interests with the public interest.

CULTURE CAUTION: It is interesting to note that Kofi Annan, the U.N. Secretary General, made a public plea in 1999 for corporations to set up their own Code of Conduct. He further stated that "markets have far outpaced societies and governments in their movements."

LEVELS OF CORPORATE CITIZENSHIP

There are four basic levels of corporate citizenship that all companies operate in at one time or another. The level at which a corporation participates is often determined by the expectations of society in a particular culture. For example, in Japan, the government has long been the main source of funding for social development, so a Japanese company is less likely to involve itself in an advanced level of corporate citizenship simply because the Japanese people do not expect it of business. The same would be true in Europe to some extent because of its socialist history.

However, in the United States, the opposite would be true. U.S. corporations face high expectations of community involvement and as a result tend to be more involved in corporate citizenship issues than corporations elsewhere. In an era of globalization, however, foreign companies seeking to do business in the United States have found that their meager corporate citizenship involvement back home has opened them to criticism in America.

The four basic levels of corporate citizenship identified by researchers in the field are:

- THE COMMON GOOD: Out of a sense of moral purpose and responsibility, a corporation involves itself in a wide range of projects simply because its corporate culture is dedicated to "the common good."

- EXPANDED SELF-INTEREST: Providing support for such programs as education and training which supports the long-term interests and success of the corporation.

An example would be a computer software company that funds a university department in computer engineering in the hopes that the university will become a future supplier of software engineers.

- IMMEDIATE BENEFITS: Doing well by doing good. An example would be a corporation getting involved in a cause-related marketing campaign. The British company, The Body Shop, is just such a company. It supports environmental actions and then uses its support of the cause to market its products.

- COMMERCIAL SELF-INTEREST: This is simply a matter of survival and common sense and involves a corporation following laws and meeting government regulation requirements.

Mainstream Corporate Citizens

A study conducted by The Boston College Center for Corporate Community Relations of U.S. multinational corporations shows that the concept of corporate citizenship is increasingly being regarded as part of a company's strategic plan. The study found that 67 percent of executives at U.S. multinationals report that their company includes community relations in its strategic plan, 73 percent say that the community relations program has a written policy or mission statement, and 56 percent say they have a community relations strategic plan. Eighty-five percent say their company encourages site management to be involved in the community and 23 percent say their company requires site management to get involved. Seventeen percent of companies include community involvement in the site manager's performance appraisal.

So, does corporate citizenship have an impact on a company's bottom line? It certainly seems to. In the United States, 55 percent of consumers say they always take into account a company's ethics and values when buying a product or service, according to a 1996 survey by the Institute of Global Ethics. On a global basis it is clear that reputation can determine whether customers establish and maintain a relationship with an organization, or turn instead to the competition. Managing a corporation's reputation through participation in corporate citizenship programs is essential as a tool in capturing market share and achieving business and public policy goals.

CULTURE CAUTION: Many emerging market economies insist that foreign corporations make significant contributions to local communities as part of any entry into the new market. These can range from training programs, to school construction, to major infrastructure improvements unrelated to the original corporate project.

Corporate Ethics

ETHICS STAY IN THE PREFACES OF THE AVERAGE

BUSINESS SCIENCE BOOK. — PETER DRUCKER

DURING THE LAST TWO DECADES business ethics was predominately a subject taught at business schools and debated by academics. It had little impact on the reality of the international business world, where the prevailing attitude was that anything goes to cut a deal. However, a much more sophisticated and socially aware consumer, along with the growth of large multinational companies, has transformed the concept from an academic

discipline into a real-life operating force. Along with corporate ethics, corruption and bribery in international business have surfaced as important issues in an increasingly interdependent world economy. No longer seen purely as a morality play, the accepted world view of corruption and bribery today is that they hinder competition, distort trade and harm consumers and taxpayers as well as undermine public support for governments. As a result, corporations see business ethics as a bottom-line issue, not one of optional morality. The acceptance of ethics as contributing to corporate operating profits or losses means it is receiving more attention than ever before.

One World, One Ethos?

Part of the problem is that business has been globalized faster than the development of a universally recognized framework for a global code of ethics and conduct. Corporations are only beginning to learn that while expanding into profitable new markets, they must also begin to take into account the social agendas of these new markets. While no global standard of ethics and conduct as yet exists, there are suggested standards being promoted from the Paris-based International Chamber of Commerce (ICC) and the U.S. Department of Commerce. And the world is seeing a convergence of sorts in what corporations and consumers from all cultures deem important. For example, although values and cultures differ, there is universal acceptance of the notion that a good corporate reputation is a competitive advantage in global business.

There is no escaping the fact that in all cultures corruption is an illegitimate and illegal behavior. In no government in the world can a politician or public official claim to be empowered by law to commit corrupt acts, accept bribes or squander resources. The logic goes that since corruption is necessarily accompanied by secrecy, the more transparent international business becomes—the faster it moves towards a global standard of transparency—the better the chance of defeating corruption and bribery becomes. Markets will work more efficiently for everyone's benefit, except, of course, those who have been taking bribes in the past. In the future, companies will distinguish themselves in the global marketplace by marketing their reputations.

CULTURE CAUTION: The reader should note that not all cultures define "corrupt" in the same way. Nor do all accept "transparency" as a virtue when it is seen as a breach of privacy and hierarchical philosophy.

Corporate Ethics Codes

To compete effectively global companies must ensure that their ethics codes and codes of conducts are culturally coherent to all employees. This is much harder than it sounds. In remote foreign locations, local management often gives its own interpretation of a company's values and ethics codes. This can be dangerous in some cases, creating an inconsistency of application and behavior that can ruin a corporation's global reputation and leave employees confused. The way to prevent this from happening is to cross-fertilize—that is, to send individual managers from head office to local offices to spread the corporate ethics gospel and to move local country employees to other company locations throughout the world so they begin to understand that the corporate ethics program is indeed a global one, consistent in application with little room for local interpretation.

While consistency is considered a vital component of a successful global ethics policy, more enlightened corporations will encourage managers to use common sense in its application. Certain circumstances require codes of conduct to be flexible and flexibility can be taught. When Italy's IVECO company moved into the Chinese market, they sent local Chinese managers back to Italy for part of their training. Besides learning basic management techniques they also became instilled with a new set of corporate ethics for potential application back in China.

CULTURE-CLASH INSURANCE

Attempting to transmit a code of conduct or ethics from one culture to another—a much more commonplace occurrence these days in the era of globalization—presents its own set of special challenges. An interesting case study presented by the Paris-based European School of Management in its publication, *Trends*, cites the case of the Japanese manufacturing and trading company, Matsushita Group (Panasonic is Matsushita's best-known corporate brand), attempting to introduce what it calls its Basic Management Objective and Seven

Principles—a corporate philosophy and basic code of conduct—to the company's French workers.

The challenge for management was to translate these rather spiritual principles, all of them based on Japanese culture and the importance of the group over the individual, into something relevant for the French culture that is far less group oriented. As you will see, the Basic Management Objective places a heavy emphasis on group well-being and the Seven Principles attempt to create the type of employer/employee relationship found in Japan. This is the opposite of the French model where unions are based on a trade, not a particular company, as in Japan.

MATSUSHITA GROUP

THE BASIC MANAGEMENT OBJECTIVE

Recognizing our responsibilities as industrialists, we will devote ourselves to the progress and development of society and the well-being of people through our business activities, thereby enhancing the quality of life throughout the world.

THE SEVEN PRINCIPLES

1. CONTRIBUTION TO SOCIETY: We will conduct ourselves at all times in accordance with the Basic Management Objective, faithfully fulfilling our responsibilities as industrialists to the communities in which we operate.

2. FAIRNESS AND HONESTY: We will be fair and honest in all our business dealings and personal conduct. No matter how talented and knowledgeable we may be, without personal integrity, we can neither earn the respect of others, nor enhance our own self-respect.

3. CO-OPERATION AND TEAM SPIRIT: We will pool our abilities to accomplish our shared goals. No matter how talented we are as individuals, without cooperation and team spirit we will be a company in name only.

4. UNTIRING EFFORT FOR IMPROVEMENT: We will strive constantly to improve our ability to contribute to society through our business activities. Only through this untiring effort can we fulfill our Basic Management Objective and help to realize lasting peace and prosperity.

5. COURTESY AND HUMILITY: We will always be cordial and modest, respecting the rights and needs of others in order to strengthen healthy social relationships and improve the quality of life in our communities.

6. ADAPTABILITY: We will continually adapt our thinking and behavior to meet the ever-changing conditions around us, taking care to act in harmony with nature to ensure progress and success in our endeavors.

7. GRATITUDE: We will act out of a sense of gratitude for all benefits we have received, confident that this attitude will be a source of unbounded joy and vitality, enabling us to overcome obstacles we encounter.

TRANSLATING AND TRANSMITTING

It is easy to see that while the principles would make sense to a Japanese worker, it would be a tougher sell to a French worker who does not share the experience of a Buddhist-oriented upbringing. The first problem to overcome was in the physical translation of the principles from the Japanese into the French language. A verbatim translation probably would not have worked because many of the powerful allegories would be lost, along with some of the uniquely Japanese ideological references. Instead, the company created a set of principles in French, based not on the verbatim translation, but rather on one that stripped out the redundancies and non-transferable references in the original and instead gave them more of a universal context that French workers would understand.

To implement the code of conduct, all workers were given seminars in the corporate philosophy and some real examples from the French workplace to show how these concepts could be applied. The French workers were taught how to understand the corporate mind-set of the company's Japanese managers in France and were encouraged to debate the value of the principles. The purpose of the seminars was to create a sense of ownership among the French workers for these "foreign" values from across the globe. The key to the success of the project was that both senior French and Japanese management provided leadership in this area and demonstrated the use of the values in day-to-day practice. Instead of just being another management fad of the month, the Seven Principles have become a part of the day-to-day dealings of all employees.

GET IT IN WRITING

Despite all the talk about the importance of corporate ethics, several studies have shown that, at least outside of the United States, surprisingly few corporations actually have a written code of conduct and ethics. In Australia, for example, 71 percent of companies do not have a written code and in Japan the figure was 70 percent. In Germany, France and Britain the figure is still under 60 percent. (Though still low compared to the United States, it is a big improvement over less than 20 percent in 1984.)

However, even those large multinational corporations that do have written codes rarely take the time and the care to ensure that it is coherent across cultures. As a result, little attention is paid to them outside of the head office. However, the marketplace is demanding that a lax attitude toward an ethics code be replaced by a functioning code that can be seen by consumers as having an impact on how a company operates.

Fighting Bribery and Corruption

The once widely held view that acceptance of bribery and the presence of corruption were somehow part of some world cultures, especially in the developing world, has been discredited. In reality, the implication that dishonesty and a lack of a moral compass was ingrained within a culture was downright insulting to these cultures. While there is no doubt that corruption is more prevalent in the emerging markets, its fundamental cause is economic, not cultural.

There has been a basic shift in thinking about the causes of global business bribery and corruption. Governments and corporations now recognize that there are two sides to the problem: a demand side, that is, the officials who accept or demand bribes, and a supply side, the multinational companies usually based in the wealthy developed nations of North America, Europe and Asia that pay the bribes to win business. To eliminate corruption, both the demand and the supply sides must be attacked.

FINDING THE WILL

The focus of the newly energized attack on international business bribery is two-fold. First: countries and corporations have come to the conclusion that fighting bribery and corruption is no longer simply a moral imperative but also a question of bottom-line economics. Second: the fastest way to eliminate bribery and corruption is by focusing not on the demand side of the equation but rather on the supply side and going after the companies and countries that feed the system of bribery by paying moneys to corrupt officials. The United States led the way with the introduction of the Foreign Corrupt Practices Act in 1977 which makes the payment of overseas bribes to government officials to win business a federal crime. But only in recent years has it managed to get real momentum for a global anti-bribery standard among the industrialized nations—many of whom allow companies to write off bribes paid to foreign officials as tax deductions.

Although all countries have laws proscribing bribery of their own officials, only the United States and Sweden prohibit citizens from corrupting foreign government officials. The U.S. stance was not motivated entirely by morality. In the 1970's the U.S. Securities and Exchange Commission revealed that over 400 U.S. companies admitted making questionable or illegal payments in excess of US$300 million to foreign governments and politicians in the previous decade. And, more recently, the U.S. Commerce Department estimates that between mid-1994 and mid-1996 U.S. companies lost US$11 billion in foreign contracts because of bribery by competing foreign multinational corporations. Further, the department says that bribery continues to be pivotal in many export competitions, with the bribing companies still winning an estimated 80 percent of the contract decisions.

CULTURE CAUTION: Even the strict U.S. law allows its citizens to make "facilitation payments" which are additional fees paid to foreign officials to get the officials to perform their regular duties.

Re-focusing the Fight

Today, countries agree that the economic costs are real: Recent studies have shown a direct correlation between the level of corruption and the amount of direct foreign investment a country receives; the higher the corruption level, the lower the investment amount. They agree that bribery leads to the misallocation of resources. Sometimes public officials are bribed to support non-essential projects. It also undermines attempts by governments to improve the overall wealth of the nation while at the same time allowing for undemocratic governments to stay in power.

As a result of U.S. efforts, the OECD and the United Nations have stepped up their efforts to eliminate bribery and corruption in global business. The UN is focusing on the laundering of illegal drug money, which it sees as one of the root causes of corruption in many countries. (The retail revenue in the illegal drug trade is estimated by the UN at US$400 billion, nearly double the revenue of the legitimate pharmaceutical industry.) The Organization for Economic Cooperation and Development (OECD) meanwhile has drawn up a Convention on Combating Bribery of Foreign Public Officials in International Business Transactions which will oblige those nations who sign it to make bribery of foreign officials a crime wherever in the world it takes place. The convention will have a global impact by attacking the "supply-side" of the bribery equation and will boost the confidence and enforcement of governments fighting the "demand-side" by re-enforcing the local anti-corruption efforts in developing countries and in those countries in economic transition in Central and Eastern Europe.

CHAPTER 16

The Cross-Cultural Team

PEOPLE ARE OUR MOST VALUABLE CAPITAL. — STALIN

THE RAPID RISE OF the use of work teams and the growth of cross-border business and global corporations are leading to the development of a new breed of corporate manager—the international cross-cultural professional. Confident in managing across cultures, these international professionals no longer use American, German, British, or Japanese management techniques to motivate cross-cultural global teams to performance excellence. Instead, they are developing a completely new skill set—one that these international managers will be able to use and adapt to any multi-national team regardless of the members' cultural origins. These skills are also transferable anywhere in the world. Going global, internationalizing activities, relocating manufacturing plants or offices and launching cross-cultural marketing campaigns are the mantras and mottoes of this new breed of business professional. To be successful they have learned how to deal with nationally and culturally eclectic teams. These managers understand the basic elements of international competition and devote time to study the culture, politics and operating style of world markets.

One Economy, Many Cultures

Perhaps nowhere else in the world is the demand for—and the shortage of— the experienced cross-cultural manager more evident than in Europe. The advent of the new single European currency (the Euro) and the further convergence of that continent's different cultures into a single business culture, complete with standardized transaction rules and transparency demands, are forcing many

European companies into developing a pan-European strategy for managing their businesses scattered throughout the continent. For a plethora of reasons, this pan-European approach has replaced the once-preferred country-by-country organizational structure. Not surprisingly, it is American multinational companies that are well ahead of European corporations in developing structures and strategies for an efficient pan-European operation.

It was the Americans who first saw the advantages of lower costs, increased operational efficiency, consistency of service and product as well as the bypassing of self-serving nationalist country managers, long before the Europeans did. Today, the problem plaguing both American and European multinationals is a shortage of these managers who possess not only the requisite language skills but the pan-European mindset. This includes the ability to build and effectively run cross-cultural teams which have become the basic building blocks of cross-border businesses.

The Global Mind-Set

The professional international manager no longer thinks in terms of one culture but rather takes a global view of each business challenge. What does it mean to have a global mind-set? It means:

- Never being content with one explanation for an event. The international manager knows that perceptions vary and that it is unlikely that two individuals from different cultures will see any one situation exactly alike.

- Accepting life as a balance of contradictory forces that are appreciated, contemplated and managed.

- Focusing on conflict management not conflict resolution. Each culture has a different approach to conflict resolution and it may be impossible to take one single approach that can satisfactorily end conflict on a cross-culture team. The international manager needs to be sensitive to this so as to limit the conflict and be resourceful in attempting to resolve it.

- Trusting the process rather than the structure to deal with the unexpected. The manager knows that an efficient process is more powerful than structure and is the key to organizational adaptability.

- Valuing diversity and multicultural teamwork as the basic form within which the team can accomplish their personal, professional and organizational objectives.

- Seeing change as opportunity and being comfortable with ambiguity.

- Emphasizing inclusion rather than exclusion in management style when circumstances call for it.

Global Teams, Global Challenges

Working in teams that span the globe poses problems not usually encountered when a group of people work together in the same city or even the same office.

Among them:

- Working across different time zones

- Being deprived of the benefit of interpreting non-verbal forms of communication; important cues and clues to real intent and commitment can be lost

- Having no direct social contact with other team members makes it difficult to develop personal relationships that help to overcome cultural differences and promote similarities

- Coordinating or minimizing cultural differences such as attitudes toward time, goals, and decision making

When cross-cultural teams work together at a single site, they will almost always create their own sub-cultures, based on the nature of the assignment, the nationalities of the team members, the organizational context of the team and the team leader's skills and attitude. In essence, the work team will develop a personality of its own—sometimes a pleasant one and sometimes, if managed incorrectly, an angry one.

Cross-Cultural Team Evolution

When cross-cultural teams work together, they inevitably come together (or, in some cases, drift apart) in one of four ways:

1. INTEGRATION: Team members realize that each culture has much to offer. The team will take the best from each culture and mold them into a team personality that reflects the diverse nature of team members. In an ideal world, all cross-cultural teams would evolve in this manner. Unfortunately, they do not. Still, an integrated team is a high-performance team.

2. ASSIMILATION: In this case, those in the minority voluntarily adapt to the majority culture. While this may avoid many of the conflicts inherent in a cross-cultural team setting, it fails to take full advantage of cultural diversity and much of the point of forming a cross-cultural team is lost.

3. SEPARATION: This happens when members of the minority culture keep their distance from the majority culture. In this case, the team never really comes together and conflicts occur. The synergy possible from cultural diversity is again lost.

4. MARGINALIZATION: This is the worst case scenario. Marginalization occurs when the minority culture members of the group are forced to give up their usual modes of behavior when the majority adopts an "either you are with us or against us" attitude. Obviously, minority members resent the majority, the team becomes dysfunctional because of dissent and production levels fall with neither the majority nor the minority feeling comfortable with each either.

CULTURE CAUTION: The term "diversity" as applied to the workplace was first popularized in the United States to describe the cultural attributes and contributions of individual workers. It is alternately a positive and a pejorative term. Majorities tend to downplay the influence of diversity while minorities use the term as a rallying cry. It is a culturally potent term and should be used only after gauging the sentiments of the workplace.

Do All Teams Succeed?

Research and the conventional wisdom state that there are several agreed upon basics on how to build and manage a high performance team. Consultants have written mountains of books and articles praising these management fundamentals. The following is a summary of Dr. Rebecca Proehl's approach to this topic on a point-by-point basis:

- **PARTICIPATIVE LEADERSHIP** Not all cultures appreciate such a style of leadership. Many cultures (Latin American, many Asian cultures) prefer a hierarchical type of leadership where the leader takes full responsibility for all major decisions of the group. They expect leaders to be all knowing and in charge. Meanwhile, there are other cultures that expect their leaders to be participative and prefer a team facilitator rather than a leader. Thus, if a cross-cultural team is really culturally diverse it is unlikely that one style of leadership will be effective. One suggestion to resolve this conundrum: separate group tasks and use different leadership styles to complete them.

- **GOOD COMMUNICATION** With such a wide variety of global communication styles among cultures, just defining what is meant by "good communication" is elusive. Team members from low-context cultures such as Germany and the United States would expect good communication to be precise, direct and detailed. However, individuals from high-context cultures such as Saudi Arabia, Brazil, and Japan, would define good communication as indirect and full of non-verbal cues. The best way to resolve this dilemma is to clarify to the team at the very start what good communication within the team means. It will probably mean that both sides will need to compromise, with low-context communicators toning down the directness while high-context team members become less subtle and more direct.

- **WILLINGNESS TO DEAL WITH CONFLICT** This is usually interpreted as meaning bringing conflict out into the open. But different cultures view and resolve conflict in very different ways. Low-context cultures tend to meet conflict head-on while individuals from high-context cultures would be embarrassed or disturbed by such a direct approach. One strategy is to use different strategies in different circumstances depending on the cultural make-up of the team. Another alternative would be to bring in an intermediary to solve conflict.

- **CLEAR GOALS AND OBJECTIVES** Team members from task-driven cultures will have a much different view of appropriate goals and objectives. They will tolerate a shorter time horizon for achievement than individuals from relationship-driven cultures. The latter tend to view time less urgently and take a longer-range view of achievement. For a manager to choose just one set of goals based on one perspective entails the risk of alienating other members of the team. The solution is to set up a combination of short-range task-driven goals combined with goals achievable in a longer, less intense time frame.

- **GOOD COORDINATION AND ORGANIZATION** This is usually interpreted to mean a clear delineation of individual job roles and individual responsibilities within the group. This might work fine for team members from individualistic cultures such as Australia and the United States. However, it clashes with the basic beliefs of those from collectivist cultures such as China and Japan. There, the welfare of the group is paramount and the emphasis is on belonging, be it to a society or a work team. To single individuals out for special responsibilities is anathema to individuals from collectivist cultures. The only solution is to think carefully about the organization of the team and to take the views of the opposing cultures into account.

- ■ CONSENSUS DECISION MAKING Decision making is influenced by a culture's approach to power and individualism. Workers from some high-power distance cultures like those found in the Middle East would not expect to be consulted on decisions, while those from a low power-distance culture would find it essential. Rather than assuming all members prefer a consensus form of decision making, adjust the decision-making process in accordance with the cultural mix.

Cross-Cultural Team Building

In cross-cultural team building one needs to be less dogmatic and more flexible than when assembling a culturally homogenous work team. Here are three basic rules of cross-cultural team building that work:

1. Identify the nature and implications of cultural differences within the team.

2. Establish a basis for building understanding and awareness of cultural differences and how they may be managed.

3. Formulate a framework for developing a high-performance team that takes account of cultural differences.

TEAM CONCERNS

As a cross-cultural team manager, you can expect your team members to have questions and concerns that need to be answered. You will probably need to have answers for at least three questions:

1. How will cross-functional cross-cultural teamwork affect them, their work process, their career status?

2. How will compensation systems work?

3. How will rewards and recognition be shared?

Domestic Challenges

The movement of workers across borders in Europe and the continuing flood of immigrants into the United States has made the development of cross-cultural management skills important not only for international projects but for domestic operations as well. German managers can find themselves in charge of a predominately Turkish or Vietnamese workforce. A Canadian manager may find himself or herself in charge of a department staffed by Indian software engineers. An Australian foreman may find that Chinese is the dominant language in the factory.

Another example is the Moslem workers at Whirlpool Corp.'s plant in Nashville, Tennessee who demanded time off from the assembly line for daily prayers (devout Moslems pray five times a day). Also under discussion is what kind of traditional loose-fitting Islamic-style clothing can be safely worn near assembly line machinery. The Council of American-Islamic relations says workplace conflicts are increasing as more Moslems immigrate to the United States and take up employment. Up to 60 percent of the council's time is spent resolving workplace disputes. Clearly, cross-cultural managers are not only needed for international assignments.

The Global Leadership Crisis

The increased emphasis on global team-building has created greater demand for business leadership. So far, companies have failed to develop enough global leaders to meet their needs, resulting in what many call a global business leadership crisis. A global study by the U.S.-based business research organization, The Conference Board, found that only 8 percent of CEOs and senior executives in multinational corporations rated their company's overall leadership capacity as excellent. Another study, by consultant Allen Morrison, found that 75 percent of executives of multinational companies believe their companies do not have enough global leaders to meet demand. Yet, less than 8 percent of those companies actually had a leadership development program in place.

The role of leadership in business is critical. Another survey of senior business executives, by the Britain-based Watson Wyatt consultancy, found that 80 percent of respondents in the U.K. believe poor leadership to be the primary cause of business failure. In continental Europe, 67 percent of executives listed it as the main cause for failure.

Developing Global Leaders

You often read about "natural born leaders" and "take-charge types" as if they were some mythical characters who had leadership in the genes. In reality, leaders aren't born, they are developed. Leadership can be taught through a careful program of mentoring, providing a wide-range of experience and a leadership development plan. This also applies to global leaders. Perhaps the most crucial aspect is for organizations to begin leadership development at the earliest levels if they wish to remain competitive in a global marketplace. The most common methods of leadership development found in global corporations today are:

- CREATION OF GLOBAL MANAGEMENT TEAMS This provides exposure to a wide range of challenges and responsibilities as well as presenting successful domestic managers with the need to develop a whole new set of management skills. The successful domestic manager may not always make a successful international manager.

- DEVELOPMENT OF LOCAL NATIONALS AS POTENTIAL LEADERSHIP CANDIDATES Corporations are looking outside their home markets for leadership candidates, thus widening the potential leadership pool. Truly global companies have no cultural or national bias in selecting leadership material.

- ROTATION OF INTERNATIONAL ASSIGNMENTS This exposes potential leaders to a wide variety of customs, cultures and market styles.

■ CREATION OF A CLEAR INTERNATIONAL CAREER PATH Previously, the domestic and international branches of corporations were often considered to be virtually different companies. Often, going abroad was rewarded upon return with career stagnation. Not any more. Corporations are creating a leadership career path that makes international experience a basic requirement. Now, those who stay home end up with the lackluster career.

■ INTRODUCTION OF A CROSS-CULTURAL MENTORING PROGRAM This re-enforces the lessons learned abroad and helps to build bridges across cultures.

Global Leadership Effectiveness

A leader is supposed to inspire great performance. So how do you measure a leader's effectiveness and contribution? Corporations now believe that traditional measures of leadership effectiveness placed far too much emphasis on a leader's individual characteristics. Not enough regard had been given to the actual goal of leadership—the success of the team. The overriding logic now is that what the team does is paramount. According to The Conference Board, 64 percent of today's companies use team performance as a measure of leadership effectiveness.

Leadership Tips

There are 10 basic leadership behaviors that differentiate between excellent and mediocre business leaders. A successful global leader should:

1. Provide clear objectives
2. Build teams
3. Achieve unit goals
4. Enhance individual and team performance
5. Make the difficult decisions
6. Gain employee/team ownership of projects
7. Generate enthusiasm and pride
8. Make the team feel important
9. Teach (and learn) from honest mistakes
10. Manage creative talent effectively

CHAPTER 17

Cross-Cultural Marketing

SMALL OPPORTUNITIES ARE OFTEN THE BEGINNING OF

GREAT ENTERPRISES. — DEMOSTHENES

CROSS-CULTURAL MARKETING is really, first and foremost, about cross-cultural communication. Consider the citizens of the Roman Empire—the first earthly civilization that was born to shop. Merchants solved the dilemma of cross-cultural marketing back then by erecting signs above their stores, displaying pictures of the wares inside. It not only served the Romans' own illiterate population but helped merchants get their commercial message across in non-Latin-speaking societies conquered by the Romans. Looking farther back we find that the fundamental principles of effective persuasion articulated by Aristotle more than 2,350 years ago can still be applied to selling products today as they could to a public debate in ancient Athens. It is clear that communication is the fundamental root of modern marketing.

Communicating with Consumers

There is no doubt that the era of global marketing has arrived. The percentage of the U.S. gross domestic product coming from international trade has ballooned from 5 percent to 20 percent in the last 25 years. Global advertising spending topped the $400 billion mark for the first time in 1998. In the United States alone, the number of companies seeking market research information on a global basis has skyrocketed. Such research is one of the first steps in taking up the international marketing challenge.

The American Marketing Association's magazine, *Marketing News*, says 32 of the nation's top-50 research firms reported revenue from work conducted outside the United States in 1998. This represents more than three times the number reporting overseas activities in 1989. Among the top-50 firms, $2.1 billion, or 41 percent of revenues, came from subsidiaries and projects outside the United States, compared with just 30.5 percent in 1989.

Why Go Global?

The most simple answer to this question: Improvements in communications technology, from global satellites to fax machines to the Internet, have made it a lot easier to closely manage a global operation than ever before. Distance, once the biggest obstacle to overseas expansion, is no longer as relevant as it once was. In essence, if you are a Paris-based company, managing and communicating with a business in Beijing is probably no more problematic than managing and communicating with a business in Lyon.

Besides the increased ease in communication, the home and regional markets of multinational corporations are becoming ever more crowded. Fearing stagnation, these corporations look abroad for growth and opportunity. And as other companies do the same, the competition has forced even the most risk-adverse multinational corporation to seek alternate methods of growth. Relying solely on a domestic market can be a recipe for death for even mid-sized firms, let along larger companies.

THE PLANETARY CONSUMER

The increasing wealth of nations has created a planet of consumers who, despite profound cultural differences, may have more in common than most marketers suspect. Besides taking care of the distance problem, the globalization of the media and the extended reach of such broadcast outlets such as America's Cable News Network (CNN) and Britain's Sky Channel have made some information universal. Magazines from America's *Time* and *Vogue* to Britain's *Economist* to Germany's *Burda Moden* to France's *Paris Match* have acted as cultural unifiers.

The world's population has new access to the same heroes, music trends, products, fashion and consumer information. This access has helped to shatter cultural barriers. Societies that were once totally self-absorbed now recognize Ralph Lauren, Dior, Mickey Mouse, Pele, and Michael Jordan. Even the staunchest communist has at one time or another succumbed to the siren call of eating at a McDonald's somewhere in the world.

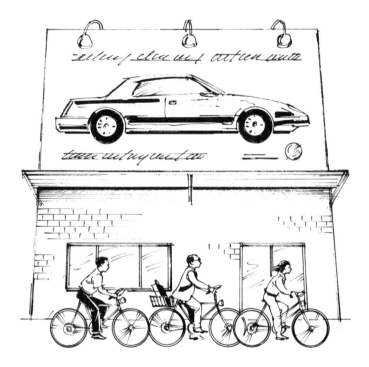

While increased customer reach is clearly a benefit of going global, it's not the only one. Companies that have taken up the global marketing challenge often come back with a better understanding of the competition. They even find new products that they can use to their advantage in their home market.

The Legendary Mistakes

Every year more than 40,000 products are introduced into the global marketplace (more than half of those in the United States alone). About 85 percent of these products fail. The road to international marketing success is built upon the debris of failed marketing and advertising campaigns. Most of them failed because of cross-cultural communication misunderstandings, others because someone in the marketing department failed to do their research. The main lesson to be learned: do your homework. At all costs, back-translate slogans and tag lines (at least twice) and watch those idioms. Here is just a short list of marketing and communication blunders:

COMMUNICATION BREAKDOWN

- Electrolux, a Scandinavian vacuum cleaner maker, thought nothing of using the same advertising tag line in the United States that met with great success in Britain. Unfortunately, "Nothing sucks like an Electrolux" had a very different meaning in America than it did in Britain. In America, the word "suck" is slang for lousy.

- When General Motors introduced the Chevy Nova in South America, it was apparently unaware that "no va" means "it won't go" in Spanish. After the company figured out why it wasn't selling any cars, it renamed the car in its Spanish markets to the Caribe or Caribbean.

- The Ford Motor Company had a similar problem when its Pinto—a big seller in the States—failed to make an impact in Portuguese-speaking Brazil. The reason: Pinto was local slang for "tiny male genitals." Ford pried all the nameplates off and substituted Corcel, which means horse.

- A translation error in Italy left the British company Schweppes highly embarrassed. An ad campaign for its Tonic Water was somehow translated into Schweppes Toilet Water.

- Kinki Nippon Tourist Company, one of Japan's leading tourist companies, found its U.S. and British offices swamped by telephone calls from folks interested in their sex tours after it launched a promotional campaign in those two countries. The company was baffled, not realizing that "kinki" (pronounced kinky) carries the connotation of unusual sexual activity in the English language. Kinki eventually changed its name in English-speaking countries.

- Coors put its slogan, "Turn it loose," into Spanish, where it was read as "Suffer from diarrhea."

- Puffs tissues tried to introduce its product in Europe only to learn that "puff" in German is slang for a brothel.

- When Pepsi started marketing its products in Taiwan, the slogan, "Pepsi Brings You Back to Life" literally translated into "Pepsi Brings Your Ancestors Back from the Grave"—obviously a marketing claim that could not be substantiated.

- Hunt-Wesson introduced its Big John products in French Canada as Gros Jos before finding out that the phrase, in slang, means "big breasts."

- Britain's Colgate Palmolive introduced a toothpaste in France called Cue. It was laughed off the shelves. It seems that the word also refers to the name of a well-established and rather infamous porno magazine—*Cue.*

The Global Consumer

Most market research has focused on the differences, not the similarities, between consumers in different cultures. This was a valid premise before the global communications explosion began merging tastes and desires. Roper Starch Worldwide, a U.S.-based market research firm, interviewed some 35,000 consumers in 35 countries to produce the Global Consumer Hot Buttons Report. It basically concludes that consumers around the world are more similar than different, with a set of shared attitudes, values and behaviors that cut across what one would traditionally think of as cultural lines. The purpose of the study was to broaden consumer research beyond traditional delineations such as geography, age and income. The report divided the world into six "global value groups" that cut across cultures. The six groups were identified as:

1. STRIVERS The largest of the six groups, strivers make up 23 percent of the world's adult population. They value material wealth and possessions, status, ambition and power. They are mostly middle-aged, more often male than female, and are mostly found in the developed and developing economies of Asia and the Pacific Rim.

2. DEVOUTS They make up 22 percent of the world's adult population and have more traditional values than strivers. They value faith, respect for elders and obedience and are found mainly in Asia, Africa and the Middle East. As consumers they would choose local brands over international imports.

3. ALTRUISTS Altruists are very outer-focused and make up some 18 percent of the world's adult population. They are well-educated, interested in social causes, older, with a median age of 44, and are predominately female. They are mostly found in Latin America, North America and Russia.

4. INTIMATES They focus on relationships close to home, family, friends, and business colleagues. They are 15 percent of the population and are most often found in the United States, Britain, and the Central European countries. They are "people people." Half of them are heavy consumers of the media, especially television.

5. FUN SEEKERS By far the youngest of the groupings, fun seekers (12 percent) seek pleasure, excitement and enjoy looking good. They hit bars, discos, nightclubs, restaurants and gobble up the electronic media. This group possesses the closest thing to a global lifestyle there is.

6. CREATIVES The smallest group at 10 percent, it includes the techno-nerds who appreciate learning and technology. Heavy users of the Internet, they are mostly found in the highly developed countries.

Battling Misconceptions

It has been recognized that consumers worldwide are much more knowledgeable than a few years ago. However, international marketers must still do battle with ignorance and cultural superstitions that sometimes defy logic. This is especially true in newly developing markets. In Uzbekistan, for example, Barbie dolls are, of course, considered the quintessential American product—one that Uzbeks have long heard much about. But the doll's American manufacturer, Mattel, found that Uzbeks rejected Barbie, not because they couldn't relate to her distinctly "to-die-for" look but because the dolls were stamped "made in Hong Kong." The Uzbeks thought they were cheap knock-offs and not the real thing. The German drug maker Hoechst AG found a similar situation with its antibiotics marketed in the same country. Local consumers thought those that were sold in packages with local Uzbek language script on the package were somehow less potent than the same drug in a package with German lettering.

Tips for Global Marketers

Obviously, the biggest obstacle to overcome with any marketing program is language. Many companies that go global believe that English can still be used as a universal language. While this may be true to some extent for senior executives and big multinational corporations, it is far from true on a retail level. Going the extra mile to address consumers in their own language can have huge payoffs. Direct-mail sellers like America's Lands End, Eddie Bauer, and Williams-Sonoma are mailing their Japanese customers Japanese-language catalogs. When the outwear catalog retailer, Patagonia, shifted to a Japanese-language catalog, its annual sales in Japan grew by 98 percent, versus the 20 percent growth shown when it used an English-only catalog.

WHEN TO GO GLOBAL

To be successful at international marketing an individual needs personal experience with cultural differences and needs to be able to identify the perceptual filters of his or her own culture. One needs to realize that communication styles and the way individuals process information vary by culture, as to behaviors, values and perceptions. What follows are some basic steps to developing a successful international marketing plan.

- First, decide why you need to market abroad.

- Once you've decided why you want to market internationally, determine where you want to market and look at the possibilities in a specific area for your product.

- Identify the potential demand for your products. Remember that some products will be unsuitable because of differences in culture, lifestyle, or preferences.

- Identify the nature of the local competition. Strong local competitors can kill a product's chances of ever gaining a foothold.

- Determine the logistical roadblocks to getting products into consumers' hands.

- Develop an organized strategy, beginning with thorough research, using both secondary and primary sources. Making it up as you go along in an international marketing campaign can spell disaster.

▪ When introducing a product, do a thorough country-by-country testing before a full launch. This can identify potential problems concerning language and packaging and provide information on potential market sizes and responses. It will allow you to tinker with details to get the main launch correct.

CULTURE CAUTION: Many nations—from developed France to emerging Vietnam—have strict legal requirements for advertising and foreign language content, as well as packaging design and recyclability. Penalties can be stiff so make sure your marketing program meets local legal standards.

RESEARCH IS THE KEY

International market research can be very difficult to conduct because of cultural constraints and customs. For example: In Islamic countries putting women in the same focus group as men is a non-starter, as is mixing social classes in Latin America or Japan. Certain political or personal questions may be appropriate in one country, but not in another. Legal and privacy issues also vary by country. In France, an adult must be present if children under age 18 are being interviewed. Privacy laws in Germany make it difficult to videotape groups or individuals being interviewed. Direct-mail marketing research techniques are also rife with regulation on a country by country basis—sometimes even city by city.

Emerging Markets: A Special Case

When entering emerging markets, foreign companies often have the misconception that their only competition is other multinationals. But local companies are gaining ground. In China, the single largest computer manufacturer is a local company called Legend, which is outselling Compaq, IBM, HP, and other major players. Multinationals also tend to overestimate the size of the consumer market.

Emerging markets are usually pyramid in structure, with a massive base of very poor people at the bottom (likely not a market) and a very narrow small point of the very rich (a likely market). What the increasing wealth of nations has led to, however, is improved potential to tap the huge middle ground as a market for consumer products. This is where the real bonanza lies. Some special considerations for entering emerging markets:

▪ BE CREATIVE ON CORPORATE STRUCTURE Companies new to a region often rely far too much on alliances and joint ventures when expanding into new markets. These have, more often than not, been a recipe for failure. Companies should be more concerned with maintaining control and setting up wholly owned subsidiaries rather than being a minority or 50/50 partner. The trend toward "going it alone" is already abundantly clear in China, where multinationals have had little success with their inefficient and none-to-honest local partners.

▪ LOOK TO EXPAND THE MARKET, CREATE NEW PRODUCTS Don't just sell to the market as it is today; create new markets. The Swiss company, Nestlé, used its skill in

food processing and its marketing savvy to create a whole new market in India for instant breakfast rice cakes.

▧ DEVELOP LOCAL MANAGERIAL AND TECHNICAL TALENT Local managers with knowledge of the region who can be taught leading-edge management practices are invaluable.

▧ BALANCE GLOBAL CAPABILITIES WITH ADAPTING TO LOCAL MARKETS Global companies have advantages in economies of scale, manufacturing, technology development, and marketing and distribution skills that should be used against competitors. At the same time, companies must localize, because too much standardization may alienate the local customer. Take a page from McDonald's book. The company localizes its menu to fit the culture. You won't see a beef patty anywhere in its restaurants in India and the big seller is the mutton-based Maharaja Mac.

International Website Marketing

The Internet is the first medium to truly deliver an almost instant global audience for marketers. Although estimates vary, the number of households on-line worldwide totaled about 24 million in 1996 and that number is expected to skyrocket to almost 70 million in the year 2000. Outside of the United States, Japan, Germany, and the United Kingdom are predicted to show the fastest growth rates in on-line households. The United States will continue to lead in the number of on-line households with 36 million in the year 2000, but its share of the total world market will drop from 62.8 percent in 1996 to 54.1 percent in 2000. Asia/Pacific Rim, Japan, Australia/New Zealand, Hong Kong, South Korea, and Taiwan have developed strong-growing on-line markets. Asia and the Pacific Rim primary markets will grow from the 3.6 million on-line households in 1996 to 10 million by the year 2000.

While this may seem to open up a sizable market for companies, current studies say that only about 1 in 10 of the households on-line has actually purchased goods or services online. People are more likely to regard the Internet as a reference library than a retail outlet. They are more interested in using it for information purposes than for making a purchase. Indeed, they are more likely to gather information such as price comparisons and then purchase products in a more traditional way. But this, too, is changing.

Building an International Website

The Internet has truly made it easier to reach a global audience. But it is not simply a matter of posting a website on the Net. To be an effective marketer internationally on the Internet, you need to ensure that your site is accessible to a culturally diverse audience.

▧ TARGET MARKET: The first decision to be made is to consider which countries you want to target as potential markets.

▧ LANGUAGE: Do you need to translate your website? Although 80 percent of the content on the Internet is in English, most people will access the Internet in their own language. Serious marketers will allow users to access material in their native language.

- KEEP IT SIMPLE: If you decide to use English only, make sure you use a simplified international style of English. Avoid jargon and local idioms that will confuse other English speakers who may not speak your "dialect" of English.

- CLEAN UP THE SITE: Make sure there are no images that might be considered offensive in another culture.

- TECHNOLOGICALLY FRIENDLY: Don't load the site up with large graphics and photo files. It will take most users too long to load them, unless they have top-of-the-line equipment. Offer a "text-only" version.

- LOGISTICS: Even before you have your website up and working, you must consider how to handle the logistics of payment, delivery and after-sales service.

- PROMOTION: It is essential to actively promote your website abroad through such techniques as print advertising, trade shows and Internet advertising.

CHAPTER 18

Cross-Cultural Consultants

WE'RE OVERPAYING HIM, BUT HE'S WORTH IT.

— SAMUEL GOLDWYN

THE EXPLOSION OF cross-border commerce has led to a sharp rise in the number of global business consultants. They offer advice on everything from good table manners to introductions to the power elite of an emerging market economy. But not all consultants are equal when it comes to quality levels and experience. There are two main types of global consultant. The first, internal consultants, are those that offer a full range of business services and marketing expertise in the country you have targeted as a potential market. The second, external consultants, are those that offer to educate you and your staff in the fine points of protocol, etiquette and international business cultures in general.

Foreign and Domestic Consultants

If you have only a rudimentary knowledge of the targeted foreign market, it is probably not the best idea to rely on local consultants alone. This is especially true in the developing world. While the locals in these new potential boom areas may walk the walk and talk the talk, they probably don't have a full grasp of what an experienced international businessperson's needs really are. A local can probably take you only so far. If you decide to go the consultant route, consider hiring not only a consultant in the target market but also a quality firm from your home country that has experience in dealing with the targeted region.

When hiring a local consultant in the target country, insist on references and do a thorough background check on the firm or its individuals. Nothing is more embarrassing to an established company than hiring a local consulting firm whose main connections are through organized crime and whose main area of expertise is bribing the prime minister's family. References are also advisable for hiring consultants from your domestic market.

Choosing a Consultant

The Institute of Management Consultants (IMC), a global organization with offices in major world cities, says that to obtain the best results from consultants, you should work closely with the individual or firm appointed, providing them with the information necessary to undertake the assignment. Experience suggests that joint assignments, bringing together consultants and members of the organization, are often the most effective. Clear communication between consultant and client is essential. The IMC offers these hard-and-fast rules for choosing and using international management consultants effectively:

1. Clearly define the objectives that you wish to achieve: Describe the job you want done and specify the things you expect from the assignment. Understand precisely how you expect your business will benefit from the work. Decide on the time, scale, scope and constraints on the assignment. Clarify your own role, which key staff will be involved, and how their time will be made available.

2. Consult with others in your organization to agree on those objectives. Jointly define your specific needs for the expertise you want. Is it a systems, human or skills problem?

3. Possible candidates should be invited to deliver a short preliminary presentation. This presentation should cover how the consultants would manage the assignment, staffing, timing, liaison and fees. Examples of previous assignments should also be provided. A final short-list of candidates should then be prepared and formal proposals solicited from which the selection would be determined. Short-list no more than three consultants, and ask them to provide written proposals, which should include:

- Their understanding of the problem

- Terms of reference

- The names and credentials of the consultants who will do the work

- Other support provided by the firm

- The work plan and time scale

- The reports and/or systems that will be delivered to you

- The fees and expenses and schedule of payment

- The inputs required from you

4. The normal method for formally engaging an individual or firm is an exchange of letters. The formal proposal should clearly define the terms of reference for the assignment which need to be agreed to by the client organization. Formal contracts should cover such matters as fees and expenses, tax payments, conditions for termination, staffing and timing, together with the facilities to be made available by the client.

5. Brief the consultants properly. They need to know and understand the background to your definition of the problem in order to produce detailed proposals that meet your requirements. Remember, the cheapest quote will not necessarily give the best value for the money.

6. Meet the individual consultant(s) who will do the job and make sure that the "chemistry" is right. Successful consultancy requires goodwill in human communications. Make sure that you see the person who is going to do the work and that the "chemistry" between you and the consultant is right. Talk through your chosen proposal with the consultant before making a final decision to ensure that you have any concerns answered. If you are not happy with any aspects of

the proposal, do not feel pressured into accepting them. Continue discussions with the consultant until full agreement on the proposal can be reached.

7. Ask for references from the chosen consultant firm and follow them up. Ask the firm or individual chosen for names or written references from former clients in order to verify the consultants' suitability for the assignment.

8. Be involved and available during the assignment. Remember that you must keep in touch with the progress of the assignment if you are to get the most from it. Consultants are likely to be most cost-effective when working with an agreed program and time scale. Make sure there are regular progress meetings and that the consultant keeps you fully briefed on progress against the program. If you and your staff need to provide input, make sure that you do it within the agreed time scale. Extra costs may be incurred if you hold up the progress of the assignment. Consultancy requires an investment not only in fees but also in client time.

9. Ensure that the consultant does not save surprises for the final report. The consultant's report is his or her most tangible "deliverable," but it must be in a format which is beneficial to you. If necessary, ask the consultant to produce a draft report so that you can discuss findings and recommendations with some of your colleagues before the final report is produced. The final report should contain no surprises. If there are very confidential or contentious issues, ask for these to be put into a private letter rather than in the report itself. Make sure the report is written in a way you and your staff can understand and use. Tell the consultant if you are not happy with it. Ask the consultant to make a presentation of the report to you and your colleagues, if this will help in a discussion on its conclusions.

10. Involve your staff in the assignment as early as possible so that they "own" the recommendations. You should aim to involve your staff in the assignment as early as possible so that they partly "own" the recommendations and have an interest in the results.

11. Implement the recommendations and involve your management as well as the consultant. You may need to make arrangements for the management consultant to help with the implementation. This can be done cost effectively by involving the consultant in regular progress meetings. Get a written fee quotation and proposal for any implementation work, even if it follows directly from an assignment. If you want the consultant to help you with training staff, make sure that attitudes as well as techniques are addressed.

CUSTOMIZATION IS ESSENTIAL

Any cross-cultural training program offered to your company should be customized to your specific needs. If the training program doesn't adequately prepare employees to do their job in-country, it probably wasn't worth the money and time. If possible, the consultant should provide customized follow-up since this provides opportunities to reinforce specific suggestions or strategies, and to communicate any areas of concern back to the company.

CHAPTER 19

Glossary

ADVERTISING A form of public notice that seeks to inform, persuade and otherwise modify consumer attitudes toward a product, with the objective of triggering an eventual purchase.

AGENDA The list of topics to be covered during a negotiation session. An agenda is usually arranged in either an ascending or descending order of importance. Control of the agenda is important to negotiation strategy.

BIG PICTURE The overall, long-term view of a business deal or transaction. To be a Big Picture thinker means you have the ability to get past the details to think ahead to see a company's overall strategy.

BONA FIDES Latin for "good faith," it refers to documents, materials and promises that show commitment by a company or individual to a particular line of business, a deal or an outcome. It is generally taken to mean that a company or individual is serious and are who they say they are. Sincerity.

BOTTOM LINE The last line in a financial statement indicating the profit of a company. Also, an American term for "get to the point."

BRIBERY Payments or concessions made to an individual holding a position of power and trust to influence the outcome of a business transaction. Morality aside, bribery is an entrenched part of doing international business, though some uniformity in the fight against it as bad economic policy is beginning to take shape by the world's more powerful economies.

BUDDHISM A religion springing from the life of Gautama Buddha (India 6th century BC). It stresses trust, kindness and generosity. And, that material desires are selfish and rooted in self delusion about an individual's importance. Suffering is accepted as an inescapable part of human existence. The religion is widely followed in Asia and has a great impact on cultural attitudes toward business.

COLLECTIVISM A cultural value that places great emphasis on the harmony of the group and appreciates individuals who cede their needs and wants to that of the group. A person thinks of the group first and follows the orders of those in charge.

CONFUCIANISM The moral system (not a religion) of China based on the teachings of the philosopher Confucius who died in 479 BC. His teachings are based on ethical precepts—benevolent love, righteousness, decorum, wise leadership, sincerity, designed to inspire and preserve the good management of family and society. It teaches that the welfare of the group takes precedent over the welfare of the individual. Its precepts are practiced in many Asian societies outside of China and form the basis of social organization and hierarchical administration in these societies.

CORPORATE CITIZENSHIP The responsibility a corporation has to employees, shareholders, customers, suppliers and the community where it conducts business and serves markets. At the minimum it entails observance of laws, regulations and accepted business practices where it operates. It goes beyond the traditional economic view of a corporation's responsibilities that included only increasing a corporation's profitability and productivity.

CORPORATE CULTURE The bond that holds an organization together. It incorporates an organization's values, norms of behavior, policies and procedures and is heavily influenced by national cultural values, ownership structure and the nature of the industry in which the corporation operates.

CROSS-CULTURAL A comparison of beliefs and attitudes of different cultures or nationalities with another set of beliefs and attitudes. In management it is a concept that deals with the challenge of managing a team of workers from different cultures.

CULTURE A set of learned core values, beliefs, standards, knowledge, morals, laws and behaviors shared by individuals and societies that determines how an individual acts, feels and views himself/herself and others.

CULTURE SHOCK A mental and physical condition that affects a traveler when everything that was once familiar to them—language, food, currency, values—suddenly vanishes because they have traveled to a new culture. The effects of culture shock are cumulative and can manifest themselves in the withdrawal of the individual from the new culture or temperamental outbursts aimed at the new culture.

DUGRI An Israeli term that means speaking bluntly, assertively and honestly with a hard edge during negotiations. When Israelis talk *dugri* there is little posturing or gamesmanship. It forces negotiations to move ahead quickly either toward resolution or failure.

ETHICS Moral principles and values of an individual or company in personal and business relationships. The word is derived from the Greek word for "character" and describes an attitude having to do with moral obligations and responsibilities. Cultural influences and attitudes usually have a great impact on ethics.

ETIQUETTE The codes and practices prescribed by social convention that govern correct behavior in all social situations and interactions from personal to business.

FACE A deeply held value, especially in Asian and Middle Eastern cultures, related to dignity, respect from others as well as self-respect and self-esteem. While in the West, losing face—being embarrassed by an error or bad behavior—is associated with personal failure, in Asian and Middle Eastern cultures it is a group concept. Shame is brought not only to individuals but to the group or organization they represent.

FEMININE CULTURE Societies with so-called feminine values that appreciate inter-personal relationships, put quality of life before material acquisition, and applaud concern for individuals and less-fortunates. A feminine culture contrasts with a masculine culture.

FIXER (see GO-BETWEEN)

FOREIGN CORRUPT PRACTICES ACT A U.S. law that makes it a federal crime for U.S. companies, citizens or their agents to bribe foreign officials to gain commercial advantage. The act is sometimes seen as an impediment to U.S. businesses whose competition does not often face similar restrictions.

GIRI NINJO One of the most powerful and fundamental principles governing personal and business interactions in Japan. It is a sense of honor, loyalty and empathy that makes business operations sometimes seem like an extended family.

GO-BETWEEN A third party that may or may not be known to one or both parties seeking to conduct a business transaction. The role of the go-between is usually to set up an introduction for a foreign business in the go-between's home country.

HIGH-CONTEXT CULTURE A culture that places great value on the intangible aspects of a negotiation or business deal. Individuals from such cultures look beyond the facts and figures and take into consideration such factors as personal relationships, atmosphere and attitudes toward respect, religion and trust. Business can never be conducted without a face-to-face meeting.

INTERNET A global network connecting millions of computers. More than 100 countries are linked into exchanges of data, news and opinions via the Internet. Unlike online services, which are centrally controlled, the Internet is decentralized by design. Each Internet computer, called a host, is independent. Its operators can choose which Internet services to use and which local services to make available to the global Internet community.

INDIVIDUALISM A cultural value that places great emphasis on the independent thinker and appreciates and honors personal success over that of the group.

LEVEL PLAYING FIELD A business environment where everyone is subjected to the same set of rules and regulations.

LOW-CONTEXT CULTURE A culture that assumes a high degree of shared knowledge on the behalf of a transaction partner and thus deals only in such tangible aspects of the deal as facts, figures and performance. The atmosphere and the personal relationship with the business partners means little. In a low-context culture, business can be conducted without ever meeting face-to-face.

MASCULINE CULTURE Societies with so-called masculine values appreciate aggressiveness and assertiveness while respecting the goal of material acquisition. A masculine culture contrasts with a feminine culture.

MONOCHRONIC A term that describes how a culture views time. In a monochronic society time is used for ordering one's life, for setting priorities and for doing tasks in a sequential order—one thing at a time. Most of the societies of the developed world are monochronic. It contrasts with a polychronic society.

NON-VERBAL COMMUNICATION Usually subtle gestures, facial expressions, posture, eye contact and body language that often subconsciously accompanies spoken communication and can reveal much about the true intentions of the communicator. Even silence is a form of non-verbal communication and can mean different things in different cultures.

ORGANIZATION OF ECONOMIC CO-OPERATION AND DEVELOPMENT (OECD) Headquartered in Paris, France, the group of 27 countries that includes the major industrialized democracies of Asia, Europe and North America was established in 1961 to promote economic and social welfare in member countries and to stimulate and harmonize relations with developing nations. The OECD is considered the leading world organization when it comes to fighting bribery and corruption in business and is a leading force in developing a global ethics standard for business.

PROTOCOL The form of etiquette and ceremony observed by businesspeople and diplomats during formal cross-cultural interaction.

POLYCHRONIC A polychronic society uses time to accomplish diverse goals simultaneously and to interact with as many individuals as possible—even at the same time. In such a society the sequential approach to tasks is seen as undesirable. Polychronism is a characteristic of emerging economies.

POWER-DISTANCE A cultural dimension that describes how individuals within a society view power and in turn how they view their roles in the decision-making process. In high power-distance cultures, people see themselves far removed from the boss and seek no decision-making role. In low power-distance cultures, workers are more empowered and hence will demand some say in the decision or implementation process. Because of respect for authority, high power-distance cultures tend to be more formal than low power-distance cultures.

PROXEMICS The formal term for the study of the amount of personal space that individuals demand or expect in their interactions with other people. How closely people position themselves to another person during a discussion can communicate what type of relationship exists between them.

REVERSE CULTURE SHOCK A mental and physical condition that results when a traveler who has spent considerable time living in a new culture returns home to his or her native culture and has trouble fitting in. This can be more severe that regular culture shock because the individual is returning to a personal and business environment they had viewed as secure and comfortable.

RELATIONSHIP-DRIVEN CULTURE A culture that relies on personal friendships and personal chemistry to do business. Because there is a lack of contract law, personal trust must be built into such a culture before any business can be conducted. The opposite of a task-driven culture.

STRATEGY The art or science of creating a plan using all the social, economic, political, legal, cultural and other forces available to achieve a goal.

STEREOTYPE To stereotype is to formulate a standardized image of a group that assigns that group a number of characteristics that helps to simplify what would otherwise be a very complex task of identification. Not all stereotypes are negative or incorrect.

TASK-DRIVEN CULTURE A culture where business is conducted on an impersonal basis and is driven by the deal, not the participants. Because of the presence of a strong legal system, personal relationships are not needed to conduct business transactions or seal contracts. It is the opposite of a relationship-driven culture.

TIME HORIZON The length of time a company or individual is willing to wait before a business deal begins to produce or make a profit. Patience with a project is directly related to the cost of the capital needed to finance it. Shorter time horizons are linked to task-driven cultures where capital bears high interest rates.

TRANSPARENCY The clear understanding by all parties of a uniform set of rules, standards and laws governing a transaction. The concept is especially important as companies seek to list shares on stock exchanges where the rules of accounting and disclosure are more rigid than in their home country.

UNCERTAINTY AVOIDANCE A cultural value that dictates how individuals and societies feel about and react to stability, ambiguity and risk. This value is often seen in business organizations and views on employment. It is in Japan, a high uncertainty-avoidance culture, where workers still cling to the idea of a job for life in exchange for ceding personal mobility.

VALUES Concepts that are important to a culture and influence social interactions or individual outlooks. The most basic value difference found in cultures is whether a society emphasizes individualism or collectivism.

WEBSITE A site or location on the World Wide Web. Each website contains a home page, which is the first document users see when they enter the site. The site might also contain additional documents and files. Each site is owned and managed by an individual, company, or organization.

WIN-LOSE (see ZERO SUM GAME)

WIN-WIN A negotiating strategy where both parties believe they will both derive equal benefit from a negotiation. It contrasts to a win-lose or zero sum strategy.

WORLD WIDE WEB (WWW) A system of Internet servers that support specially formatted documents. Not all Internet servers are part of the World Wide Web. There are several applications called web browsers that make it easy to access the World Wide Web.

ZERO SUM GAME (aka win-lose) The concept that one side's gain is directly offset by another side's loss. When the gains and losses from each side are totaled, the sum is zero.

CHAPTER 20

Resources

A GOOD STARTING POINT for researching resources about cultural differences in business is the Internet. There are literally thousands of country-specific sites providing a range of information from basic economic and political facts to the intricacies of the most obscure cultures. Of course, more traditional sources can also provide a wealth of information on how to do business in a new culture. The local library is obvious but also the local trade missions, embassies and consulates of your target country are usually cooperative, if not flattered by your interest. Also, many governments sponsor cultural institutes in foreign countries to promote both business and culture of their home country. Among the largest:

- THE GOETHE-INSTITUTE, funded by the German government, promotes German business and culture abroad. The institute maintains about 150 locations in more than 70 countries. Among these are large institutes with up to 70 employees, in New York, London, Paris, Tokyo, Moscow, Cairo, Jakarta, and Rome. The institute has a total of about 3,600 German and foreign employees worldwide.

- THE ALLIANCE FRANÇAISE is the largest network of French language and cultural centers in the world. There are 1,300 Alliance chapters established in 112 countries serving more than 400,000 students.

- THE JAPAN FOUNDATION maintains two Japan cultural institutes, five Japan cultural centers, and 11 offices in 17 countries. The Japan Foundation was established in 1972 under the auspices of Japan's Ministry of Foreign Affairs for the purpose of promoting mutual understanding and friendship on the international scene. Its activities are financed by operational profits from government endowments, aid from the Japanese government, and funding from the private sector.

- THE UNITED STATES INFORMATION AGENCY: The U.S. federal government operates cultural centers, including libraries and multi-media resources, in over 90 countries. Its aim is to promote U.S. business and culture throughout the world.

Internet Resources

This is by no means meant to be an exhaustive list of international-related culture and business links. Most of the sites have their own set of additional web links and most were used as resources for this book.

BUSINESS AND CULTURE

- THE WEB OF CULTURE: http://www.worldculture.com/
  This site is primarily designed to educate and entertain you on the topic of cross-cultural communications. Nicely illustrated and fairly comprehensive.

- RELOCATION AND REAL ESTATE NEWS: http://www.relojournal.com/main.htm

Don't let its pedestrian title fool you. This site has extensive links to literally hundreds of sites about national cultures. There is a link for just about every country in the world conveniently organized in alphabetical order.

- INTERNATIONAL BUSINESS NETWORK: http://www.ibnet.com
  This site bills itself as an electronic version of the "silk road," the ancient trade route that linked China with the West. The network is dedicated to the exchange of business information and the facilitation of international trade and is a global partner of the World Network of Chambers of Commerce and Industry. Allows you to register and search its data base for specific global business opportunities. It also has a small business site link.

- INTERNATIONAL BUSINESS RESOURCES: http://ciber.bus.msu.edu/busres.htm
  One of the best and most comprehensive indexes of international and globally focused business and cultural resources on the Internet. The site is maintained by the Center for International Business Education and Research (CIBER) at Michigan State University in the United States.

- INTERNATIONAL CHAMBER OF COMMERCE: http://www.usa1.com/~ibnet/icchp.html
  This site points to information about world business and investment in the free market system. Also provides a link to its own electronic business publication.

- ISLAMIC CHAMBER OF COMMERCE AND INDUSTRY: http://www.ave.net/~icci/
  This site is dedicated to encourage and help Moslems to network and assist advancement of Moslems in corporate and professional careers. It also educates those unfamiliar with Islamic business practices. Good links to other Islamic business sites are included.

- INTERNATIONAL TRADE ADMINISTRATION: http://www.ita.doc.gov/
  The ITA falls under the umbrella of the U.S. Department of Commerce and is responsible for implementing a national export strategy. This site provides lots of detailed trade information organized by industry, region and country.

ETHICS

- TRANSPARENCY INTERNATIONAL: http://www.transparency.de/
  This is probably the best site to catch up on the latest in the fight against international business bribery and corruption. Transparency International is a German-based not-for-profit, non-governmental organization, founded to counter corruption both in international business transactions and government contracts. It produces a World Corruption Index ranking countries for their honesty in business.

- INTERNATIONAL SOCIETY OF BUSINESS, ECONOMICS AND ETHICS
  Société Internationale d'éthique, d'économie et de gestion: http://www.nd.edu/~isbee/
  The aim of the Society is to facilitate the dissemination of information and to foster mutually fruitful interaction among businesses, academics, professional societies, and others interested in the ethical dimensions of business and economics on the international level.

- BEST GLOBAL BUSINESS PRACTICES PROGRAM: http://www.ita.doc.gov/bgp/
  The U.S. Department of Commerce established the Best Global Practices (BGP) Program to promote President Clinton's Model Business Principles relating to

corporate conduct abroad. The objective is to encourage U.S. businesses to implement voluntary codes of conduct and serve as models of exemplary corporate citizenship in their operations overseas. The BGP Program provides a clearinghouse of existing corporate and non-governmental organizations' (NGOs) codes of conduct, as well as information about programs on global ethics and related issues.

■ INTERNATIONAL BUSINESS ETHICS INSTITUTE: http://www.business-ethics.org
Plenty of references and ethics code examples.

■ BUSINESS ETHICS FROM AN ISLAMIC PERSPECTIVE: http://www.islamist.org.ethics.htm
What you see is what you get but an important site for anyone doing business in the Middle East.

WOMEN'S ISSUES

■ ADVANCING WOMEN: http://www.advancingwomen.com/
An international directory of information for women in the workplace. It is one of the best sources for women's business links and networks on a global basis.

■ CANADIAN WOMEN'S BUSINESS NETWORK: http://www.cdnbizwomen.com
Directories provide an opportunity to promote your business and make connections throughout the world. The site also offers a wide range of business articles and resources.

■ ANNUAIRE AU FEMININ: http://www.iway.fr/femmes/
Listing all the women's organizations in France, including Business and Professional Women's Groups, American Women's Clubs Abroad, and online magazines dealing with women. In French and English.

■ DAS OSTERRETCHISCHE FRAUENNETZWERK: http://www.telecom.at/womennet-frauen/index.html
The Austrian Women's Network—in German only.

■ THE INTERNATIONAL ALLIANCE: http://www.t-i-a.com/
It serves worldwide as the umbrella organization that unites, supports and promotes professional and executive women and their networks in the business, not-for-profit and government sectors.

BUSINESS LEADERSHIP

■ THE CENTER FOR CREATIVE LEADERSHIP: http://www.ccl.org/
The center is an international, nonprofit educational institution that, through research, develops models of global and international managerial practice.

CHAPTER 21

BOOKS

Axtell, Roger E. (ed.) *Do's and Taboos Around the World*. New York: John Wiley & Sons, 1990.

Axtell, Roger E. (ed.) *Do's and Taboos Around the World for Women in Business*. New York: John Wiley & Sons, 1997.

Blake, Terence, Danielle Medina Walker, and Thomas Walker. *Doing Business Internationally: The Guide to Cross-Cultural Success*. New York: Richard C. Irwin Inc.,1995.

Country Business Guide Series, 12 country-specific texts on doing business in major emerging markets. Novato, CA: World Trade Press, 1994-1999.

Curry, Jeffrey Edmund, *A Short Course in International Marketing*. Novato, CA: World Trade Press, 1999.

The Global Road Warrior, 85-country handbook (106-country CD-ROM) for the international business communicator and traveler. Novato, CA: World Trade Press, 1999.

Hall, Edward T. *Beyond Culture*. Garden City, NY: Anchor Press, 1977.

Hofstede, Gert, *Cultures and Organizations: Software of the Mind: Intercultural Cooperation and Its Importance for Survival*. New York: McGraw-Hill, 1997.

Hofstede, *Cultures Consequences: International Differences in Work-Related Values*. Sage Publications, 1984.

Lewis, Richard D. *When Cultures Collide: Managing Successfully Across Cultures*. London: Nicholas Brealey Publishing, 1996.

Niemeier, Susanne, Charles P. Campbell, and Rene Dirven. *The Cultural Context in Business Communication*. New York: John Benjamins Pub. Co., 1998

Passport to the World Series, 24 country-specific books on the business culture of countries, Novato, CA: World Trade Press, 1996-1999.

Schell, Michael S. and Charlene Marmer Solomon. *Capitalizing on the Global Workforce: A Strategic Guide for Expatriate Management*. New York: Irwin Professional Pub., 1996.

Schneider, Susan C. and Jean-Louis Barsoux. *Managing Across Cultures*. Englewood Cliffs, NJ: Prentice-Hall, 1997

Shippey, Karla C., *A Short Course in International Contracts*. Novato, CA: World Trade Press, 1999.

Yip, George S., *Total Global Strategy: Managing for Worldwide Competitive Intelligence*. Englewood Cliffs, NJ: Prentice-Hall, 1992.

Biography

Charles Mitchell has worked as a foreign correspondent for U.S. and European wire services, newspapers, and magazines for over 20 years, reporting from more than 45 countries on four continents. He has lived and worked in South Africa, Kenya, and Russia and remains a frequent visitor to those lands. As foreign editor of the Detroit Free Press newspaper, he carried out roving world reporting assignments in the Middle East and throughout Europe.

Currently he is the Director of Publishing for The Conference Board, a New York-based non-profit business and economic research organization whose aim is to enhance business's contribution to society.